T0340063

Communism and Consumerism

Eurasian Studies Library

HISTORY, SOCIETIES & CULTURES IN EURASIA

VOLUME 7

The titles published in this series are listed at *brill.com/esl*

Communism and Consumerism

The Soviet Alternative to the Affluent Society

Edited by

Timo Vihavainen and Elena Bogdanova

BRILL

LEIDEN | BOSTON

Cover illustration: 'Kapron stockings. Pretty, durable, hygienic. Advised by the Ministry of Light Industry.' Glavshveisbyt, 1952. (Главшвейсбыт МЛП СССР). Designer Viktor V. Pimenov.

Library of Congress Cataloging-in-Publication Data

Communism and consumerism : the Soviet alternative to the affluent society / edited by Timo Vihavainen and Elena Bogdanova.
    pages cm. -- (Eurasian studies library, ISSN 1877-9484 ; volume 7)
    Includes index.
    ISBN 978-90-04-30396-6 (hardback : alk. paper) -- ISBN 978-90-04-30397-3 (e-book) 1. Consumption (Economics)--Soviet Union. I. Vihavainen, Timo. II. Bogdanova, Elena.
    HC340.C6C65 2015
    339.4'709470904--dc23

2015027397

This publication has been typeset in the multilingual "Brill" typeface. With over 5,100 characters covering Latin, IPA, Greek, and Cyrillic, this typeface is especially suitable for use in the humanities. For more information, please see www.brill.com/brill-typeface.

ISSN 1877-9484
ISBN 978-90-04-30396-6 (hardback)
ISBN 978-90-04-30397-3 (e-book)

Contents

Abbreviations

CPSU	Kommunisticheskaia Partiia Sovetskogo Soiuza (Communist Party of Soviet Union)
GARF	Gosudarstvennyi arkhiv Rossiiskoi Federatsii (The State Archive of the Russian Federation)
LOGAV	Leningradskii oblastnoi gosudarstvennyi arkhiv v Vyborge (Leningrad Regional State Archive in Vyborg)
RGAE	Rossiiskii gosudarstvennyi arkhiv ekonomiki (The Russian Government Archive of Economic History)
RGANI	Rossiiskii Gosudarstvennyi arkhiv noveishei istorii (Russian Government State Archive of Contemporary History)
RGASPI	Rossiiskii gosugarstvennyi arkhiv sotsial'no-politicheskoi istorii (Russian State Archive of Social and Political History)
TsGA SPb	Tsentral'nyi gosudarstvennyi arkhiv Sankt-Peterburga (Central State Archive of St. Petersburg)
TsK	Tsentral'nyi komitet (Central Committee)
TsMAM	Tsentral'nyi munitsipal'nyi arkhiv Moskvy (Central Municipal Archive of Moscow)
TsSU SSSR	Tsentral'noe statisticheskoe upravlenie SSSR (Central Statistic Administration of the USSR)
TsUM	Tsentral'nyi universal'nyi magazin (Central Department Store in Moscow)
VAZ	Volzhskii avtomobil'nyi zavod (The Volga Car Factory)
VLKSM	Vsesoiuznyi Leninskii Kommunisticheskii Soiuz Molodiozhi (All-Union Leninist Communist Union of Youth, Komsomol)
VTsIK	Vserossiiskii Tsentral'nyi Ispolnitel'nyi Komitet (All-Russian Central Executive Committee)

Acknowledgements

My gratitude is due first of all to the three ladies, who contributed to this volume and preserved their patience through the several years, which were needed until this book appeared.

I thank also the editors-in-chief Sergey Bogatyrev and Dittmar Schorkowitz for their kind attitude towards this manuscript. I am also grateful for MA Godfrey Weldhen for his professional language-checking and witty remarks. Any remaining bad language is due to my later additions. I also thank Ph.D. Marina Vituhnovskaja, who took care of the interviews, on which the chapter on *meshchanstvo* and *intelligentnost'* is based.

I also thank the journal Anthropology of East Europe Review, which kindly allowed to reprint parts of the article by Olga Gurova, which had been published there in 2006, Vol. 24, No 2.

Helsinki October 19, 2012
Timo Vihavainen
Professor of Russian Studies
University of Helsinki

About this Book

The American scholar Gary Cross has concluded that consumerism has been the 'ism' that won the battles of the 20th century despite the fact that it never had any formal philosophy, no party and no obvious leaders.[1]

Cross seems to believe that consumerism, as it had developed by the end of the 20th century, was first of all a product of American culture. Even there, it had to overcome many kinds of attacks and restraints.[2]

The British historian Niall Ferguson has called consumerism one of the seven 'killer apps', which made Western civilization the dominating force in world history.[3]

According to Ferguson's epic story, the 'rest' of the world was only able to catch up and challenge the West after they adopted those victorious 'killer apps' themselves.

That they would do so was not obvious just one generation ago. At various times, the West was challenged by Soviet Communism, then by Chinese Communism. The North Korean Juche idea, Cambodia's 'popular' rule, Cuban Socialism, and other less well-known ideologies also purported to build another kind of civilization.

As a rule, consumerism was conspicuously absent in these projects; sometimes they were even quite rigorously anti-consumerist. Now they seem to us history's blind alleys. As against just a couple of decades ago, almost all of those countries now seem to have been conquered by consumerism, the super-ideology of our time.

The road to the present state of things was not so simple, even in America. It was much more complicated in Russia, where the state did its best to keep people's consumerist instincts in check and tried to build an alternative civilization.

Just about fifty years ago it was declared that there was an alternative to the kind of modern consumerism which was already flourishing in America. This happened in 1961, when the Communist Party of the Soviet Union solemnly declared that within twenty years both production and consumption per capita in the Soviet Union would be vastly superior to that of the most advanced capitalist countries.

---

1 Cross (2000), 1.
2 Ibid., 145–191.
3 Ferguson (2011), 196–255.

But this was not the main thing about the program. It was also declared that every Soviet citizen would receive everything that he/she wanted, free of charge. In other words, every consumer in the country would be fully satisfied. Even money would no longer be needed.

This was an open challenge to the West. The Soviet Union not only proclaimed its moral superiority, it even boasted superiority in material terms, in tomorrow's standard of living.

This promise proved to be a gross miscalculation. In fact, the inability to fulfil the needs of consumers would become a major factor in destroying the Soviet regime, perhaps even the chief one.

But the Soviet program of building a communist society is a remarkable example of the ways in which states and societies have tried to cope with human behavior and the consumerist instincts of citizens.

The story of the Soviet experiment in the field of social and cultural engineering has been told many times, but, astonishingly, the ideological aspect has received little attention.

There are lots of books about consumption in the Soviet Union, especially concerning the 1930s.[4]

This, however, is not a book about consumption as such. This book concentrates on the ideological aspect, the efforts to contain the spirit of consumerism. The focus is on Russia proper within the Soviet society in the 1960s, which was the crucial period when the Soviet Union really tried to create a new kind of consumer without the consumerist mentality. This topic has been very little studied so far. There are books which deal with the world of Soviet consumers in the 1950s and the perestroika era, but the crucial years of the 1960s have not received much attention.[5]

The articles in this book devote much interest to clothes and fashion. These have been studied previously to some extent, notably by Susan Reid (2000), Djurdja Bartlett (2010) and some others. However, the approach of this book is different.

Nowadays, we easily forget that society without consumerism seemed to exist for decades in Russia and China, for instance.

The present situation, where markets are ready to cater to all the whims of the consumer and where the spirit of consumerism prevails in all materially

---

4 Notably, there are the outstanding books by Osokina (2001), Hessler (2004), Randall (2008), Gronow (2003), Hilton (2012), Siegelbaum (2007) and several others.

5 For instance, Hessler (2004), Barker (ed.) (1999), Moskoff (1993), Humphrey (2002), Roth-Ey (2011), Reid (2000), and Bartlett (2010), Ledeneva's (1998) book about *blat*, the Russian economy of favours, deserves special mention for its relevance for our theme.

well-off states, is something which few people could have even imagined just half a century ago. Even in America as late as 1900, only a few people expected that the new century would be one of consumption.[6]

Communist society, which the Soviet Union claimed to be constructing, was first sketched by the theorists of the mid-19th century and updated later in the mid-20th century. Such a society was supposed to provide all of its citizens with all the necessities of everyday life but, first of all, it would be a society where greed and egoism had vanished and things material would not be the major concern. Instead, people would concentrate on developing their personal talents and actively take part in altruistic cooperation with their fellow citizens.[7] In other words, there would be an affluent society without the consumerist mentality.

In the West, the upsurge in consumerism in the second half of the 20th century coincided with and probably to a large extent even caused a veritable cultural revolution. Within a couple of decades, the material and spiritual situation of modern man was revolutionized.[8]

Whatever the mechanism of the process, the role of religion in western culture has declined apace with the progress of consumerism after World War II and especially since the 1960s. At the same time, Communism, another surrogate religion, gradually lost its support in the West. In Communist countries, this happened somewhat later.

It is still too early to assess the impact of this process for our civilization as a whole. The change has probably been qualitative, not just quantitative. It is worth remembering here that these processes did not take place simultaneously in either Russia or the West.

The Soviet economy also purported to satisfy the consumer's needs, but, in the Soviet Union, those needs and their satisfaction were determined and conceived in a specific way which did not exist in the West. The authors of this book analyse how this was done.

In assessing Russian life over the last few decades, it is also important to remember that extremely rapid changes have taken place in the western world itself during this period. The western consumer's world in, say, the 1930s or even the 1950s was very different from that of the 1970s and subsequent decades.[9]

---

6 Cross (2000), 5–6.
7 *Scientific Communism* (1983), 395–398.
8 Marwick (1998), 16–20.
9 See: Cross (2000), 145–191.

Soviet living standards did not necessarily look very low to a western tourist in the 1930s or even in the 1970s. The Soviet urban scene was certainly grey, with very few advertisements and luxury items visible, but there were few signs of real poverty. At the same time, conspicuous signs of poverty were still easy to find in most European cities, especially in southern Europe.

Since the 1960s, a new consumerist revolution took place in the West which has raised consumption to a new level. To a degree, this happened simultaneously with the stagnation and even absolute regression in the level of consumption which took place in the Soviet country.[10]

The Soviet Union was never able to enter this new wave of consumerism which boomed in the Western world. Only after the collapse of the Soviet Union did the Russians suddenly encounter it. What was new for them was not just the abundance of consumer goods, but also the unabashed consumerist mentality.

The consumerist mentality had emerged gradually in the West. In fact, the very concept of 'consumerism' in its contemporary sense is of quite recent origin. Gary Cross has aptly stated that in America consumerism "the belief that goods give meaning to individuals and their roles in society" was the 'ism' that won after a hard battle, despite repeated attacks. The victory of consumerism meant, among other things, that the very idea of the primacy of things political has receded. Instead there is a consuming public and its needs, which dictate the political agenda.[11]

It has often been maintained that Russia never was culturally part of the West. Such ideas are nowadays quite popular in Russia itself and they deserve some attention.

While Russia was undoubtedly part of the Western cultural sphere and even economically closely connected to it, it also had certain specific traits.

To some extent, Russian specificity was due to the fact that the industrial revolution came rather late to Russia and the vast masses of its population remained rural up to the middle of the 20th century.

Even though they had been liberated from serfdom in 1861, they still continued to live in the village communes, which must be characterized as archaic.

But peasants were not the only ones left outside the modern exchange economy and its industrial psychology, which incited consumption. It is also interesting to note that an outspoken anti-consumerist mentality *avant la lettre* was popular in 19th century Russia both among the Slavophiles and the narodniks as well as hugely popular and influential radical writers, such as Maxim Gorky

---

10   Ibid., 193–232.
11   Ibid., 1.

and Leo Tolstoy. Loathing of the conspicuous consumption of the leisured class also pervaded Bolshevik ideology.

While pre-revolutionary Russia was obviously not immune to a consumerist mentality, its intellectual climate was inimical to it. It may be assumed that just a tiny portion of Russians, both physically and psychologically, had entered the world of modern consumption before the Bolshevik Revolution put an end to the capitalist development of Russia for many decades to come.

The articles in this book do not concentrate on the political importance of the Soviet consumer or consumption. The authors do not try to survey the whole sphere of Soviet consumption or its countless aspects, from *blat* and the black market to special shops and the role of tourism and information flows concerning commodities in the West. Instead, the authors will concentrate on certain specific aspects of Soviet consumption both in terms of ideology and practice.

In Chapter 1, written by Professor Timo Vihavainen, the author tries to pose some of the most fundamental questions relevant for our understanding of the revolution of consumerism, both in the West and in Russia. The task is not to chart the world of the Russian consumer, but to explore the outlines of the specifically Russian intellectual tradition and its attitudes to the growth of the consumerist mentality, which was already taking place both in the West and in Russia itself since the late 19th century.

In Chapter 2, Vihavainen explores the Bolsheviks' mission to build a new kind of society, which was supposed to satisfy everybody's material needs to the fullest extent. Unlike Capitalism, at the same time it very earnestly purported to avoid the consumerist mentality, which was supposedly morally inferior.

The Communist Party's attitudes towards consumption, affluence and luxury goods changed considerably during the 75 years that the party ruled the country. From outright egalitarianism and praise of asceticism, which prevailed in the 1920s, the ideology veered into an apology for affluence for the 'best people' in the 1930s, both for those who worked in production and for those who occupied a high place in the party and state hierarchy.

When Nikita Khrushchev promised to 'bury the West' in the 1950s, he had in mind the supposedly inescapable victory of socialist society in the struggle for leadership in living standards, among other things. Communist society, where no scarcity would exist, was to be built in the Soviet Union by 1980. American living standards were to be left far behind even earlier.

One is forced to ask whether the solemn promise of the party concerning the construction of the communist society was sincerely believed by the majority of Russians. There are some clues which indicate that the answer was positive for a certain time.

It is also interesting to notice that when the moment of truth came, the party lost its popularity very rapidly. This seems to imply that the collapse of the Soviet system caused a very abrupt and severe revolution in values.

The ideological scene of post-perestroika Russia will raise many questions. At first, the consumerist mentality, which was suddenly rehabilitated after having been the main public enemy for decades, was not accompanied by any real opportunities for fulfilment. There was not much to consume for the great majority of people. After the collapse of the Soviet economy, the average Russian citizen had to wait until the 2000s in order to enjoy material well-being for the first time in Russian history. How did the popular masses react to massive frustration, which seemed to imply that those accomplishments which had been represented as the main glory of the Russian people, were actually worthless?

In Chapter 3, Dr. Olga Gurova explores the awkward issue of the public discourse on consumption and official attitudes to consumer goods, especially clothes, in Soviet Russia from 1917 to the 1980s.

In this chapter, the ideology of consumption is understood as a 'set of dominant discourses which contain ideas about consumerism and attitudes to consumption and consumer practices represented in the media in Soviet society'. Her article is on the ideas and concepts which contained information about and attitudes towards clothes, fashion and everyday consumer practices in Soviet Russia from 1917 to the 1980s. The author has defined four main periods in the ideology of consumption as reflected in attitudes concerning fashion and clothes on the basis of media discourse analysis.

Karl Marx had concluded that under Capitalism the cult of goods transforms the relationships between people into the relationships of things. In the Soviet Union of the 1920s, ideologists criticized things, that is, material objects, as the source of a philistine obsession. They actively condemned an individual's desire to obtain more material things than was deemed necessary. To have a lot of things, especially those produced and obtained before the revolution, meant that one was loyal to the reactionary past, and to the values of the old world. The very word 'fashion' was derogatory.

In the 1930s, 'culturedness' (*kul'turnost'*) became a watchword of the day. It was everybody's duty to become 'cultured'. In the material sphere, this meant a relatively high standard of individual consumption. On the ideological level, material goods were now given a legitimate right to appear in the daily lives of the Soviet people. They even became the subject of consumer worship. The category of 'consumer' was increasingly often accompanied by the category of 'Soviet man' in the mass media. In real life, the objects of 'consumption pornography' that were represented in the press rarely became available to the ordinary consumer.

In the 1950s and 1960s, the production of consumer goods became a priority for the Soviet leadership. The author concludes that ideologically this meant that the Soviet middle class adopted life styles similar to those of post-war America's middle class.

In Brezhnev's time, it became clear that victory over the West in the consumption race was not imminent if possible at all. In this situation, the leadership resorted to a policy called the 'Little Deal'.

The 'Little Deal' was an unwritten agreement between the Party and the middle class in which the Soviet middle class would support the authorities in exchange for financial security, a differentiation in wage levels, and a readiness to turn a blind eye to the black market and the good life. The purpose of this deal was to ensure the stability of the existing social order. The aim of the Soviet state remained the creation of a socialist post-materialistic world in which there would be plenty of consumer goods. However, these would not be of excessive significance for the individual. Soviet people would not and should not be obsessed with the adoration of things, which should be used mostly in a functional way.

Ideas about de-materialization along with criticism of fashion started to disappear by the beginning of the 1980s, because of the visible contradiction between official ideological statements and the growing demand, production and import of consumer goods. From the end of the 1970s to the 1980s, official discourse was filled with modern-sounding terms such as 'culture of consumption' and 'consumerism', and by the middle of the 1980s this discourse was reoriented away from the socialist values of the USSR to what would become the values of the new post-socialist Russian materialism, as the author concludes.

In Chapter 4, Dr. Larissa Zakharova's article concerns patterns of Soviet clothing consumption in the 1950s and 1960s. She asks how the Soviet state evaluated the consumers' needs for fashionable clothes and which of them it intended to satisfy. In 1961, the Soviet Communist Party solemnly promised to catch up with and surpass the West in the production of consumer goods within ten years, that is, by 1970. The idea of constructing a society of abundance legitimized consumption ideologically.

Olga Gurova's article, referred to above, shows that changes in ideology were always quickly reflected in the field of fashion. But what were the actual results of the new ideological orientation in the field of clothing consumption? What did the State do to provide the population with clothes and what kind of clothes were they? How did it evaluate the consumers' needs for durable goods and which of them did it intend to satisfy? And how did the consumer behave in reaction to the policy of production and the system of distribution of these goods?

Zakharova attempts to evaluate the efficiency of the State's program to satisfy the people's material needs by studying legal and illegal consumer strategies and the State's actions to promote the former and to constrain the latter. One of the methods is to analyze the correlation between socio-economic factors and the choice of consumer strategies, essentially on the basis of materials on people's incomes from the Leningrad Department of Statistics.

The author also takes into account the influence of cultural factors on consumer strategies. Based on interviews with consumers of the 1950s and 1960s, this part of the research aims to find some 'patterns' of consumption, or consumer, cultures combining different strategies. Finally the author considers the relationship between the mechanisms of fashion and 'patterns' of consumption.

The Leningrad Department of Statistics conducted an ongoing budget survey for the population of Leningrad. This survey had enormous theoretical and practical significance. It was necessary both for the evaluation of consumption in different professional milieus and for the elaboration of plans for consumer goods production. It was also used for the formulation of the theory of socialist consumption.

The Department discovered that expenditure on clothes did not increase proportionally to income growth. When income reached a certain level, expenditure on clothes stopped increasing and became stable. It seemed possible to elaborate a 'rational norm' of clothing consumption characteristic for 'healthy, cultured, conscious members of the communist society with reasonable needs'.

From the point of view of ideology this was encouraging: even though the material needs of the Soviet people had a tendency to exhibit constant growth, according to Khrushchev's frequent statements, they could not increase endlessly. According to this theory, social and economic differences could disappear.

Thus the III party program, adopted at the XXII Party Congress, declared that one of the targets for the near future was the satisfaction of the Soviet people's 'reasonable needs', which was equated with the complete satisfaction of the needs of citizens in a communist society. In practice, the quality of goods and their relation to so-called fashion were not taken into consideration.

Soviet economists, who were obsessed by volumes of consumption, underestimated the importance of the question 'how and what to consume?' In this case, they did not attach any real significance to the question of fashion when it came to clothes.

Although clothing designers invented the concept of socialist fashion, economists continued to stigmatize fashion as a strictly bourgeois phenomenon related to the mechanism of market competition, whereas the socialist economy 'respected the products of human labor and could not permit the idea of throwing out some goods because they had become obsolete'.

An attitude to clothes based upon following fashions was considered a luxury: 'the task of providing all the population with the most fashionable clothes cannot be imposed on industry because the communist society has as its aim the satisfaction not of all the needs, but only of reasonable needs. The premature withdrawal of huge material values from the field of consumption due to the specificities of changes in fashion is out of the sphere of the reasonable'.

Deficiencies in the system of clothing production and distribution created a vicious circle: the lack of some goods aggravated shortages and resulted in the complete disappearance of such goods from the shops. Clerks and commercial managers organized special 'closed' networks for the distribution of these goods among their relatives, acquaintances and special clients able to pay more than the State price for these goods. An informal system of distribution based upon *blat*, was the origin of private enterprise in the Soviet Union and involved a constant reselling of goods for ever higher prices. This was officially stigmatized as speculation and was punishable by five years in prison.

Because fashionable clothes remained scarce, given that Soviet industry was not interested in producing them and retailers were not interested in selling them, people resorted to different strategies in order to obtain scarce goods. These included the private production of clothes with individuals sewing items for sale, and contraband goods obtained through the black market.

The State was not categorically against private production and even tried to produce more sewing machines. Fashion as such was tolerated and even Western fashions to some extent. But, in spite of the lofty principles concerning the satisfaction of 'reasonable needs', society remained divided on this issue.

The differences in how and what to consume were determined by inequalities in resources and ways of accessing scarce goods. The State itself maintained such distinctions by establishing dressmaking establishments catering for various levels: from ordinary workshops to institutions of a higher category, the so-called 'luxe' shops (with higher prices). Some consumers wanted to be up-to-date, profited from the partial opening up of Soviet society to the West and became rather detached from official Soviet fashion. They looked at trends in fashion abroad, using specific mechanisms for the spreading of fashion: foreign films, the presence of foreigners in the USSR, trips abroad, contraband, etc. So the official orientation to the field of consumption legitimized the construction by Soviet people of their own consumer cultures by combining different strategies for obtaining clothes. Without this activity, the results of Khrushchev's program would have been even less striking than they actually were.

In Chapter 5, Dr. Elena Bogdanova surveys the world of the Soviet consumer in the light of the system of complaints available in the late Soviet period. Approaching ideas concerning consumption from several angles provided by the system of complaints, enables the author to draw a many-sided and incisive analysis.

As the author remarks, the very word 'consumption' as ambiguous in Soviet ideology and several consequences stemmed from this fact. Consumption in a general sense was an important element in Marxist-Leninist theory and Socialist ideology. According to these, production develops the need for produced goods and entails consumption, which finally determines the level and structure of production.

According to the Marxist understanding of consumption, the word 'consumer' was used almost synonymously with the words 'citizen' or 'worker' and went far beyond the limited understanding of consumption as simply the satisfaction of personal needs. The understanding of consumption as the satisfaction of personal needs existed in Soviet discourse as well, but bringing it into conformity with the official, overarching theory of Marxism-Leninism caused Soviet ideologists no small amount of effort. In particular, they created the concept of 'reasonable needs', which could be divided into two groups. In the first group were reasonable needs which could be regulated by using scientific standards. These standards were to be worked out scientifically by institutes of hygiene and medicine. In the second group were reasonable needs which could be regulated by bringing material needs into line with the level of production so far attained.

The basis for defining the level of need in both cases was an artificially created standard, determined by Soviet production capacity. The standards set out what quantity of meat, milk, bread, refrigerators, pairs of winter boots, and so on should be required by the average Soviet citizen over a certain period of time.

Using levels of consumption as a guide, a clear ideological position was worked out which was used to make sure that these standards were observed. The ideology encouraged consumption, but only as long as it did not exceed certain limits.

A level of personal consumption that exceeded state norms was presented as a pathological desire for enrichment and the acquisition of material goods. In the Soviet lexicon, this was denoted either as 'consumerism' or *veshchizm*, materialism (in the sense of excessive devotion to material objects).

As a consequence, in Soviet discourse the words 'consumption' and 'consumer' had negative meanings. The existence of such a contradiction within one discourse explains the variety of concepts which were used to define personal consumption in the Soviet period. The word 'consumer' was often substituted with 'buyer', 'visitor', 'client', 'citizen', 'customer', and so on. Depending on the context it could be interpreted as good or evil.

The Soviet consumer's situation vis-à-vis the mighty machinery which professed to satisfy his needs was, in principle, not an easy one. Complaints were his weapon and sometimes they helped, if the strategy was aptly chosen.

A lack of competition between state-owned retailers, the consumers' dependence upon the retailer, and a number of other factors often left consumers defenseless. Sending complaints directly to retail employees turned out in most cases to be absurd or useless. In addition to complications in searching for or acquiring goods consumers regularly ran into problems with shop service. The standard, characteristic behavior of Soviet shop assistants and service personnel was rudeness and boorishness.

The Soviet consumer of the 1960s was not only seduced by novelties. Oleg Kharkhordin, a researcher into Soviet society, notes that, roughly at the beginning of the 1960s, material objects began to play an important stratifying role in society.

Making a complaint was a legitimate and widespread means of exposing violations of the Soviet citizen's interests in Soviet times. As a means of addressing a superior person, complaints displayed, in the clearest fashion, the traditional hierarchical relationship between citizens, on the one hand, and agents representing the authorities in Russian and Soviet society, on the other. Moreover, complaints displayed the paternal dependence of citizens on the authorities, which was an organic part of the idea of Soviet societal structure.

Complaints from citizens were interesting for the authorities in so far as they provided valuable informal information 'from below' for the state administration, and gave citizens the illusion of taking part in important political processes. The reasons for such complaints were many: 'rudeness, being given short change, an incorrect weight or measurement, badly prepared food, slow service and a refusal to give the customer the book of complaints'.

As complaints were a universal means of interaction, it gave citizens the opportunity to enter into a dialogue with the authorities when their civil rights and interests had been violated. It was this interaction which led to the defining peculiarity of Soviet complaints – their pragmatism.

In theory everyone had the right to complain and the means to do so. At the same time the options for expressing criticism and dissatisfaction with the existing system were severely limited. As a rule, complaints informed representatives of authoritative structures about failures in the system or cases of social unfairness.

Dealing with shop assistants and customer service authorities sapped one's strength. Everyday consumption became something more than simply buying things. For some it was a problem which complicated their everyday. For others it was like a hobby or sport. For both it represented a system of relations, structured according to certain rules. Every Soviet consumer found himself caught up in a number of complementary hierarchies: the consumer as opposed to the shop assistant, or the consumer who was in a network of unofficial distribution as opposed to the consumer who was not, and so on.

In order for a complaint to be successful, the consumer needed to know which authority he should address his complaint to, so that it resulted in his request being satisfied. The consumer also had to have a detailed knowledge of the rules (such as the existence of hierarchical relationships, the system of moral and ethical norms which were current, and the difficult and contradictory theses of Soviet ideology) in order to speak the same language as the authorities. In comparison with any other type of complaint, a consumer's complaint needed to demonstrate that the complainant was moderate in his or her consumption, and to include additional explanations and justifications connected with the ambivalent status of consumption, the consumer and problems of consumption in Soviet society.

In Chapter 6, Timo Vihavainen investigates the discourses and attitudes towards *meshchanstvo*, or petty bourgeois mentality, as it has mostly been translated. The chapter is largely based on interviews conducted in the early 2000s. The concepts of *intelligentnost'* and *meshchanstvo* (often translated as 'philistinism') and their mutual relations have played a prominent role in Russian intellectual history. The author seeks to point out the special role which this discourse played in Russian culture at the time of the great transition to Capitalism.

It happens that *meshchanstvo*, which was defined as the most severe moral defect in the human personality by the pre-revolutionary *intelligentsia*, was considered to be the absolute opposite of or negation of *intelligentnost'*, which in turn was held to be the embodiment of everything that was lofty and respectable in a human being.

Whereas *meshchanstvo* in the discourse of the Russian *intelligentsia* was very much the same thing as the psychology of the proprietor in bourgeois society, it was assumed that its influence would be overcome in a socialist society. Maxim Gorky, who was the highest cultural authority in Stalin's Soviet Union, concentrated much of his work on attacking *meshchanstvo*.

The psychology of a *meshchanin* was that of the 'ideal' bourgeois consumer, who was interested not in the public good, but only in selfish goals, who hoarded goods for their own sake and whose whole psychology was based on self-centered individualism and egoism. Obviously, he was the very opposite of the ideal Soviet citizen, who was living in Socialism and building Communism.

Interestingly, informants in post-Soviet St. Petersburg and Petrozavodsk, with ten years' experience of post-communist life and society, largely paid homage to the Soviet – and partly even pre-Soviet – ideas and appraised the consumption-oriented *meshchanin* for the most part in very negative terms, while *intelligentnost'* was mostly held in high esteem and understood as the direct opposite of *meshchanstvo*.

However, the full picture of the interviewees' ideas about the concepts was more complicated. Some thought that these concepts were already old-fashioned and belonged to the Soviet past. People also understood the concepts in a variety of ways; for instance, some identified a high level of education or a leading position in society with *intelligentnost'*, while moral qualities were primary for others.

In general, the ideas of the pre-revolutionary Russian *intelligentsia* concerning consumption, which had later been inculcated under the Soviet regime, seemed to be very much alive in the informants' minds ten years after the collapse of the Soviet regime.

To sum up, in order to understand the origins of the unique Soviet project of building a radically new kind of consumer heaven we will, in this book, not only point out the importance of classic Marxist theory but also that of the Russian intellectual heritage. Conspicuous consumption and luxury were very much present in pre-revolutionary Russia and they were also very much disliked by both the *intelligentsia* and the masses.

We will assume that pre-revolutionary Russia differed a lot from Western Europe in several important respects.

On the eve of the Russian Revolution of 1917, modernization in the Russian countryside had only just begun and, although it was progressing rapidly, especially in the years which preceded 1917, the social situation and intellectual constitution of the heavily peasant-dominated and archaic Russia was slow to change.

We will also point out that Russian intellectual tradition was fiercely anti-bourgeois. The main ideas of the leading moral authorities of pre-revolutionary Russia are essential reading if one wants to know the intellectual background of the attitudes towards consumption during the Soviet era.

It will be assumed that the communists meant it seriously when they said that they intended to build a society which would satisfy man's natural and 'reasonable' material needs.

The idea of 'reasonable' needs is particularly interesting and deserves to be assessed by the measures of the epoch.

Ideology is the central subject matter of this book. Ideology was ubiquitous in the USSR. Clothes were not just clothes, but reflected the political aspirations of both their users and their producers. The flaws in the theoretical framework of the party and its fantasies concerning people's 'rational needs' became obvious when the state tried to put up with fashions. If the client remained unsatisfied, the problem concerned not only consumers but also producers, who were the heroes of the state.

The problems which arose in solving the problems and which the official ideology forced on the people will be discussed in this book at some length.

The current development of the standard of living in the Soviet Union of the 1960s, which was experienced both in absolute and relative terms, will also be discussed as one of the relevant background factors contributing to the credibility of the program of building communist society within twenty years.

This is a short book, in which these fundamental problems cannot be thoroughly discussed, let alone resolved. However, we believe that it is also an important task to point out those problems, which may give important clues for understanding Russian history during the past one hundred years.

Bibliography

Barker, A. (ed.) (1999): *Consuming Russia: Popular Culture, Sex, and Society since Gorbachev.* Durham, N.C.: Duke University Press.

Bartlett, D. (2010): *Fashion East: The Spectre that Haunted Socialism.* Cambridge, Mass.: The MIT Press

Crowley, D., Reid S. (eds.) (2010): *Pleasures in Socialism. Leisure and Luxury in the Eastern Bloc.* Evanston: Northwestern University Press.

Ferguson, N. (2011): *Civilization. The West and the Rest.* London: Allen Lane.

Gronow, J. (2003): *Caviar with Champagne. Common Luxury Goods and the Ideals of the Good Life in Stalin's Russia.* Oxford, New York: Berg.

Hessler, J. (2004): *A Social History of Soviet Trade: Trade Policy, Retail Practices, and Consumption, 1917–1953.* Princeton: Princeton University Press.

Hilton, M. (2012): *Selling to the Masses: Retailing in Russia 1880–1930.* Pittsburgh: University of Pittsburgh Press.

Humphrey, C. (2002): *The Unmaking of Soviet Life. Everyday Economies after Socialism*. Ithaca & London: Cornell University.

Ledeneva, A. (1998): *Russia's Economy of Favours: Blat, Networking and Informal Exchange*. Cambridge: Cambridge University Press.

Marwick, A. (1998): *The sixties: Cultural Revolution in Britain, France, Italy, and the United States, c.1958–1974*. Oxford: Oxford University Press.

Moskoff, W. (1993): *Hard Times. Impoverishment and Protest in the Perestroika Years*. M&E Sharpe.

Osokina, E. (2001): *Our Daily Bread. Socialist Distribution and the Art of Survival in Stalin's Russia 1927–1941*. London & Armonk, New York: M&E Sharpe.

Randall, A. (2008): *The Soviet Dream World of Retail Trade and Consumption in the 1930s*. Palgrave, Macmillan.

Reid, S. and David Crowley (eds.) (2000): *Style and Socialism. Modernity and Material Culture in Post-War Eastern Europe*. Oxford New York: Berg.

Roth-Ey, K. (2011): *Moscow Prime Time. How the Soviet Union Built the Media Empire that Lost the Cultural Cold War*. Ithaca: Cornell University Press.

Scientific Communism (1983): Moscow: Progress Publishers.

Siegelbaum, L. (2008): *Cars for Comrades, The Life of the Soviet Automobile*. Ithaca, New York: Cornell University Press.

CHAPTER 1

The Spirit of Consumerism in Russia and the West

Timo Vihavainen

The Problem of the Consumerist Mentality

'Consumerism' is a word, which has several meanings. It has been used to de-note variously just a high degree of consumption, the practice of increasing consumption, opulent, or conspicuous consumption. It has also denoted the protection of consumers' rights[1] and it has been used to denote the belief that an ever-expanding consumption of goods is advantageous to the economy.[2] It has also meant attachment to materialistic values, addiction to consumption or the belief that consumption is the meaning of life.[3]

Gary Cross has defined consumerism as a kind practical ideology, as 'the belief that goods give meaning to individuals and their roles in society'.[4] This kind of consumerism was triumphant in the late 20th and early 21st century, but it may have been not common in earlier epochs.

Obviously, using different definitions as one's starting point, it would be possible to write several books about the topic 'consumerism and the Soviet Union' all different from each other.

Historians who have dealt with western consumerism have mostly under-stood their subject as an interest in acquiring produced goods. If defined in this way, consumerism began in the 18th century or even earlier. Sometimes consumerism is also found in antiquity.

In Europe, colonial expansion and the industrial revolution certainly pro-vided new opportunities for consumption and the cultural phenomenon called consumerism, which can be considered a cultural novelty.

Over the centuries, the nature of consumerism and the preconditions for it have radically changed. There are authors who maintain that, as regards con-sumerism, there was simply nothing more to happen, technical modifications aside, after 1800. But this can be contested. If we take as a point of departure

---

1 For instance, Hilton (2003); Cohen (2003).
2 'Consumerism'. Merriam-Webster dictionary. Available at: <http://www.merriam-webster.com/dictionary/consumerism>.
3 For instance, Barber (2007), 42–54; Bauman (2008), 58–59.
4 Cross, (2000), 1.

© KONINKLIJKE BRILL NV, LEIDEN, 2016 | DOI 10.1163/9789004303973_002

that society is consumerist if it '(makes) human wants, desires and longings into the principal propelling and operating force in society',[5] it will be obvious that the role of consumerism in society has changed significantly since the 18th and even the 19th century. These changes can be considered qualitative.

Peter N. Stearns thinks that a second stage of consumerism began in the late 19th and early 20th century. There was a much greater diversity of commodities to consume, more shops and advertisements, and even the tenor of the messages of the advertisements had changed. The emotional significance of acquisition was increasing. Obviously, consumption was also fulfilling some emotional functions, perhaps filling the void left by social change which had made self-fulfillment at work less and less possible.

Stearns believes that it is possible to argue that yet another consumerist phase began sometime after World War II. This seems plausible. At least it is obvious that the volume of consumption has massively expanded since the war, and particularly after the oil crisis of the 1970s had passed.[6]

Some scholars support the idea that western civilization has entered a qualitatively new epoch of postmodernity. In the postmodern condition, it has been argued, consumption has assumed a central role in human life.[7] Paraphrasing the Communist Manifesto of Marx and Engels, Zygmunt Bauman has depicted the postmodern world as a place, where 'solid' modernity has given way to 'liquid' postmodernity. Bauman stresses the fact that in this new world, an increased freedom to enjoy and consume has been accompanied by a sense of insecurity in a society where the consumer and not the producer is the central figure.[8]

The Special Case of Russian and Soviet Consumerism

If we assume that the bourgeois western world entered a qualitatively new phase in the development of a new kind of culture, namely that of consumerism at some point in the late 20th century, then Russia, after the collapse of the Soviet Union, entered the same cultural community quite suddenly and with a very different cultural baggage.

---

5   Bauman (2007), 28.

6   For clues concerning these discussions; see: Stearns (2001), vi-x, 1–26.

7   For instance, Barber (2007), 54; Bauman (2007), 12.

8   Bauman (2007), 28–31.

Until the early 1990s, Soviet society and culture differed very strongly from the western capitalist world, where consumerism was rapidly developing.[9]

Like the history of Russia in general, the history of Russian consumerism has developed in a specific way. Before the Bolshevik Revolution and even up to the middle of the 20th century Russia was a predominantly peasant country.[10] Even a great part of the urban work-force was of peasant origin and preserved its rural ways of life.[11]

The history of consumerism in Russia in some sense certainly began in the 19th century, maybe even before. However, its dimensions as a cultural phenomenon necessarily remained restricted for a long time.

By the late 19th century, Russia experienced a period of industrial development and consumption, at least in its major cities.[12] New department stores were built and a huge amount of previously unknown goods and products were widely advertised.[13] The conspicuous consumption and culture of the elite was not shared by the masses, however, and even the 'brain of the popular masses', the *intelligentsia*, loathed those who were obsessed with hoarding material goods instead of selflessly serving the people and concentrating on spiritual values.

Under Soviet rule, the Party had a troubled relationship with consumerism. It bore the legacy of anti-bourgeois and anti-consumerist Marxist tradition, which also had its proponents in the West. Later, from the mid-1930s, even the consumerist instincts of the Soviet people were courted by the party to some extent. Clearly consumerist lifestyles were advertised and encouraged on a small scale but they were only made available for a selected few in the Soviet Union.

This new trend in the official ideology was linked with the supposedly accomplished advent of the promised land of Socialism, which was proclaimed in 1936. New ideas were reinforced by the state-sponsored production and advertisement of luxury goods. In practice, however, official attitudes towards consumerism always remained ambivalent.[14] It was really proclaimed that the good life meant not only a materially secure life, but an affluent life. The future communist society was supposed to give material goods to everybody; each would have as much 'as he needed'.

---

9   Cross (2000), 193–232.
10   Lewin (1985), 38–41.
11   Bradley (1985), 105–117.
12   Smith and Kelly (1998), 107–113.
13   Hilton (2012), 31–72.
14   See: Stearns (2001), 86–87.

On the other hand, the new communist man would not have superfluous material interests. Satiated materially he would be emancipated to fulfill his true mission as a human being: develop his talents to the maximum and to use them for the common good of the people.[15]

In other words, the future affluent society would not have a consumerist culture. Acquiring goods would not be the purpose of life. On the contrary, the effortless availability of material goods would make them wholly uninteresting. Thus in Communism material interest would be overcome, it could no more determine man's relation to work or to his human brethren. Man was supposed to be satiable materially and insatiable only spiritually. Only as long as there was no communist society as yet, but just a socialist one, material concerns remained important.[16]

Western scholars could classify Soviet society as consumerist, because it fulfilled certain criteria required of such a society.[17] But, on the other hand, the culture of Soviet socialist society was not consumption-oriented, but production-oriented. While market economies could afford open selfishness and freedom of choice for their citizens, Soviet society had to try to make people obey rules that they most probably would have liked to disobey. The official ideology (which was supposedly 'materialist') maintained that the Soviet man's main interests were not material (quantitative) but social and spiritual (qualitative) in nature.[18]

In fact, in the Soviet Union, the public's interest in material goods was immense.[19] In reality commodities in the Soviet Union always remained scarce and frequently they were very scarce. This happened in spite of the official ideology, which praised the socialist system for its superior talent for production and held out the promise of an end to scarcity for everybody in the future.

Moreover this future land of Communism was said to be a qualitatively new stage in the history of humanity.[20] Even socialist society, which supposedly had been established in 1936, was claimed to have already introduced a new kind of relationship between man and society. The 'developed socialist society', which it was claimed had been reached sometime after the late 1950s, was proclaimed to have been yet another and higher stage in the development of human society.[21]

---

15   *Scientific Communism* (1983), 246–251.
16   Ibid., 244–254.
17   Randall (2008), 179.
18   *Scientific Communism* (1983), 246–247.
19   See: Grushin (2001), 145.
20   *Scientific Communism* (2003), 296–303, 395–417.
21   Ibid., 227–228.

As we know, socialist prosperity never became a reality, except for a small privileged group, such as the *nomenklatura,* which, it was said, already lived in Communism.[22] But can we call Soviet society consumerist? Certain necessary elements of consumerism existed. There were factory-made goods in shops, and there was the urge to attain them, but is this enough to constitute a consumerist society? Compared with western consumerism, Soviet everyday culture remained strikingly different.

If we compare Soviet society of, say, the 1960s with the western world, we will realize that in spite of certain analogous 'consumerist' elements, there were also very serious cultural, material and institutional differences.

In the early 1960s, the level of consumption, and indeed the level of needs seems to have been very low in the Soviet Union.[23] Water taps, central heating, WCs or telephones were still rare, but most people had enough to eat, which was a very precious privilege in the light of the country's recent history. On the other hand, the means to satisfy other needs were still scarce, but growing.

Not only did the soviet consumer not have much money, he also faced quite specific difficulties. Often scarce goods could not be bought at all even if one had money. Advertisements were rare and hardly alluring. The consumer was not faced with the constant temptation to buy some new and 'unnecessary' things. On the contrary, it was often not easy even to obtain daily necessities. It was a shortage economy, where commodities constantly fled from the consumer.[24]

Moreover, anti-consumerist and leveling sentiments among the masses were common.[25] Sometimes these sentiments were directed against the *nomenklatura* and its lifestyle.[26] The whole issue of consumption was rather awkward from the point of view of the state. Though it was not wise to incite anti-consumerist sentiments too much, it was obviously necessary to fan them to some extent.

If there were no goods to buy, it was best from the state's point of view to keep the people thinking that this was a good thing and not the result of any shortcoming of the system. Soviet tourists, who visited capitalist countries and saw masses of consumer goods in shop windows but no queues, were told that the poor work-slaves of the capitalists had no money to buy them. In Soviet Union of the 1970s, it was the opposite, people had more money than they could use.

---

22 See: Voslensky (1980).
23 Grushin (2001), 154.
24 See: Kornai (1992), 228–234.
25 Grushin (2001), 147.
26 Fitzpatrick (1992), 227–233.

It could also be maintained that the state of things in the Soviet Union was morally superior to that in the capitalist West. As long as the basic everyday needs of the people remained unsatisfied, it was in principle better not to waste resources on the production of 'unnecessary' things. Elements of modern consumerism existed, but, for a long time, they remained restricted to a small minority.[27]

To an outsider it might appear that the Soviet Union resembled a kind of penitentiary for the would-be consumer. The main difference with the West would then be restricted to the different opportunities to satisfy one's consumerist desire prevent it.

This may be a superficial approach. Soviet society and western societies did not experience the same stages of material affluence simultaneously, but were in effect living in different 'epochs' at any given moment. It may be that all societies are destined to become consumerist at some point in time, but, even so, there has at least been a 'diversity of trajectories to consumer modernity'.[28]

Popular attitudes concerning consumerism also developed in a specific way in the Soviet Union, which was separated from the West by the iron curtain. It has been maintained that the arrival of consumerism as the everyday culture of the middle class was a major revolution in the West. Obviously, in Russia this revolution was much sharper, when it took place as late as the 1990s.

For comparison, it is necessary to have a quick look at the history of western consumerism. How did the consumerist revolution happen in the West?

Consumerism and Rationality in Europe

Consumerism has been defined in various ways. In some sense it can be considered an eternal phenomenon. Human beings have always been prone to acquire an abundance of goods which satisfy their primary, physical, or secondary, social, needs. Moreover, like many other species, homo sapiens obviously is also prone to hoarding. The possession of unnecessary amounts of goods is a resource, which is not only a guarantee against future need, but also an asset in social life.

But what about the propensity to obtain expensive and unnecessary goods; that is, the desire for luxury? Ancient scriptures such as the Bible, Greek authors like Aristotle or Roman ones like Tacitus provide ample testimony that the temptations of luxury were understood to pose a challenge to human

---

27   Hessler (2004), 11–12.
28   Randall (2008), 158.

virtue. Human frailty would frequently lead to indulgence in luxury, which would rapidly cause the ruination of both peoples and states. It was no accident that most states used to restrict the trade in luxury goods. This happened even in the 20th century.[29]

Consumerism, if understood as the propensity of an individual to acquire unnecessary goods, is *prima facie* not rational. Such a mindset used to be considered evil. The concept of luxury itself points to something that is not necessary, something that is too much, superfluous.

Luxury has traditionally been understood as the decay of mores. Seen from the Aristotelian point of view, indulgence in luxury, like all vices, is a deviation from the golden mean, *aurea mediocritas*. An excess of any good thing becomes in the end a bad thing. All developed and prosperous societies can at some time be expected to indulge in periods of excess consumption, which, in modern terms, can be understood as outbursts of consumerism. But it is also true that different kinds of goods may be classified as luxury goods depending on the productive capacity of the state in question.[30]

In times when labor productivity was low, the dearth of resources inescapably made periods of affluence short-lived, and moralists, like Tacitus in Roman times, kept condemning them. The hard reality behind such attitudes was that in a pre-modern society superfluous consumption was not sustainable; it really was the road to destruction.

The Bible told how in Egypt seven prosperous years were followed by seven years of need. Every peasant would, in principle, understand the wisdom of this rule at any moment of history. Nature has always taught the peasant that a good harvest is not a reason to buy superfluous things. It's better to put the extra grain aside. Someday the harvest will be poor and if there are no savings, people will perish.

But consumerism can also be understood as a socially constructed mindset, not just as the mere indulgence in vice during weak moments of society by weak human beings. It has been maintained that the mere availability of goods did not cause consumerism. It was no automatic companion of upper-class status.[31]

The emergence of modern European consumerism, in this sense, seems to have had many specific traits and can perhaps be considered an important innovation in history. Whatever the causes, it happened that in Europe, after the industrial revolution, both a new abundance of goods and a new propensity to

---

29   Ibid., 161–162.

30   Ibid., 31–32.

31   Stearns (2001), 2–4.

consume developed simultaneously. Increased labor productivity made new levels of consumption permanently sustainable and a permanent readiness to obtain more and more commodities of secondary importance emerged.[32]

The Birth of Consumerism as a Moral Revolution

It has been pointed out that this new attitude towards things, that is, commodities was, in fact, a moral revolution. Ironically, it spread first in England, where the protestant ethic had also created a vibrant Capitalism by means of preaching abstinence from instant gratification. Strangely enough, it proved possible to move from puritan asceticism to consumerist hedonism within a short time-span. This apparently puzzling phenomenon has been explained by the emergence of Romanticism. Romanticism was the all-important cultural phenomenon which put the individual self and its satisfaction at the center of attention.[33]

Colin Campbell, who has stressed the importance of Romanticism for the birth of consumerism, believes that even the teachings of social philosophers as influential as Adam Smith or Jeremy Bentham were, after all, secondary. He believes that the real conduct of people is hardly guided by the theories of social philosophers. For Campbell, utility and hedonism are different things; the former, unlike the latter, being compatible with asceticism.[34]

This distinction seems plausible. Utilitarianism, as a mentality had a rationalist basis. It put an accent on the usefulness of things, but did not necessarily give license to plain hedonism, which could easily have degenerated into non-productive parasitism.

The 18th century, also known as the Age of Reason in Europe, was the Age of Utility in social philosophy. As Adam Smith pointed out, the wealth of nations did not stem from the possession of precious metals, but from industriousness. Work was essential for the creation of value. This was one of Adam Smith's most important ideas, which Karl Max would also adopt as an axiomatic truth. In the USSR it became the official truth for over seventy years and it still had its proponents quite recently.[35]

The idea of economic dynamism, the possibility of augmenting the sum total of commodities, also stemmed from Smith and was something new and

---

32   Judt (2005), 324–353.

33   Campbell (2005), 202–227.

34   Ibid., 28.

35   *Kansantaloustiede* (1960), Chapter 3.

revolutionary. This idea made it possible to think about constantly rising consumption, and, by implication, it also granted new dignity to the worker, the producer, who had earlier been confined to a humble role. Traditionally, the lot of the producer had lacked prestige.

The French Revolution was an uprising of 'useful' people against people who were considered to be unfairly privileged. Those formerly honored uppermost layers of society could now be deemed worthless. They were useless because they were *unproductive*. It has been pointed out that the 'third estate' originally denoted something residual: those who were neither clergy, nor noble nor serfs. The spokesman of the rebellious French people, the Abbé Sièyes in his famous pamphlet 'What is the Third Estate?' characteristically answered that it was 'nothing' but that it wanted to be 'something'.[36]

It also deserves attention that the ideas of the third estate regarding the rightful order of things were now believed by them not to be just a matter of opinion, but a scientific fact stemming from the nature of things.

Earlier, such a conclusion would not have been possible. Still less had it been self-evident that the productive layers of society deserved respect, or that they could be given the reins of state. As Plato had written, they were not the head of society, but its hands and feet.

Eighteenth-century French society had both a sizable and potentially significant contingent of people who were socially and politically confined to the institutional limits of the third estate. Outstanding thinkers had created a philosophy which argued that 'utility' was something basic in society and that production, the kind of activity which the third estate was pursuing, was, in fact, the most important occupation, if not the highest calling of humanity. Accordingly, the natural order of things required that those who were useful for the material well-being of society, the representatives of the third estate should be held in the highest esteem and have the corresponding degree of political power. 'Take away the privileged orders, and the nation is not smaller but greater ... (the) privileged class is assuredly foreign to the nation by its do-nothing uselessness', the Abbé Sièyes proclaimed.[37]

Later, the workers' movement, especially Marxist social democracy and its Bolshevik offshoot always depicted the 'working people' as 'useful', while the consuming classes, capitalists, clergy and soldiers were idling on the backs of the exploited working classes. The working classes, in Marxist jargon, were not just the workers, the proletarians, who were exploited by the capitalist indus-

---

36   Cit. by Gouldner (1970), 62.
37   Ibid., 63.

try. To be sure, the proletariat was understood to be the vanguard class, the decisive element, whose historical mission was to overthrow the old order.

However, the sphere of 'working' people also encompassed the majority of the peasantry, whose consciousness was restricted and distorted by their social status, but who were also a socially 'useful' element and exploited by the 'useless' categories of the landlords, the bourgeoisie, and even the more prosperous peasants. Marx spoke about the 'idiocy of rural life',[38] referring to the pre-modern and pre-capitalist form of living outside the modern market system of production and class-struggle. It could be added that the peasantry was also outside the sphere of modern consumerism.

To define something as 'useful', obviously presupposes some idea of value, which is promoted by activity defined as 'useful'. From the 18th century defining something as 'useful' was understood in terms of a person's or a class's productive contribution to the material well-being of society. The flourishing business of the industrialist and the merchant obviously added something to the common welfare and the sum total of happiness could only be greater if the consuming privileged classes were not there, taking their undeserved share of production.

The term 'utilitarianism' was coined by Jeremy Bentham and James Mill, who systematized some of the central social ideas of the Enlightenment. The doctrine was later developed by John Stuart Mill and it may be said that most moral philosophy in the West ever since has just been a modification of the central idea of utilitarianism, 'the greatest happiness of the greatest number', pleasure and pain being understood as the prime movers of human conduct.[39]

Rational Hedonism as the Ethical Norm in the West

It has been pointed out that when determining the idea of goodness that which is good, utilitarianism amounts to supposing that 'desirable' simply refers to the thing or quality that is being desired. Thus it does not really tackle the ethical problem, which might be formulated as 'what should be desired?' In this sense, utilitarianism seems to give free rein to hedonism. 'Pushpin (a children's game) is better than poetry' if it brings more pleasure, Jeremy Bentham famously remarked.[40]

---

38   Marx and Engels (1848): (1–14).

39   Mill (1863).

40   See: <http://www.ucl.ac.uk/Bentham-Project/who/quotations>.

The central idea of utilitarianism can be said to be the rational defense of hedonism and, consequently, of the phenomenon that we call consumerism. The principle of utilitarianism has by and by become deeply attached to the mainstream moral thinking and practice of modern Europe. It can be maintained, as Alvin Gouldner does, 'that utilitarianism is and has been not just moral philosophy, but rather a real mentality and way of life, central part of the popular, everyday culture of the middle class'.[41] Its built-in license to promote consumerism has become more and more manifest during its two centuries old history. Nowadays it is the core of modern western everyday culture, the way of life of the dominant middle class.

Utilitarianism has also had another important cultural consequence, which is of interest here. Its primary concern was with the consequences of actions, not their intrinsic worth or intention. Here, utilitarian culture inevitably clashed with Christianity and diminished its credibility. Questions about human behavior became factual rather than moral issues.[42] Utility, the main thing pursued in modern middle-class society, is rather a matter of knowledge than morality.

Utilitarianism was at odds with traditional morals with their stress on conforming to given rules and established moral values. Facts and values became separated, morality divorced from law. Utilitarian morality was, first of all, a private matter. Law, on its part, registered the public interest, Alvin Gouldner remarks.[43]

The utilitarian revolution took place first in urban Europe, only later in the countryside, where most people went on living as they had always done. But by and by this new mentality sapped the roots of religion and its place in society. If duties did not derive from God, but from man's own nature, then religion became superfluous. Alvin Gouldner considers that, encountering utilitarian culture, Christianity 'contracted a terminal illness', and it was no surprise when Nietzsche pronounced the death of God at the end of the 19th century.[44]

Modern western society became more and more de-moralized, indifferent to moral issues in everyday life. This process did not take place in traditional societies. Marxist societies were left outside this development.

---

41 Gouldner (1970), 62.
42 Ibid., 67.
43 Ibid.
44 Ibid., 66–72.

The Moralizing Anti-Hedonist Heritage of Marxism

Marxism was born within bourgeois utilitarian culture as a reaction against it. While claiming to be dictated by reason, Marxism in fact also exhibited a moralistic pathos, which strongly resembled the reactionary invectives of the premodern or early modern critics of Capitalism, like Thomas Carlyle.[45] Later this moralizing anti-bourgeois and, simultaneously, anti-consumerist Marxist legacy would become very important in the Soviet Union.

For the 19th-century bourgeoisie, the accent on 'usefulness', which it used in order to fight the nobility, soon became a two-edged sword. From the point of view of the bourgeoisie, the old privileged classes might have been superfluous and non-conducive to the general well-being, but what else could one say about the capitalist renter, who gathered immense profits with no direct contact whatever with the process of production?

Apace with the growth of the opulence of the bourgeois classes, blatant cases of bourgeois uselessness-cum-hedonism multiplied. The riches of a nation could now be wasted in spectacular spending by the bourgeois parvenus no less outrageously than by the nobles. The producer did not receive his fair share. In Russia, as well as elsewhere, the nobility rapidly lost its social position and its riches during the 19th century. The bourgeoisie became the new 'useless' class, which concentrated on consumption, while the producers had to abstain from it.[46]

Socialism, or the principle that society itself should own capital, looked like a morally tenable solution for millions of people and scores of diverse socialist doctrines in the 19th century. The moral ethos of Socialism remained much the same as that which had been used by the bourgeoisie against the nobles: social utility, not heredity, is important.

In general, socialists supposed that consumption had to be earned by a comparable contribution to the fundamental task of production. The place of honor in society belonged, in principle, not to the superfluous consumer, but to the producer. This, they believed, was not a matter of opinion, but a scientific fact, stemming from the nature of things. Karl Marx and Friedrich Engels, in their Communist Manifesto depicted the bourgeoisie as a vicious class: a wrongly privileged and morally dissolute layer in society, exploiting the real producers, namely, the workers.[47]

---

45   Carlyle (1843), 75–77.
46   Tian-Shanskaia (1993), 146–150.
47   Marx and Engels (1848).

It is worth noting that the bourgeois way of life was not depicted by Marx and Engels as simply the inescapable result of economic laws. It was also branded as dissolute and immoral. These unproductive people were hoarding riches by stealing the worth of the work and sweat of the true producers. It was they, who lived in vice and luxury, while the workers went hungry and lacked the most basic necessities of life.[48]

The founding fathers of 'Scientific Socialism' did not share the utilitarians' understanding towards satisfying any desire in principle, but displayed genuine moral indignation when describing the lifestyle of the bourgeoisie. This cast of mind resembles the pre-bourgeois world. Moral rules were not considered to be a private matter, but to stem from the nature of things. Obviously, while the founding fathers of Marxism shared the value theory of Adam Smith, they did not share the utilitarians' approach to morals. In fact, they attacked the emerging new bourgeois mentality with arguments which stemmed from the past, obviously supposing that they would prevail in the future.

In a way, Marxism was a mirror image of Christianity: the producer, that is, the majority in society created the riches, but was doomed to live without the opportunity to enjoy them. The working class was the collective great sufferer, but also the great liberator, who would restore righteousness.

The bourgeois were morally inferior, because their consumption was underserved. But was life in production intrinsically nobler than consumption? In the 19th century the question about the moral perils of consumerism for the workers did not become an issue of the day. The proletarian was treated just as a producer.[49]

Still a century ago it was obvious in any country that if the fruits of production were evenly distributed, there would hardly be any luxury at all. Probably the utilitarian ideal of the happiness of the greatest number would thus have been realized in the form of a decent subsistence for everybody and no surplus for anybody. It seems that this was more or less what was expected in Russia in 1917–1921.[50]

It can be asked, what 'affluence', before the invention of the 'affluent society' could have meant to the emerging socialist masses. The answer cannot be found in the discourse of the programs of the socialist parties. For instance, the Gotha (1875) and Erfurt (1891) programs of the German Social Democratic

---

48   Ibid.

49   Lafargue's argument concerning the right to be lazy is a notable exception to the rule, see: Lafargue (1883).

50   As suggested in Lenin's texts in that year, for instance, see: Lenin ([1918] 1964); Lenin ([1917] 1972); MacAuley (1991), 280–304.

Party only spoke about the abolition of privileges and exploitation. While it was stressed that labor was the only source of wealth[51] and that inherited wealth should be subject to progressive taxation,[52] no hint concerning the intrinsic value of this wealth as realized in consumption was given. Obviously this wealth, at least, was enjoyed by the wrong people for the time being and this state of affairs would continue until the socialist revolution restored the morally rightful order.

Wealth, which working people were creating, was stigmatized. It had been consumed up to now by the capitalists and their lackeys. In fact, that wealth had to be destroyed by repartition in order to satisfy the working people as V. I. Lenin understood.[53]

A socialist revolution would liquidate undeserved wealth, ignorance, superstition and religion. It would create better work conditions and a shorter working day, which would give time for self-development and social participation, including self-rule. The paradise of the Russian Bolsheviks as reflected in the party's programs of 1903 and 1919 gave no hint that an affluent society was the goal, even a remote goal. Rather, it had something of the austerity of the Old Testament, which condemned the children of Israel, who had begun to worship the golden calf as their idol.[54]

It is hardly possible to find any acceptance of hedonism or consumerism in these programs. The idea that critique of hedonism might apply to the masses may have sounded frivolous at a time, when people were starving. The workers, in the discourse of the Marxists, resembled a very ascetic and morally austere people.

However, according to Marx, there was a minority group of asocial members of the lower classes, which indulged in hedonism, drinking, gambling and prostitution. This depraved layer of poor people was the *Lumpenproletariat*. In his article *The 18thBrumaire of Louis Napoleon*, Marx depicts this motley crowd as being the 'refuse of all classes', including 'swindlers, confidence tricksters, brothel-keepers, rag-and-bone merchants, and other flotsam of society'. Unlike the proletariat proper, this element was vicious and easily bribed by the bourgeois.[55]

---

51   The Gotha Program ([1875] 1906), 617–619.

52   *The Erfurt Program* (1891).

53   Lenin: ([1917] 1972); Lenin (1971), 365–371.

54   *Programmy i ustavy* (1969), 19–62.

55   Marx ([1852] 1998), Chapter 7.

This is to say that, theoretically, lower-class origins were no guarantee against having a bourgeois (petty bourgeois) cast of mind and propensity for pleasure-seeking. Also in real life, in Russia in the revolutionary atmosphere of 1917 the epithet 'bourgeois' (*burzhui*) became a general word of abuse for moral outcasts, meaning 'something between 'scoundrel' and 'swine'. Such moral qualities as egotism and cupidity in the members of any class were called 'bourgeois'.[56]

Obviously, the Marxist heritage, especially in its Russian form, was in conflict with the utilitarian world view, which did not pay homage to moralism and considered the search of individual gratification to be in the nature of things.

The Bolsheviks claimed to be the only orthodox Marxists at the beginning of the 19th century. Obviously, the Marxist heritage really played a central role for the Bolshevik discourse, and the texts of the founding fathers were always treated with the utmost reverence by Lenin and his successors. In order to justify their claim of orthodoxy, the Bolsheviks were constantly obliged to refer to the founding fathers. Marx and Engels, for their part, always depicted the bourgeoisie as vicious and dissolute sybarites, while the proletarians were presented as champions of classical virtues.

Among the central proletarian virtues were tenacity and endurance. If the proletarians wanted to take riches away from the bourgeois bloodsuckers, who did not deserve them, it did not mean that they aspired to the sweet life themselves, if one is to believe the masterpieces of Bolshevik literature. Ostrovsky's 'How the Steel Was Tempered' (*Kak zakalialas' stal'*) was a classic, loved and learned by generations of Soviet youth. The author was careful to show that the proletarians, unlike the representatives of other classes, always personified or embodied high moral standards. They were neither indulgent hedonists nor calculating utilitarians, but fiery soldiers of their cause. In fact, paradoxically, they very much looked like puritan moralists.[57]

Their mirror image was the bourgeoisie, who worshipped the false god of mammon and was driven by self-interest. This was something of a paradox in a philosophy which claimed to be materialist. In principle, after all, it was not morals, but the logic of capitalist production which gave rise to the opulence of the rich and to the poverty of the workers.

Why the proletarians were supposed to be righteous, is not clear, but, of course, at least the workers were not rich, and were not likely to be. Therefore,

---

56   Figes and Kolonitskii (1999), 178–79.

57   Ostrovsky, Nikolai (////): How the Steel Was Tempered. Available at: <http://www.cpa.org. au/resources/cpa-presents/how-the-steel-was-tempered-book-1.pdf>. Ostrovsky (1972).

in a capitalist society, they did not even have the opportunity of being corrupted by luxury. Marx also refers to the class-struggle of the proletariat, which 'was boiled in the kettle of the factory'. This experience had taught the workers to value collective and in fact, objective thinking, which made possible the unselfish solidarity and endurance of the proletarians.

Alvin Gouldner is probably right in considering that in the western world, utilitarianism become the mentality and way of life of most people, even the proletariat. This was perfectly suited for the growth of consumerism.

On the other hand, history would make Marxism the official philosophy of Russia for over seventy years. This certainly meant that consumerism would be regarded *prima facie* as something very suspect.

But Marxism was only one of the many currents of the Russian intellectual tradition, which disapproved of utilitarianism and hedonism.

'Russia's Specific Path of Development' and the Question of Consumerism

In Russia, a country with almost no bourgeoisie in the western sense, there developed a domestic anti-bourgeois tradition, which became quite influential and co-existed with the local varieties of Marxism and other kinds of Socialism.

Usually this tradition has been associated with the *narodniks,* also called the populists. This is true, but the anti-bourgeois pathos was not restricted to this group. It was preached by many more social thinkers, from conservative Slavophiles to liberal authors and violent revolutionaries.

Alexander Herzen can be considered the founding father of the antibourgeois tradition in Russia. As Adam Walicki points out, his attitudes in this matter stemmed from his aristocratic background rather than from his pity for the martyred people.[58]

Herzen loathed the bourgeoisie with an aristocratic contempt as a class of vulgar upstarts. He was against capitalist development in Russia precisely because he expected that Russia, if it became a capitalist country would transform the hitherto unspoiled Russian peasants into wretched proletarians and, thereafter, into a bourgeoisie, which was no better from the moral point of view.[59]

---

58   Walicki (1969), 11.
59   Ibid., 11–12.

Unlike the *narodniks*, Herzen expected that Capitalism would ultimately yield an increased and growing level of material welfare, but, he argued, this would not be worthwhile, as it would come at a terrible price.

A world of plenty did not mean a good world, for cheap goods and standardized consumption would be obtained at the cost of quality: 'Everything – the theatre, holiday making, books, pictures, clothes, everything has gone down in quality and gone up terribly in numbers. The crowd ...is bursting through all the dams, overflowing and flooding everything; it is content with anything and can never have enough'.[60]

Like Herzen, the *narodniks* also wanted to save the Russian peasant from the perils of Capitalism, which was threatening to annihilate his morally superior way of life. The Russian peasant, as the prominent *narodnik* Nikolai Mikhailovsky thought, lived a life, which was 'poor, but full'. Being economically self-sufficient, he was an independent and 'total', 'all-round' man, liberated from the machinery of Capitalism and its division of labor.[61] Capitalism, Mikhailovsky thought, with its 'system of maximum production' could not make even the rich happy, because it set in motion a frantic race of desires and needs without offering any real possibility of satisfying them.[62]

Like Herzen and the *narodniks*, the early Slavophiles of the 1840s were also appalled by the prospect of an arising Capitalism, because of its obsession with things material. For Ivan Kireevsky, as Abbot Gleason concludes, the western world was ridden by 'the cluster of qualities which we associate with the rising entrepreneurial middle class: greed, low cunning, the dirty business of politics, 'enrichissez-vous'.[63]

For the Russian anti-bourgeois *intelligentsia*, the growing Capitalism of the West thus meant spiritual decline. Somehow, Russia should be saved from it. America, the new world, where remnants of the past did not restrain new social developments, became a kind of dystopia for the anti-bourgeois Russian *intelligentsia*.

America became familiar to Russians largely through the works of Tocqueville. As Abbott Gleason has shown, for the Russian *intelligentsia*, it became the quintessential example of the perils of modernization, 'the Republic of Humbug', as Petr Lavrov called it.[64] Of all the western countries, America came to embody extreme individualism, greed and vulgarity for people as different

---

60   Cit. by: Walicki (1969), 12.
61   Walicki (1969), 53.
62   Ibid., 59.
63   Gleason (1972), 163.
64   Gleason (1992), 12.

as Feodor Dostoevsky, Vladimir Korolenko, Petr Lavrov, Konstantin Aksakov and Maxim Gorky. Paradoxically, the idea that material comfort was the highest goal of man was deeply resented by the Russian *intelligenty,* who struggled for the freedom and happiness of the poor.[65]

While it is obvious that a prominent part of the Russian *intelligentsia* was afraid of the development of Capitalism in Russia and such modernization, which would bring about the dissolution of the Russian peasant commune, one may still ask, if this meant opposing consumerism in the modern sense. Of course, the question is anachronistic, because the consumerism of the affluent society did not exist and could not be foreseen. However, the Slavophiles and the *narodniks* could foresee a world where the 'organic' unity and collective way of life of the Russian village would be replaced by a society of individuals, whose relations to other human beings would be determined by money and not by morals. For them, material welfare was no substitute for the spiritual damage, which would be caused by a way of life, which was determined by the search for money.

Political and social thinkers seldom determine the thinking, let alone the practical way of life, of the broad masses. How did Russian peasants, the large majority of the Russian people, actually see the modern, urban way of life, which was emerging in Russia in the 19th and 20th centuries?

Traditional Ideas Concerning Luxury and Opulence in a Land of Peasants

It seems that every traditional society has disapproved of luxury, that is, superfluous consumption. Sometimes it has even been sanctioned. Such opposition to luxury had religious grounds in Europe, but mercantilist considerations have also played their part in various countries.[66]

The Dictionary of the Russian Academy published at the end of the 18th century defined luxury (*roskosh*) as the 'excessive satisfaction of alleged (*mnimykh*) needs, preferring things in rarity and paying much for them'. Luxury was said to be the consequence of and sometimes the reason for decay of morals. It was also the reason for the ruin of states, and raised the level of prices.[67]

Of course, the very concept of luxury presupposes that it is possible somehow to assess how much is enough and what is superfluous. At any given time,

---

65   Gleason (1992), 4–6, 9–10.
66   Stearns (2001), 2–14.
67   'Roskosh'. *Slovar' Academi Rossiiskoi* (1789–1794), 164.

it also has to be asked what is too much *for whom*? The Russian encyclopedia of Brockhaus and Efron in 1890 stated that luxury was that part of the belongings (*obstanovki*) of a person which did not conform to the ethical and economic interests of a certain person at a certain time.[68] The Malaia Sovetskaia Entsiklopediia of 1930 also noted that items of luxury at one time may later become necessities, like electric light. In class societies luxury items were used only by members of the ruling classes. In the Soviet Union, luxury was being fought by means of restrictions like higher prices and taxes.[69]

Obviously, lustre and pomp had in past centuries been considered right and proper for tsars and nobles, for churches and even for high-ranking members of the clergy when performing their offices. On the other hand, they became sinful and perverse when usurped by the wrong people, especially by the productive classes. According to mercantilism, the wealth of the whole nation was in danger if the use of expensive imported items spread widely among the lower classes. This had been the argument against conspicuous consumption by the masses of society not only in Russia, but also in Scandinavia during the 18th century, and analogous views were common throughout Europe.

In addition to the rational condemnation of luxury, there were also religious and moral arguments. Had not Jesus Christ warned that it was virtually impossible for a rich man to enter heaven? 'It is easier for a camel to go through the eye of a needle than for someone who is rich to enter the kingdom of God'.[70] In the Bible, Mammon was presented as an idol which diverted man from the worship of God.

Orthodox Christianity laid stress on the simple life and abstinence. Everybody was to fast several times during the year and the saintly ascetic was respected as the exemplary Christian. Abstinence from gratification of the cravings of the body manifested a person's care for his soul. The flesh was a source of temptation and it was called feeble in the Bible. In its aversion to hedonism the Orthodox faith was, in principle, not unlike other varieties of Christianity. However, it can be pointed out that unlike Protestantism, it stressed fasting and other forms of asceticism as *podvizhnichestvo* – a fight of faith. Many popular saints of the Eastern Church were ascetics.

As regards Russia, it is important to note that up to the 20th century, Russia was a country of peasants. Amongst the rural masses, religion was a serious

---

68   'Roskosh'. *Entsiklopedicheskii slovar' Brockhausa i Efrona* (1890).
69   'Roskosh'. *Malaia Sovetskaia Entsiklopediia* (1930).
70   Mark 10:25.

factor, and in Russia the peasants were a more dominant social component than in any other major European country.[71]

Was there any remarkable difference between Russia and the West as concerns criteria of the 'proper' degree of material well-being and luxury? It has been suggested that there was.

The Russian peasant has had a reputation of having been extremely simple as regards appearances or daily comfort.

In the deep past, at least, remaining poor could make sense as a survival strategy. Nikolai Kostomarov gave a historical example: 'The Russian of that time (i.e. the time of Ivan the Terrible), if he had any surplus, tried to look poorer than he was. He was afraid of putting his money in circulation in order to avoid becoming the object of denunciations … the Russian lived as he could, he earned the resources for life as he could, always being in danger of being robbed, cheated, or ruined by treason. Himself, he was not slow to take notice of the dangers which loomed in front of him, and he also cheated, robbed, and, where he could, he lived at the cost of his nearest in order to ensure his always fragile existence. That is why the Russian excelled in untidiness in his house, in laziness at work, and in relations with people in treachery, perfidy and heartlessness'.[72]

Of course, Ivan the Terrible's reign was in the 16th century and it is hard to prove that it left a permanent legacy for centuries to come. At the time of collectivization the same strategy could have been effective once again.

One remarkable document from Ivan IV's time, the *Domostroi,* also warned of luxury, referring to both religious and practical considerations: 'someone who does not consider his means …and control his expenses, who imitates other people, living beyond his means by borrowing or acquiring ill-gotten gains, will find his honor turn to great dishonor. Such a person will find himself subject to ridicule and scorn; in bad times no one will help him. His behavior is a sin before God and deserves the reproaches of others'.[73] The *Domostroi* was a handbook for the potentates of society.

As regards the mentality which Kostomarov described, it had many things in common with the serf's plight in general. The serf also knew that any of his riches that became known to his landlord could soon be taken away. Thus, it was better to look poor, stupid and submissive in order to keep one's livelihood at a reasonable level. In the early 20th century, the legacy of serfdom was still far more alive in Russia than it was in other European countries.

---

71   Lewin (1985), 49–56.

72   Cit. by: Kostomarov ([1874] 1996), 302.

73   The Domostroi (1995), 123.

The myth about the Russian peasant which was developed in the 19th century declared that he was both a real *Christian* and a born collectivist. The main virtue for an *Orthodox Christian* is humility. The Slavophiles considered the Russian peasants to be exemplary in this respect.[74] The Slavophiles were keen to take notice of the Russian peasant's aversion to luxury: Ivan Kireevsky asserted that the Russian respected more the rags of a beggarly and weak-minded man of God than the golden brocade of a courtier. In his opinion, luxury used to penetrate Russia as an infection from the neighbors. People apologized for it; they succumbed to it as a vice, and always felt its unlawfulness, not only in religious terms, but also in moral and social ones.[75]

The Slavophiles were romantics, who were prone to idealize the peasants. But the peasants' aversion to luxury seems to have been real. At least it can be noticed that the peasant uprisings in Russia during the Revolution of 1905–1907 were notoriously vandalistic. Several thousand manors were burnt and vandalized. The same kind of conduct was widespread in 1917.[76] This may suggest that the lower classes had no aspirations of someday becoming like the upper classes. The void between them was too deep.

It can also be pointed out that the majority of the Russian peasants, up to the beginning of the 20th century, even to the early 1930s, lived in the *mir*, where land was repartitioned every now and then.[77] This gave rise to a remarkable degree of leveling. It also happened that the whole collective was responsible for paying taxes. This may also have worked against individual peasants' will to excel by conspicuous consumption.

Peasants who showed signs of becoming well-to do were resented by their neighbors, some studies tell us. Arson was traditionally used against neighbors that were seen to be flourishing too much. Olga Semionovna Tian-Shanskaia, who observed Russian village in the 1890s, also argues that the peasant practically never had money. If he got some, he drank it. The peasants believed that 'it is a sin to pile up money'.[78] This kind of propensity to consume instead of saving, however, can hardly be called consumerism in the modern sense of the word.

---

74   Riasanovsky (1965), 120.
75   Cit. by: Riasanovsky (1965), 122.
76   Figes (1996), 182, 520–536.
77   Lewin (1985), 79–86.
78   Tian-Shanskaia (1993), 144, 153.

By the end of the 19th century, however, we are told that well-to-do peasants could show off their wealth by wearing expensive clothes. The fashions to be found in the towns also began to exert their influence in the village.[79]

Some ethnographers of the late 19th century tell us that the well-to-do peasants were respected by the less prosperous villagers.[80] In turbulent times, however, such as the Civil War and collectivization, the wrath of the poor peasants was directed towards the well-to-do peasants, the kulaks, whose wealth was expropriated by their neighbors.

Under Bolshevik power, dekulakization (*raskulachivanie*) was certainly organized policy and does not necessarily prove that the Russian peasants had a special propensity for leveling.

The anti-kulak campaigns in Russia, however, seem to have few parallels in modern history. Russia's specific circumstances may have created a mentality where riches were understood to belong to the whole collective by right. One, who had hoarded riches for himself, was understood to have done so at the cost of others. He was sometimes called a *miroed*, the 'eater' of the *mir* – the common good.

The Russian peasant way of life does not seem to have had the élan of consumerism in spite of the tradition of *otkhodnichestvo* – going to town for seasonal work. By and by, more and more peasants went to town to work and also began to settle in the town, but as we know, until the 1930s, Russia remained very rural. After 1917 modernization of the countryside in fact took several steps backward, and even the *mir* was reinstated. It was liquidated only at the time of collectivization, in 1929–1932.[81]

As Alexander Chayanov's theory of the peasant economy presumed, the peasant's consciousness was not capitalistic. He tended to produce just 'enough' for his own needs and was not interested in producing surpluses.[82]This habit or tendency was to be acutely felt later on, in the Soviet economy of the late 1920s, when the peasants stopped selling their grain.[83]

Given the social structure and the pace of social development in Russia, it may be concluded that the mentality of Russia's toiling masses in 1917 and even much later, was more alien to bourgeois hedonism and utilitarianism, than was the case in most of Europe, which was more urbanized.

---

79   Firsov and Kiseleva (1993), 89–91.

80   Ibid.

81   Lewin (1985), 17–18, 86–87.

82   See Chayanov (1986); Shanin (1985), 84–86.

83   Nove (1992), 146–152.

But Russia did not consist of just peasants and the tsar. There were also the nobles and the townsmen, amongst them both merchants and the *meshchane*. The latter can be described as the petty bourgeoisie. They also were understood to be the quintessential champions of consumerist appetites.

It goes without saying that consumerism in its early form also arrived in Russian cities in the 19th century. In St. Petersburg and in Moscow, more and more 'unnecessary' items of consumption were available and new department stores were opened.[84] The population of the cities multiplied and a new kind of consumer appeared. He was neither the rural *barin*, nor the traditional urban *kupets*. In the eyes of the radical *intelligentsia*, he stood out by his lack of refinement and by his pretensions in trying to look respectable.

The term *meshchane,* originally denoted city-dwellers who were neither peasants nor merchants or nobles. These people were given the honor of becoming the symbol of bourgeois vices, avarice being the worst of them. The Russian antibourgeois tradition began with Alexander Herzen and it was soon adopted by the whole of the radical *intelligentsia*. It was not only the *narodniks*, Slavophiles and socialists who professed it, so too did the Russia's great writers from Leo Tolstoy and Feodor Dostoevsky to Anton Chekhov, Maxim Gorky and others.[85] The Russian *intelligentsia*, unlike their French colleagues, did not despise the toiling masses, but adored an idealized variety of them. For the *narodniks*, the peasants even deserved adoration, while others, like Gorky and the Bolsheviks preferred the workers and loathed the peasants. But all agreed that the *meshchanin* was the moral inferior.

Obviously, the 'ideal' *meshchanin*, whom the *intelligenty* demonized, was a bearer of the modern, utilitarian cast of mind. He was the practical utilitarian, who could pay lip service to morality and common good, but would, in fact, pursue his own selfish goals. The *meshchanin* was, in fact, the man of the future, whom neither the socialists nor the Slavophiles would tolerate in Russian society.

The Antibourgeois Tradition in Early Twentieth Century Russian Culture

Maxim Gorky's views on this issue are illuminating. Gorky, the future pope of socialist realism, was already at the beginning of the 20th century one of the great names of Russian literature. He was also genuinely popular and famous

---

84   Hilton (2012), 83–87, 132–143.
85   See: Vihavainen (2004), 18, and the sources mentioned there.

for his revolutionary feats. According to a contemporary survey, even workers widely read Gorky. Tolstoy and Gorky were the two most popular writers several years before the Bolshevik Revolution (Read 1990:31).[86]

For Maxim Gorky, the struggle against philistinism was always a major theme, even the main one. His early play 'The Philistines' (*Meshchane*) was a major success. Before the Bolshevik Revolution, Gorky had also written essays on this topic and engaged in polemic a couple of times, in 1905 and 1908–1909. They deserve some closer examination.

In his essay 'Notes on Philistinism' (*Zametki o meshchanstve*) of 1905, Gorky defined and described the philistine in several ways and gave some concrete examples of representatives of this quality. Philistinism, he wrote 'is the cast of mind of a representative of the contemporary commanding classes'. The main characteristic traits of philistines were a morbidly developed sense of property, an intense craving for inward and outward tranquility, a gloomy fear of everything that in one way or another could disturb that tranquility, and a constant urge to explain away, for oneself, everything that could disturb one's precious balance of mind. This 'explaining away' was necessary in order to rationalize one's own ways, one's passivity in the struggle of life.[87]

Gorky's concepts were somewhat unorthodox from a Marxist point of view: for him the petty bourgeois was not just a would-be big bourgeois but a representative of the 'commanding classes' and he also had property. He had created the state in order to guard his property, yet, on the other hand, property could guard him against the state.[88]

In fact, it seems that Gorky is using the word petty bourgeois (*meshchanin*) here as a synonym of the spiritual qualities of both the philistine and the bourgeoisie as a social group, which comprises both small holders and big proprietors. Representatives of the petty bourgeoisie, like the protagonist of Gorky's novel 'Foma Gordeev', were morally crippled by their property, which separated them from the *narod*.[89]

It seems, however, that for Gorky, the oppressor was not so much the inert bourgeois class as such, but the sinister force of philistinism, which kept the 'people' in its grip and diverted it from the revolutionary struggle. This force can be interpreted as the new utilitarian world view, which was practically oriented and remained complacent towards the moralizing of the *intelligentsia*.

---

86   Read (1990), 31.
87   Gorky (1953), 341–344.
88   Ibid.
89   Gorky (1970a), 214–224.

In fact, Gorky argued, the philistines were Lilliputians and the *people* (*narod*) were Gulliver, tied down with threads of lies and deception. When the giant awakened in 1905, the philistines ran to the forefront and declared themselves the victors, as representatives of the people.

Gorky's extremist moralizing and his apparently unwavering faith in the necessity of a drastic final solution to the philistine question pleased Lenin, who gave a positive appraisal of Gorky's views. The philistine (*meshchanin*), for the early Gorky, was a person, who lacked radicalism and was afraid of the ultimate doomsday which was to settle the scores between tortured and torturers.

In another essay Gorky developed further the portrait of the *meshchanin*.[90] Here the philistine was not just a representative of the 'commanding classes', and not even just a political being. For Gorky, the philistine was apparently an eternal principle: the philistine represented the inferior part of man. He was the quintessential consumer, who could not be a creator. Only by overcoming philistinism would it be possible to emancipate *Man* (*Chelovek*, with a capital letter), who, when stripped of the filth of philistinism, embodied all that was brave and great in a human being.

'Man –chelovek–, the conqueror of the earth, wrote Gorky, burns in the darkness of life like a lighthouse, like a flower of fire, born of thought. 'Man' – with a capital letter – burns bright and walks in front of the people and shows them the way to perfection. But far from him, carefully looking for his every step ... comes after him the real lord of the whole earth, the sensible and respectable philistine'.

The hands and feet of the philistine were bound with the chains of property, Gorky declared, and all the time he was trying to bind himself still more tightly. The philistine was sensible, he did not know what inner freedom was, and his small heart was full of yearning for comfort, rest, nourishment and respect. He wanted to fill his stomach and his soul, and in this he saw his happiness.

The wretched philistine followed 'Man' from afar and utilized his accomplishments. When 'Man' conquered fire from the skies the philistine lit his bedroom lamp with this fire. If 'Man' explored the essence of sound, the philistine used his work to make a gramophone for his entertainment. The cryptic x-rays, which 'Man' had discovered, he used for guarding his property. In everything, the philistine made the existence of 'Man' useful or entertaining for himself. He himself liked stable truths, behind which he could hide from new currents of Thought.[91]

---

90   Gorky (1970b), 383–384.
91   Ibid.

As we can see, for Gorky, 'Man', with a capital M was no utilitarian. He was both the divine creator and the paragon of virtues. In his novel 'The Mother' (*Mat'*) (1906), Gorky depicted conscious proletarians as the *intelligenty* of a new era, as non-philistine heroes, who forsake the petty-bourgeois life and dedicate everything to the great cause of the liberation of Man.

Gorky expected that the rising proletarian 'Man' would bring about a renaissance of morals, which the bourgeois philistines had destroyed. Gorky considered that not only greed and fraudulence, but also any kind of excessive or queer sexuality, were signs of bourgeois decadence. They belonged to the bourgeoisie, which was to cede its place in world history to the proletariat.[92]

The worst element in Russian society, from Gorky's point of view, however, was the peasantry. In his opinion, peasants were the quintessential philistines, who cared only for their petty property. They were the very opposite of culture.[93] The torch of culture was born by the proletariat. No wonder that Gorky hailed collectivization, which would emancipate the peasantry by liberating them from the burden of petty property.[94] Peasants cannot be equated with consumers, rather the contrary. In Gorky's eyes, however, they belonged essentially to the same category because of their allegedly excessive interest for the material sphere of life.

The ethos of this 'anti-materialist' moralizing, which was so typical for the early Marxists and, later, for the Bolsheviks, can also be found in other moral teachers and writers of the late 19th and early 20th century.

Leo Tolstoy is generally recognized to be one of the greatest writers of all times. His novels bear witness to an artistic and moral genius, which is so multi-sided that it is almost impossible even to classify him as a representative of this or that literary tradition. Tolstoy was no 'hedgehog', but a 'fox' as Sir Isaiah Berlin said. A fox knows innumerable things, while a hedgehog knows only one great trick.[95]

With all due respect to Berlin's general conclusion, it is also true that Tolstoy, the prophet, who in his old age sought the charms of the simple life, was also a great proponent of egalitarianism and asceticism in late imperial Russia. Tolstoy's later pamphlets in particular, which put him into sharp conflict both with the state and the church preached against all kind of luxury and dissolution. It was these texts and not the epic novels, which made Tolstoy one of the most popular moral teachers of the era.

---

92   Gorky (1931).
93   Gorky (1919), 172–173; Gorky (1923).
94   Gorky (1932), 26–27.
95   Berlin (1982), 22–23.

The good and worthy life, for Tolstoy, was the simple life of the peasant, who worked in the fields and did not hoard unnecessary things. Individualism, obsession with material riches, as well as sexual dissolution was, for Tolstoy, the origin of evil and of suffering. Epicureanism was evil and the way to salvation went through renunciation of personal welfare.[96]

No wonder that Tolstoy has been considered as one of the most important harbingers of the Russian Revolution of 1917. Even Lenin recognized his importance in this respect.[97]

The revolutionary process of 1917 was triggered by the World War I, but in the background we can see the sharp conflict between the lifestyles of the rich and the poor, between those who concentrated on consumption and those who produced. This conflict was probably greater in Russia than in many other countries and it was probably sharpened by the fact that a demographic explosion produced ever greater numbers of rural poor, who lived near a subsistence minimum at precisely the same time that a new wave of consumerism swept over the great cities of Russia.[98]

---

96   Walicki (1979), 329–333.
97   Lenin ([1909] 1963), 353.
98   Nove (1992), 10–16.

CHAPTER 2

Consumerism and the Soviet Project

Timo Vihavainen

The Ideology: Focus on Leveling and Producing

In his moralizing pictures, William Hogarth showed how a decent young man was turned into a 'rake' and how an innocent maiden become a whore. In both cases, glorious promise was turned into nasty practice and in the end the protagonists died in disgrace. The Bolsheviks began with a modest reform program in 1903, veered into over-zealous leveling at the time of the revolution and then tried to reinstate a kind of rational consumerism. Their rule ended when there was nothing more to consume.

The first program of the Bolshevik Party from 1903 concentrated on practical demands, concerning the main political and material rights of the workers. It greatly resembled other social democratic programs. From the point of view of the 21th century it looks rather modest and even realistic. Its most conspicuous points, concerning suffrage, working conditions and social insurance are commonplace in many countries of modern Europe.[1]

The next program, from the year 1919, which was supposed to give the general outlines for the construction of a socialist society, was much more radical and utopian. For instance, it proclaimed the idea of total leveling, although higher wages for specialists were to be permitted for some time.[2] The tenor of that party program was very production-oriented and egalitarian. It also stressed everybody's duty to take part in administration.[3] Speaking about wages and the distribution of goods, it stressed the importance of leveling and the distribution of goods and services free of charge.[4] Affluent society was not yet the order of the day, liquidation of privilege was more important.

To be sure, even before World War II, the Bolsheviks did not aspire to build just an egalitarian society for its own sake. Apart from those almost puritan and egalitarian goals, which were presented in the Bolshevik Party's program in 1919 (which was in force until 1961), more refined ideas concerning the

---

1 *Programmy i ustavy* (1969), 19–28.
2 Ibid., 52.
3 Ibid., 41.
4 Ibid., 57.

© KONINKLIJKE BRILL NV, LEIDEN, 2016 | DOI 10.1163/9789004303973_003

growth of the human personality in the future socialist society were popular within the Bolshevik Party.

Maxim Gorky was just one prominent representative of a curious current which predicted the emergence of a Nietzschean superman out of the ranks of the proletariat. Humanity would reach new heights when emancipated from the capitalist yoke. Also Nikolai Bukharin and Leo Trotsky had such ideas.[5]

This kind of high-brow speculation may have had little popularity among the mass of Bolshevik supporters. But resentment against 'bourgeois' instincts or *meshchanstvo* (philistinism) was obviously shared by both the leaders and the masses.

According to Marxist logic, it was concluded that because of his class position, the small proprietor was likely to be a *meshchanin* (philistine). Obviously he did not want the revolution, because he had in this world other things to lose besides his chains, as Marx famously said. The proletarian for his part had a different class nature.

For some reason, Marx and Engels seemed to believe that proletarians did not even want to become proprietors; instead, they wanted to annihilate the whole institution of private property. So, in a certain sense, the ideal proletarian, whom Marx depicted as a paragon of virtue, was also a hero of virtue, who did not indulge in the imminent gratification of his needs – a quality considered to be typical of the underclass.[6]

The ideal Bolshevik was not supposed to be a utilitarian calculator of pain and pleasure. Paradoxically, although he was supposed to be a materialist par excellence, he had to keep his soul above material things. In Russia, the classics of socialist realism depicted the proletarian as the moral opposite of the selfish *meshchanin*. Maxim Gorky demonstrated this in several of his works, notably in the novel 'Mother' (*Mat'*), which became the great standard work of socialist realism. In the novel, the hero is a young worker, Pavel Vlasov, who puts his personal advantages at the service of the revolutionary cause. His personality resembles that of a Christian hero of faith.

Other exemplary Bolshevik heroes of Soviet literature like all *Komsomol* youths' idol, Pavel Korchagin in Nikolai Ostrovsky's cult novel 'How Steel was Tempered' (*Kak zakalialas' stal'*) or Gleb and Dasha Chumalov in Feodor Gladkov's *chef d'oeuvre* of socialist realism, the 'Cement' (*Tsement*) also combined the virtues of asceticism, personal prowess and collectivism.

Personal well-being was absolutely unimportant for these altruistic heroes. Ultimately, it was altruism, the well-being of the masses which drove them

---

5   Sesterhenn (1982), 119–127; Stites (1989), 168; Guenther (1993), 40–41.
6   Marx (1978), 62–63.

forward. Heroes of their class, the model communist materialists were driven by moral ideals, not by material gain or calculation.

It is curious that precisely this variety of ethics, which laid the main stress on moral intentions and not on the results of deeds, was adopted in the Bolshevik Soviet Union and prospered there at the very time when a utilitarian (and truly materialist) ethics of consequences was making its triumphal march in the capitalist West, where traditional morals and religion were rapidly decaying in the face of this new cultural enemy.

By the beginning of the World War II, the Soviet Union had developed into a deeply moralistic country with puritan ethics, where the establishment assiduously fought the demon of 'petty-bourgeois' greed and hedonism, which, paradoxically, was still somehow threatening socialist society.[7]

It has been said that *anomie*, or normlessness, is the 'normal pathology of utilitarianism',[8] meaning that utilitarianism organically tended to reduce the sphere of morality to a pleasure calculus, whereas it was almost exclusively concerned with the outcome of deeds, and not with their intrinsic value.[9]

In other words, if it was true that man is a creature driven by the craving for personal pleasure, a utilitarian disposition obviously functioned without coercion, and therefore a minimum of moral rules and coercion was needed in a rational society. In this sense, utilitarianism was supposed to stem from the nature of man and could claim to be the natural ethics of a modern capitalist society.

Bolshevik society for its part also claimed to conform to the true nature of man, and to satisfy to the maximum his most fundamental cravings, which stemmed from his Aristotelian essence.[10]

Unlike capitalist society, which functioned for the benefit of the exploiting classes, socialist society was supposed to be objectively just, for it remunerated everybody according to his work. No capitalist was stealing part of the value which the worker produced. In principle, the most just of systems, when really established, would work without any coercion whatever, as Lenin in his famous booklet 'State and Revolution' had presaged.[11]

Unfortunately, Soviet propaganda did not adequately reflect the realities of society. Everyday life in the Soviet Union obviously did not contain much coercion, but it was not easy to convince those in doubt that this was not due to the ubiquitous surveillance and threat of punishment.

---

7   See: Vihavainen (2006), 267–295.

8   Gouldner (1970), 65.

9   Ibid., 67–68.

10   *Scientific Communism* (1983), 244–250.

11   Lenin ([1918] 1964), 390–497. *Scientific Communism* (1983), 411.

Vladimir Shlapentokh, an outstanding specialist on Soviet society, has stressed that 'all-consuming fear (was) a necessary ingredient of Soviet normalcy'.[12] In 1932, for instance, a new law introduced capital punishment for the pilfering of state property, for example, collecting corncobs from the kol-khoz fields for one's own nourishment. This punishment could even be meted out to children, 12 years of age.[13] It was admitted on an official ideological level that socialist society 'combated with determination' breaches of labor disci-pline, which obviously continued to exist, after all.[14]

The system thus was obliged to ensure its members' public spirit and altru-ism by threats. They complemented the functioning of the official moralizing. This need not necessarily mean that the average Soviet citizen normally con-sidered the system unjust. Still less does it mean that he tried to oppose it.[15] Any pre-modern social systems were obliged to resort to analogous means to ensure their functioning.

The Soviet ethos of production-oriented ethics, with its puritan stress on self-sacrifice and its moralistic stress on the intrinsic value of collectivist be-havior persisted right up to the end of the system. The worker, the creator of material values and the champion of collectivism, remained on his pedestal as the hero of production. The credibility of such an ideology was not always in doubt, as the one-time popularity of Communism in Western European coun-tries indicates.

The Practice: From Scarcity for Everybody to Well-Being for the Best

The Soviet command economy was best suited for military purposes. Its pref-erences were determined by the central authorities and the consumption of the masses remained a very low priority until the late 1950s. For decades, Soviet industry concentrated on producing investment goods and weapons, and the material well-being of the people remained a secondary goal. However, the all-powerful state had somehow to explain what it was doing and why it was doing it. The official ideology took care of this. A mighty machinery of indoctrination explained every day to everybody why things were as they were in the Soviet Union, and that this was the best possible society in the world.

---

12   Shlapentokh (2001), 99.
13   Conquest (1968), 86–87.
14   *Scientific Communism* (1983), 298.
15   Shlapentokh (2001), 127–152.

In fact, 'Soviet ideology', which persisted throughout the Soviet period and always claimed to represent the unchangeable truths of Marxism, changed considerably during the 75 years that the Bolsheviks were in power. The CPSU always pretended to be the guardian of the one and only true version of Marxism for the entire world. After the appearance of the 'Short Course of the History of CPSU' in 1938, the official ideology came to be labelled '*Marksizm-Leninizm*' (Leninist Marxism), which stressed the importance of Lenin's interpretation of Marxist ideas.[16] In fact, the true mastermind of this Soviet ideology was Stalin, who had, by 1937, destroyed all possible ideological competitors and was now the sovereign legislator of the so-called 'general line' of the CPSU.

By 1938 the doctrine of the CPSU had already come a very long way from the utopian egalitarian ponderings of Lenin, who, as early as 1917, had forecast the imminent transition to a community of communes, which would harmoniously coexist in a voluntary union under the dictatorship of the armed people.[17]

At that time Lenin still professed his faith in the panacea of confiscation. Expropriation of the well-to-do and the repartitioning of their property among those in need were proclaimed to be the secret weapon of the Bolshevik Party.[18] The process of confiscation of the well-to-do's wealth would mobilize the masses, the have-nots against the haves, and the new regime's incitement of such plundering would convince the masses of the truly popular nature of the new regime. Confiscation, for Lenin, was the 'bridge to Socialism', to the social system where everybody would be rewarded according to his labor.[19] Soon thereafter, the communist society would give everybody goods according to their needs, receiving in exchange from everybody according to their abilities.

In 1917 Lenin was speaking about a repartition of housing, clothing and food, the essential means of survival. True, the peasants and workers also repartitioned much else: even parts of pianos and other articles of luxury. However, the simple truth is that by proceeding in this way, there was never any likelihood of even remotely achieving general well-being. The expectations of future affluence, which the Bolsheviks had also very vaguely promised – were based on ideas about achieving a vastly greater level of production in the near future.[20]

During so-called War Communism, the Bolsheviks tried to make all trade, including retailing, a state monopoly. Draconian punishments were put in

16   *Kratkii kurs* (1953), 99–127, 337, 340.
17   Lenin (1971), 277–291.
18   Ibid., 365–371.
19   Lenin (1971), 300–309; Figes (1996), 520–536.
20   Ibid., 304–305.

place for the usurpers of this prerogative of the 'people's state'. A certain kind of 'Communism' was reached during the civil war, when people received their rations (*poiok*) but no wages, but this was still very far from the communist utopia and still farther from affluence. We must remember that the scarcity of all kinds of goods was terrible during the Civil War years, when millions died of hunger and two thirds of the inhabitants of St. Petersburg left the city.[21]

Millions of people either lived on the margins of subsistence or perished of cold and starvation during War Communism. Feodor Gladkov's novel 'Cement', which came to be seen as one of the masterpieces of socialist realism, described the extreme scarcity and ruination of the economy. It praised the heroic struggle of communist believers, who sacrificed their personal happiness and even the life of their children for the idea of Communism and turned down all temptations of acquiring an easier life.

The Bolsheviks also had to thank the *narodnik* tradition within the Russian revolutionary movement for their legacy of leveling and asceticism. The quintessentially Russian hero in Nikolai Chernyshevski's famous novel 'What is to be done?' (*Chto delat'*?) Rakhmetov, led a modest life (even though he ate only beef) and even slept on a bed of nails in order to temper his character.[22]

Would the heroes of Socialism continue this kind of lifestyle in the future? The standard Soviet textbook taught that material values were created by work and only by work. In Capitalism, the employer stole part of the worker's produce. In Socialism this would not happen. It followed that in a post-capitalist, socialist society the real wages of working people would be constantly rising. This would also lead to a constant rise in people's consumption.[23]

In 1960, it was proclaimed that the worker in a socialist society was deeply interested in the material outcome of his work, because work really produced (general) well-being. Luxury, that is to say such commodities which belonged only to the exploiting classes, did not exist in a socialist economy, because all consumption goods went to the working masses. In 1960 it was concluded that such things, which 'formerly had been considered luxury goods and had been consumed only by capitalists will more and more go to satisfying the consumption of the broad masses'.[24] So, instead of luxury for the few, a kind of mass luxury phenomenon would develop. This was somewhat of a contradiction in terms. But some items of affordable luxury were already being produced in the 1930s.[25]

---

21   Nove (1992), 57–68.

22   See: Chernyshevski (1975).

23   Bukharin and Preobrazhensky (1969), 102–105; *Kansantaloustiede* (1960), Chapter XXVI.

24   *Kansantaloustiede* (1960), Chapter XXXIV.

25   See: Gronow (2003), 21–30.

Marxist economics supposed that prices in Socialism would have an objective quality. They would be determined according to the amount of socially necessary work used in the production of a certain item. The same principle determined the salary of workers. Because 'salaries were emancipated from their capitalist restrictions, it became possible to raise them to that level, which was rendered possible by the production capacity of the society and which was necessary for the perfect development of the individual'.[26]

In principle, but not in practice, in the 1920s, the skilled worker's wage became some kind of norm for all other salaried individuals. No communist should had received a salary which was higher than that of a skilled worker, but this had nothing to do with the turbulent reality with mass unemployment and delayed payments. For various reasons, the years immediately after the revolution, even the 1920s, were not the time to indulge in conspicuous consumption. One of the reasons for this was the general exhaustion of the economy, which, for instance, was reflected in the fact that millions starved to death in the Volga region in 1921–22.[27]

In the 1920s, luxury was, in principle, left for the much-hated 'nepmen', the nickname for the new bourgeoisie, which was tolerated during the New Economic Policy in 1921–1928. In practice, instinct for consumption and private property persisted even then, even amongst the Bolshevik elite.[28]

But these were deviations from the norm. The temptations of the petty-bourgeois, hedonistic lifestyle came under attack from the *Komsomol*, which started an offensive against 'philistinism' (*meshchanstvo*) in the 1920s.[29]

The general trend in the 1920s was towards leveling. Lenin at the time of the revolution had already made some concessions to the principle of higher salaries for bourgeois 'specialists', who would in this way be recruited to the task of reconstructing Socialism. This exception from the general rule was also mentioned in the Bolshevik program of 1919.[30] Leveling became even more acute during the First Five-Year plan, when Stalin in effect declared war on the old 'specialists'. For a couple of years, this gave rise to a campaign where all and any 'petty-bourgeois' elements in society were attacked. The kulaks were liquidated, the poor and middle peasants collectivized and remnants of the 'exploiting classes', like the merchants, were destroyed in a few years in a 'class-war' that was unleashed for some years.[31]

---

26   *Kansantaloustiede* (1960), Chapter XXVIII, 492–502.
27   Carr (1954), 80–81; Nove (1992), 81, 110–114.
28   Lebina (2000), 7–26.
29   Gorsuch (2000), 87–95.
30   *Programmy i ustavy* (1969), 52.
31   See: Fitzpatrick, (1978), 8–40.

A Farewell to Leveling

However, despite the initial ethos of this campaign, the process did not lead to leveling. On the contrary, when overzealous policies, such as the founding of agricultural communes, threatened to ruin the economy, Stalin suddenly condemned the whole idea of leveling in March 1930. He declared that nobody needed leveling, and he granted every peasant household a house, a plot of land and a cow of its own.[32]

Before the revolution, working people were generally poor and most of them did not have much opportunity to indulge in 'petty bourgeois' consumerism, let alone luxury proper. The same was true up to the 1930s. In practice the living standards of the vanguard class of proletarians as a whole only hovered around the minimum required for subsistence.[33]

This, however, was not the ideal promised by Socialism. It had always been supposed that the new social system would emancipate the workers from poverty. In a socialist society, life would be better for the workers than in Capitalism, but what would the well-to-do socialist worker be like? He would hardly resemble the archetypal greedy *meshchanin* or the dissolute hedonistic bourgeois, who had been so hated in pre-revolutionary society.[34]

By 1936, when Socialism was proclaimed to be a reality, much had happened as regards the Bolsheviks' attitudes towards consumption in general and leveling in particular. After the horrors of the famine of 1932–1933, which claimed millions of victims, the state finally ceased exporting grain abroad. The rationing of bread could also now be discontinued. This gave Stalin reason to declare in 1935: 'life has become better, life has become merrier'![35]

This was, in fact, just a partial recovery from an exceedingly dismal situation, but there must have been a need to show that the much advertised socialist construction had something better to offer than just misery. The top echelons of society also seem to have grown tired of asceticism.

Proclaiming the advent of the good life in his speech, Stalin also stressed that the socialist system of production would be more effective and thus would produce more goods than Capitalism. Obviously, it would make people richer. The newly founded Stakhanovite movement heralded this new epoch and prepared the transition from Socialism to Communism.[36]

---

32   Stalin (1954), 197–205.
33   Osokina (1998), 120–127.
34   Figes and Kolonitskii (1999), 167–182.
35   Stalin (1967), 89.
36   Ibid., 81–82.

Indeed, Stakhanovites, record-breaking producers, were given the opportunity of obtaining luxury items, from pianos to cars. In this respect they
obviously served as a window into the future communist society for their fel-
low-workers.[37]

In fact, a socialist society had not yet been proclaimed a reality in 1935. That
was done in the following year. The new Soviet constitution was adopted in
1936 and it proclaimed that the country had constructed a new type of society,
where two friendly classes the workers who, by the way, were no longer proletarians, as Stalin was at pains to stress, because they did not live in misery, and
the peasants. They were living in mutual harmony and material well-being. In
addition to these two classes, there was also a stratum (not a class) of *intelligentsia*. All of these social groups were in a friendly relationship with each
other. Moreover, the borders between these groups were disappearing. All the
people had obtained the chance of a well-to-do and cultured life.[38]

Now, in the dawn of Socialism, it was time to determine what this well-to do
and cultured life would be in practice and who would enjoy it in the name of
the people. Clearly, the emergence of well-to do people implied that leveling
had to be abandoned. In fact, by the mid-1930s this had already been done on
the ideological level. Since his famous letter 'Dizziness from Successes', published in March 1930, Stalin had been combating leveling in various ways. The
logical culmination of this process came in 1934 when Stalin declared that leveling was an 'anti-Marxist petty bourgeois' phenomenon.[39]

The new heroes of work, the Stakhanovites, who had emerged in 1935, excelled not only at work, but also at consumption. From the end of the 1930s
until the early 1950s, differences of income in the Soviet Union were bigger
than in some capitalist countries. Moreover, living standards in the Soviet
Union were still generally so low that only a very thin, privileged layer of society was really able to 'consume' beyond the most elementary needs of daily
subsistence.[40]

The Stakhanovite, the new human type, which was introduced to the public
at large in the mid-1930s, was a new kind of producer who also consumed in a
new way and did not suffer from the vicious greed of the bourgeoisie. He was
supposed to be materially well-off, because, in Socialism, he was remunerated
according to his labor, freed from capitalist exploitation. It was also important
that he was not corrupted by his new wealth, not obsessed with his albeit de-

---

37   Siegelbaum (1988), 210–246.
38   Konstitutsiia SSSR (1936); Stalin (1967), 142–148.
39   Stalin (1954), 361–364.
40   Osokina (1998), 127–137, 195–206.

served salary, which provided him with the opportunity to enjoy a good and cultured life.[41]

Ideological tracts argued that work in socialist society was of a new kind, that is, creative work, free of exploitation, where manual and intellectual elements were amalgamated, which was indeed its own remuneration. In communist society it would become the first need of people, regardless of material gain for the worker. Material prosperity was obviously a necessary outcome of work, but essentially of secondary importance. This advertising of the Stakhanovites as living representatives of the future was what Sheila Fitzpatrick has called the 'discourse of socialist realism' – the tendency to view the present through the prism of an imagined future.[42]

The mid-thirties marked the beginning of a new era as regards attitudes towards consumption as such. The new ideal of Soviet man was no longer the ascetic producer who frowned on the 'petty bourgeois' pleasures of a materially good life. Now, the new ideal combined the 'proletarian' stamina of the shock worker and the 'cultural' skills and tastes of the old engineering specialists. The ideal Stakhanovite could have a car and a piano, he could behave in civilized company and he certainly knew some Pushkin by heart. 'Harbinger of the future' as he was, he had liquidated the difference between intellectual and manual physical work.[43]

Under Communism this is what would happen throughout society, as there would be affluence for everybody. So far, the pleasures of the 'cultured life' were available to the great masses only virtually: in film and the printed word. 'Consumption pornography' created images of numerous different kinds of cheeses and sausages, although in reality none were available in large parts of the Soviet Union.[44]

For the political leadership this new accent on consumption may have been due to practical considerations. After all, it would probably be good for the efficiency of production, if the worker had some prospects of future personal well-being and not just abstract promises of wonders to come. Material well-being and a comfortable life had also loomed large in the utopias of the early socialists. In the phalansteries of Fourier, the best cooks would acquire the importance and prestige of ministers of state.[45]

But Fourier's communes belonged to the world of utopia. In fact, they had been banned in the Soviet Union since Stalin's speech of 1930. This new

---

41   Siegelbaum (1988), 210–214.
42   Fitzpatrick (1992), 217.
43   Ibid., 223–227.
44   Gronow (2003), 123–128.
45   Riasanovsky (1969), 75.

interest in material well-being in Soviet ideology did not really mean that the ideal Soviet man would become a consumer instead of a producer. The heroes were still the producers, but now, in a socialist society, the producers were entitled to enjoy the fruit of their work, not just to work unselfishly for others. Moreover, the idea of a higher standard of living for political cadres and other representatives of the higher echelons was also rehabilitated.[46]

After the early 1930s, there was no return to the *partmaksimum* of the 1920s, which had forbidden granting party cadres salaries higher than those of skilled workers. As the rising personality cults of the leaders indicated, the leading comrades were now ideologically even more worthy than the workers, although the latter – as a class –were supposed to be the leading element in society. The party program of 1919 had presented the granting of higher wages to bourgeois specialists as a concession and a temporary deviation from the egalitarian ideal. Now it was, in essence, proclaimed that a good life for the elite was its deserved prerogative.[47]

In spite of their lifestyles, there was nothing bourgeois, it was claimed, about these new heroes of socialist society; they were simply a new variety of *intelligenty*.[48] They were cultured, and to become cultured was everybody's duty. Since the new well-to do Soviet *intelligentsia* did not have a bourgeois class nature, but a working-class nature, it was wrong to envy them. On the contrary, everybody, including the workers, had to emulate them. Besides, having an impeccable class nature, the Soviet intelligent was the most developed kind of human being and, therefore, everybody should do their best to become more and more like a Soviet *intelligent*. This epithet was no longer reserved for the radical critics of society, now it was used even of administrators.[49]

In the light of socialist theory, a member of the Soviet *nomenklatura*, who was now included in the group of *intelligentsia*, and was a worker by class nature and an intelligent by education and profession, was obviously entitled to a reasonable level of financial compensation for the 'socially necessary work' which he was doing. In practice, it must have been difficult to make objective comparisons between the relative worth of the work of a party secretary and a miner.

The size of this new elite was very small. It has been estimated to have comprised just some tens of thousands of people in the 1930s. In the 1970s its size may have been about a couple of hundred thousand.[50]

---

46   Fitzpatrick (1992), 216–219.

47   Stalin (1967), 398–399.

48   Fitzpatrick (1992), 218–219.

49   Stalin (1967), 398–399.

50   Osokina (1998), 134–137.

But in principle the novelty was very important. This was the 'Big Deal' which provided justification not just for the lifestyles of the worker Stakhanovites, but first and foremost, to the so-called 'new class'. It has been said that despite the pretentious lifestyles of the highest echelons of Soviet society, their numbers were so few that they did not really count when it came to the statistics of the national economy. This may be true, as regards the *nomenklatura*. However, the income of the highest paid 10% of the Soviet population was more than seven times that of the income of the lowest paid 10% at the end of Stalin's reign. This was more than in many capitalist countries. One should not forget the miserable state of the peasants, who had hardly any money income at all. In 1948–1950, a peasant had to work sixty days in order to buy a kilogram of butter. In order to buy a poor-quality suit, more than a year's work was needed.[51] True, the *kolkhoznik* could get most of his foodstuffs from his private plot, but this standard of living did not leave much room for consumerism.

From 'Virtual Consumerism' to a Hunger for Goods

We could call the first period of Soviet ideology concerning consumption, in which leveling and the requisitioning of other people's wealth for redistribution amongst the masses (or repartitioning, to use the terminology of the Russian commune) was highlighted the 'time of asceticism'. It lasted, roughly, from 1917 to 1935. The second period, from the mid-1930s to the early 1950s could be called the time of 'virtual consumerism'. During this time, the material well-being of the masses was praised in slogans and glorified in posters and works of art according to the code of 'socialist realism'. But the leadership understood perfectly well that items of consumption, beyond the primary necessities of everyday life, were available only for the very few. Heavy industry had little to offer for households and the individual consumer interested in durable goods. But a hunger for goods had been awakened.[52]

The situation, from the point of view of the potential consumer, was only worsened by the fact that prices for many goods were lowered, which in turn raised their demand to a level that Soviet industry could not meet.[53]

This was a conscious policy. Stalin himself proclaimed that it was one of the chief virtues of a socialist economy that the incomes of the consumers grew faster than the production of commodities. This was the very opposite of a capitalist economy, where surplus production caused dreadful depressions,

---

51   Nove (1992), 307–308, 355–356.
52   Hessler (2004), 306–08.
53   Zubkova (1999), 86–89.

when the workers lacked purchasing power. Anyway, surplus purchasing power created queues. In principle this was considered to be a good thing, a sign of
a new prosperity, and this attitude probably inhibited any effort to overcome
the situation.[54]

After the early 1950s the picture begins to change again. By the mid-1950s,
the semi-starvation and forced saving of the postwar years had been overcome,
and shops had more and more to sell. And it was not just foodstuffs (whose
availability notoriously suffered from interruptions), but also clothing and increasing numbers of durable commodities, including radio and television sets,
refrigerators and washing machines. Even cars were sold. All this relative abundance appeared quite abruptly, in a situation, where the national economy,
after the severe damages of the war, had barely been restored.

However, the legacy of the past's misery was felt for a long time. As late as
1971, most people still lived in primitive conditions. More than 64% of the population had less than 10 square meters of living room. Sixty three percent had
no running water at home, 75% had no shower or bathroom, and about 90%
had no telephone.

Only somewhat more than 2% had a car of their own, but more and more
household goods were available. Fifty nine percent already had a television set,
54% had a washing machine and 28% had a refrigerator. According to Boris
Grushin, a few people also told about plans to buy durable commodities.[55]

The very low standard of living did not give rise to popular discontent, so
argues Boris Grushin.[56] People had learned to accept poverty as the norm and
we should also remember that the improvement of living standards had been
very rapid. The situation had never been so good and very few people could
make any comparisons with the rest of the world. They had also grown up with
an unabashed leveling psychological outlook and it can be concluded that the
majority did not consider material consumption as the main thing in their life.
Moral values were also more highly esteemed and the principles of Communism were almost unanimously supported, Grushin argues, even though he
does not seem to have very relevant material at his disposal.[57]

Grushin's view of the Soviet scene at that time is interesting. Even if we remember that social research has also found that practically all of the Soviet
people were strongly interested in the material betterment of their lives, as the
results of a 1961 survey established, it may really have meant nothing more
than the attainment of decent housing, clothing and nourishment. This does

---

54   Hessler (2004), 308.
55   Grushin (2006), 348–350.
56   Ibid., 355–358.
57   Grushin (2001), 138–158, 410–422.

not really amount to consumerism, which implies some kind of luxury; not just satisfaction of primary needs. Fashionable goods and conspicuous consumption were obviously something which most Soviet people could still hardly afford or even imagine. This may have suggested, for the leadership that satisfying the people's material needs was not, and would not be, so difficult.

However, the genie had been released from the lamp. After all, Soviet fashion houses had existed since Stalin's time, and that meant a clear concession to the idea of superfluous consumption. Fashionable clothing, which Larissa Zakharova discusses in this book, proved to be one kind of luxury for which the masses continued to long in spite of the ideas of the leadership. However, in the 1960s, affluence was still largely virtual; promised and awaited, but still a thing of the near future. Scarcity, it was proclaimed, would completely disappear soon, but was still all-encompassing, and practically no advertising was needed in order to sell factory-made products. However, advertising did exist, although on an extremely modest scale, as every tourist to the Soviet Union will remember.

In the Soviet Union of the 1960s and 1970s, there was very little incitement to purchase items of secondary importance, such as cars. Rather, it was made very difficult and unattractive. Even if one had the money, it would not have sufficed. Later, the 'happy' owner of a private car had to be prepared to hear insults on part of such comrades, who did not have one. [58] Very few cars for personal use were available until the VAZ company began production. Buying and keeping a car was also a formidable task, impossible to solve without a lot of toil and drudgery.

There was also the question of quality, which socialist production was never able to solve. The hapless consumer was often obliged to struggle for his right to receive products which were worth the asking-price, as Elena Bogdanova shows in her article in this book.

But the Soviet people lacked opportunities to make comparisons. According to several surveys, the Soviet people considered the quality of their life to be fairly good in international comparison. In 1976, they believed it to be much better than in the USA although somewhat lower than in Czechoslovakia![59]

The often complicated process of obtaining scarce goods, the lack of advertising catering for the consumer and the information gap between the Soviet Union and the outside world created for the consumer a milieu which sharply differed from the western capitalist scene, where everything seemed to be within close reach. When asked how much they thought their salary should be

58   Andreeva (2009), 26–28.
59   Shlapentokh (2001), 122–123.

increased, Soviet citizens demanded no more than 10% even though their salaries were among the lowest in the country.[60]

At the beginning of the 1960s, there seem to have been some signs of genuine optimism, if not enthusiasm among the people as regards their prospects of material well-being. The rise in living standards after the war was now clear, so in that sense there was reason for such optimism. Such factors as the spectacular successes of the Soviet Union in space technology fuelled this optimism. But sudden shortages, like that caused by the bad harvest of 1963, made people question the wildest promises of the party. The notorious riot and massacre in Novocherkassk showed that the system was vulnerable to working-class discontent.[61]

Grande Finale: 'The Party Solemnly Declares: the Contemporary Generation of the Soviet People Will Live in Communism!'[62]

In 1961 the Communist Party declared that the final battle between Capitalism and Socialism had begun. Socialism was to 'bury' Capitalism, to become its lawful heir as the more advanced and humane social system. The 'program of constructing Communism' was launched very pompously, and the party solemnly swore that the present generation would live in a communist society.

Within 20 years, that is, by 1980, communist society was to be constructed 'in the main', as the party program put it, leaving the door open for some minor amendments if required.[63] However, the party also made certain quite concrete promises which concerned both the volume of production in general and future living standards in particular.

The standard of living in the Soviet Union would be highest in the world. At the same time, the Soviet worker would have the shortest working day in the world: six hours by 1970. This was not quite congruent with the assumption that work in Communism would be transformed into the foremost need of Soviet man, but it was in line with the tenor of the earlier program, which promised to liberate the Soviet worker from the overwhelming burden of work, and proclaimed that efficiency was the hallmark of a socialist economy. The program promised unheard of amounts of grain and meat, cotton fabric and leather shoes. Also housing production was boosted by launching the construction of the *khrushchevkas*; simple and quickly built town houses. In the

---

60   Ibid.
61   Baron (2001).
62   *XXII s'ezd* (1962), 227.
63   *Programmy i ustavy* (1969), 135.

beginning of the 1960s, the needs of the people were still rather simple in the Soviet Union. Obviously, the material basis for a good life in Communism consisted mainly of good housing, decent clothing and wholesome food. Cultural needs and recreation were also supposed to be guaranteed by society.

The III program of the CPSU declared: 'Communism is a highly organized community of free and conscious working people, where social self-rule is established, work for the society will become the first vital need of everybody, a conscious necessity, and everybody's abilities will be maximally used for the good of the people'.[64]

It also declared that the relations within society and between individuals would be harmonious. The demands of the people, greatly varied as they were, reflected the 'normal and sensible needs of fully developed human beings'. The highest standard of living in the world was to be realized through a dual strategy: on the one hand, salaries were to be raised, while the prices of commodities were to be reduced and taxes abolished. On the other, 'social reserves of consumption' would be raised. These were commodities and services which were distributed to the population free of charge, and not dependent on the amount or quality of their work.[65] These included education, medical care, pensions, the maintenance of children and communal services. The general standard of living in a communist society would be higher than in capitalist society even though their national income might be the same. This was because it was distributed according to the interests of everybody and there were no groups of 'parasites', which in capitalist societies stole and wasted the immense riches created by the work of millions. The characteristics of a communist society were taught to all students in obligatory classes of 'Scientific Communism'.

For the next 20 years, salaries based on the amount of work done would still be the basic means for the satisfaction of material and cultural needs. However, the difference between high and low salaries was to be reduced. The salaries of low-income groups such as the peasants were to rise faster than those of the rest of society.[66]

What, exactly, were the commodities which would be abundant within 20 years? The CPSU program mentioned 'good quality and varied diet' including meat, fats and milk products, fruits and 'good quality vegetables'. 'All layers of society' would get 'enough good quality consumer goods, good and beautiful clothes, footwear, goods which enrich and adorn the everyday life of Soviet citizens, comfortable and modern furniture, better household furnishings and

---

64   Ibid., 131.
65   Ibid., 164–165, 172–175.
66   Ibid., 164–165.

many kinds of cultural goods and so on'. It also announced that 'in the interests of the people, many more cars will be produced'.[67]

It is worth noticing that the old idea of liquidating the individual family household was the order of the day once again. Women were to be liberated from household work so that they could more fully contribute to more effective forms of production. This would be achieved by putting children into kindergartens and boarding schools and by offering free meals in communal canteens.[68]

But what if some people took more than their fair share of the common product? Would there not be people, who preferred to work less than the norm and take more? This was in fact admitted.

In principle, the worker was the hero of the country and of the whole socialist system. He was the creator of all commodities, because all value was based on work, as socialist political economy taught.[69]

As late as the 1980s 'Scientific Communism' explained that 'The individual sees work at a socialist enterprise as serving the good of the people, as the highest meaning of life'. The moralizing pathos of intentions is obvious and the stress is on production, not consumption. According to the theory of 'Scientific Communism', this new attitude towards work was already becoming the norm in Soviet socialist society, even though the material interests of the worker still played a role.

Later, in Communism, when distribution according to work was to be substituted for distribution according to need, material interest would cease to play any role at all.[70] From the 1930s it was argued that features of the Communism of the future were already present in socialist society. In the early 1960s, a movement of 'communist work' was begun. 'Shock-workers of communist work' over fulfilled their norms and expected no extra reward for doing so. To some extent, work was already supposed to be its own reward. In Capitalism it was, supposedly, a curse.[71]

This moralizing pathos regarding intentions and rules was very different from utilitarian complacency, which regarded morals as a private matter. Moralizing rhetoric played a very conspicuous role in Soviet culture. The 'Moral Code of the Builder of Communism', which resembled the Decalogue in its

---

67   Ibid., 167.

68   Ibid., 172–173.

69   *Kansantaloustiede* (1960), Chapter 3.

70   *Scientific Communism* (1983), 246–48, 397.

71   About this concept, see: <http://www.cultinfo.ru/fulltext/1/001/008/062/831.htm>; Grushin (2001), 278–279.

stress on rules and personal moral qualities, was officially approved by the XXII Party Congress in 1961. It consisted of the following twelve commandments:

- Devotion to the cause of Communism, love of the socialist Motherland and of the socialist countries.
- Conscientious labor for the good of society: He who does not work, neither shall he eat.
- Concern on the part of everyone for the preservation and growth of public property.
- A high sense of public duty; intolerance of actions harmful to the public interest.
- Collectivism and comradely mutual assistance: one for all and all for one.
- Humane relations and mutual respect between individuals: man is to man a friend, a comrade and a brother.
- Honesty and truthfulness, moral purity, unpretentiousness and modesty in social and private life.
- Mutual respect in the family, concern for the upbringing of children.
- Irreconcilability towards injustice, parasitism, dishonesty, careerism and profiteering.
- Friendship and brotherhood among all peoples of the USSR, intolerance of national and racial hatred.
- Intolerance towards the enemies of Communism, peace and the freedom of nations.
- Fraternal solidarity with the working people of all countries, and with all peoples.[72]

Here, it is the moral duties of the individual that clearly set the tone, while the central duties are those towards the state and society and not towards other individuals. The importance of 'intolerance' as a moral quality is also interesting from our point of view. This kind of moralizing approach was not only in sharp contrast with the libertarian ethos of the 'affluent society', which was beginning to develop in the West during the 1960s.

In fact, it was a far cry even from the indulgent and tolerant popular culture of utilitarianism, which had been growing in the West since the early 19th century. 'Really existing Socialism' insisted that it functioned without coercion, because people in this system wanted to behave according to its rules. In fact, it smelt strongly like regimentation and surveillance.

---

72   *Programmy i ustavy* (1969), 198–199. See also: *Moral Code of the Builder of Communism* (1961).

The new socialist norms of life always existed more on paper than in reality. The campaigns which purported to prove the existence of a new, communist culture in society ('communist work' for instance) seem to have left no permanent traces.

At the same time, a system of privileges was built and it had a blatantly administrative character. 'Extra-economical' coercion and privileges for a chosen few had been typical for feudal society, so children learned at school in communist countries. Now, in fact, they had become typical of socialist society, which was 'building Communism'. Every citizen had some personal experience of this. The 'special shops' for the *nomenklatura* were just one flagrant example of this reality.[73]

'Remnants of the Past' or Products of Socialist Society? Consumer Attitudes without Consumerism?

'Remnants of the past' were to survive for some time, Soviet ideology famously supposed.[74] Everybody's consciousness was not on the level of development of the production forces. However, 'fully developed' people would understand their own true worth and submit freely to the necessities of society. In general, people would learn that there was no point in taking more than one's share. Why should somebody buy three tickets to the theatre, if he could be sure that one ticket is sufficient to get admittance? Soviet man in a communist society would not be materially insatiable; he knew that taking more than one's share does not make sense.

The communist level of material well-being, which the party program had promised, does not look very impressive by the standards of the 21st century. Most of the social services, which the program promised have been realized in welfare states like Finland or Sweden. In today's world, at least in the advanced economies, there are also enough 'good quality foodstuffs' and clothing, not to mention household appliances or 'cultural services'. It must be inferred that the top leaders of the Communist Party did not expect that any normal and 'fully developed' human being would need the quantities of consumer goods people nowadays actually use in many societies.

One interesting example is the car. It seems that the average household in communist society would not own a car. The party did not intend to produce that many of them. At the time of the creation of the III party program, ideas about leasing cars and dachas were presented. Why should somebody have a

---

73   Fitzpatrick (1992), 221–237; Hessler (2004), 199–200.

74   *Programmy i ustavy* (1969), 200–201.

car of his own? Did anybody have a theatre of his own or a train of his own? Cars and dachas as communal property would have the advantage of being used more effectively and liberate the average user from the troubles of maintenance.[75]

The time spared by using communal property and not one's own, could be used for the general development of everybody's human capabilities. This was expected to be the natural calling of the human being, instead of indulgence in alcohol, narcotics, sex and debauchery.

Human growth, the full development of the personality, indeed, was considered the real ultimate goal of social development, material things were just a means to that end.[76] Communism would realize the freedom of the human personality more fully than Capitalism, which had, in fact, turned the state into a prison for the working majority.

Millions of people were supposed to believe in these dogmas and we have no reason to doubt that the program would not really have strongly affected the attitudes of the Soviet people, at least for some years.

Polls, as late as 1998 and 1999, established that more than a half of those polled reported that they had believed in Communism. This was three times more than the number of those who did not believe in Communism at all. True, just 35–37% said that they had also believed that it was possible to achieve Communism according to the timetable that was set by the xxii Party Congress.[77]

Only during perestroika did the policy of *glasnost'* open up some channels for criticism of the 'really existing' worker. Valentin Rasputin's novel 'The Fire' (*Pozhar*), which presented a group of workers as primitive lazy drunkards, was a startling instance of new attitudes towards the central tenets of the official ideology. This type of worker smacked of Marx's *Lumpenproletariat*. It was scandalous to suppose that it could survive in 'developed Socialism'. Alexander Zinoviev, living abroad, in the 1980s, claimed that Soviet socialist society encouraged people to minimize their output for society and maximize their 'input' for themselves. It was a falsely moralizing society, where supposedly good intentions, which produced bad consequences, were hypocritically praised. Zinoviev depicted Soviet workers as reluctant slaves, who tried to shun work as best they could. This did not mean that they opposed the regime, on the contrary, it suited them perfectly well. The balance between work and remuneration was excellent.[78]

---

75   Pyzhikov (2002), 299–300.
76   *Programmy i ustavy* (1969), 134.
77   Aksiutin (2004), 333–340.
78   Zinoviev (1984), 100–117.

Valentin Rasputin's novel 'The Fire' (*Pozhar*), which was published in 1985[79], was in effect a literary description of Zinoviev's theoretical musings. This book, like some other novels by the same author, immediately aroused great interest. It was rightly interpreted as public criticism of Soviet society. This kind of criticism had always been taboo outside the sphere of *belles letters* and it was hard to discover even in those 'problematic' (*problemnye*) works of art that were allowed to be published every now and then.

This time the criticism hit a very sensitive target. It happened that the scoundrels of the story were representatives of the Soviet working class. Instead of being paragons of the new, communist virtues of voluntary work (*kommunisticheskii trud*) and social enthusiasm, the antiheroes, a brigade of loggers was shown to consist of lazy drunkards, who terrorized their fellow-citizens and were totally disinterested in their work and their environment. These people respected nothing, took care of nothing. All that was important, for them, was how to exploit others for their own benefit. This 'benefit' did not include trying to make life better or care for the future. The only thing that mattered to these prototypical lumpenproletarians, was to get their daily portion of vodka and *zakuskas*.

Rasputin's antiheroes were remarkable in many respects. They had unpardonable 'consumer' attitudes towards society and nature. But those attitudes were far from consumerism in the modern sense of the word.

The same kind of psychology was represented in a cartoon in *Literaturnaia Gazeta* at about the same time. In the cartoon a drunkard in a shabby *vatnik* was telling another that he had no car and no dacha. Instead, he asserted, he was 'spiritually rich' (*bogat dukhovno*).

It is not easy to say, how large a problem this kind of lumpenproletarianism actually was in the Soviet Union. Statistics about alcoholism, mortality and poverty in Russia's villages, which at the time were secret, suggest that the issue was far from negligible and had only got worse during the period of 'developed Socialism'.[80]

It is hardly an overstatement to say that, for a long time, Soviet Communism achieved a remarkable degree of success in its struggle against consumerism. However, at least to some degree, this was the kind of success that nobody wanted or envied. When the Soviet project came to an end, it was found that the system had created a situation in which for many people in rural areas there were simply no prospects of a better life. They did not have any reason for

---

79   Rasputin ([1985] 1990).
80   Takala (2002), 254–263.

believing that things would get better, and they had no prospects concerning personal enrichment or social mobility: they did not even have hope.[81]

The same kind of problems also plagued the cities, but to a lesser extent. When luxury goods, and even everyday goods, such as quality food and clothes, were at the same time both scarce and underpriced, attaining them was often only possible by means of *blat*, the system of mutual services. People who had no social capital that could be used in *blat* could easily drop out of the wheel of consumption.

Earning more money was not a sensible option, if one knew that money could not pay for much in a world where *blat* was the hardest currency.[82] In *Pozhar*, when a fire breaks out in a shop, the flames reveal that many much sought after goods had in fact been lying hidden inside. The shopkeepers had kept them for themselves instead of selling them to the public. As their retail price was much lower than their real worth in a society where such goods were in short supply, they could exchange them for something else, also in short supply, which was worth much more than their retail price.

Alexander Zinoviev, the illustrious logician and eccentric critic of Soviet society, made some startling conclusions concerning the nature of the Soviet system. Soviet 'Communism', he said, was the perfect social system from the point of view of human nature. By nature, man was inclined make the minimum amount of effort for the maximum advantage. This was not possible in the West, but it was possible in the Soviet Union, where people could live virtually without working at all. 'Communist' society, according to Zinoviev, was a product of 'human communality', a natural inclination for unworthy conduct: 'Civilization is effort; communality is taking the line of least resistance. Communism is the unruly conduct of nature's elemental forces'. [83]

Zinoviev inferred that the Soviet system was consequently extremely stable, because it corresponded with human nature, which tended towards the inertia and effortless stagnation described above. He even maintained that the social evolution which had taken place in the Soviet Union was 'irreversible'.[84]

As we know, on this point Zinoviev was not right. The Soviet system proved to be extremely fragile and it collapsed suddenly. It can hardly be said that people made much effort in order to cling on to their Soviet past. Rather, the majority was quick to forsake the Communist Party and its teachings as soon as the blind alley up which it had taken them became economically obvious. This happened during the year 1991, when people began to flee the party.

---

81   Moskoff (1993), 109–119.
82   Ledeneva (1998), 70–72.
83   Zinoviev (1984), 27–30.
84   Ibid., 252–259.

Victory in the Wrong Race?

We know that Soviet Communism did not conquer Capitalism. On the contrary, it lost the battle. It seems to be that it had built-in flaws. What looked good in theory did not work in reality. What was proclaimed to be freedom was, in fact, hardly more than slavery. What was to be the highest quality and highest standard of living in human history proved to be substandard quality and constant shortages. In its final stage, the system drove a whole people into semi-starvation.

However, it has sometimes been said that the Soviet Union did win the race that it had proclaimed in 1961. Indeed, as it had promised, it produced bigger amounts of certain key raw-materials than its chief capitalist rival, the USA. However, it obviously won the wrong race. Large amounts of material products were created, but this did not bring well-being.[85]

It also turned out that at the same time as the planned economy of the Soviet Union finally managed to produce a considerable amount of consumer goods, they often proved to match the standards of yesterday, not contemporary world standards.

It happened that in the western world, a new epoch of consumerism had begun at the very time when the regime in the Soviet Union was still trying to 'satisfy the moderate and rational needs of people' according to the standards of the early 1960s. In the West, consumerism entered a qualitatively new level and, compared with the new standards, Soviet achievements and even plans for the future, which had looked very bold in 1961 were rendered hopelessly obsolete.

The story seems to have a parallel in the building of the welfare state. The ideas which the Bolsheviks presented in 1903 were very impressive at the time. Seventy years later it could be safely said that they had been realized in many European countries to a greater extent than in the Soviet Union.

In other words, for any well-informed judge, it was obvious that the Soviet project was not fulfilling its promises in the late 1980s, but was lagging more and more behind the most advanced countries.

It may be worthwhile to do some international comparison. Certain material for this is available. While Russia proved to unable to catch the West in material terms, let alone to surpass it, it also was left outside a new kind of value-orientation, which was beginning in the developed western countries.

People in the developed countries, where material well-being was on a high level, were more and more adopting a set of 'post-materialist values', as the

---

85   Nove (1992), 384–388.

World Values Survey[86] indicates. This meant a shift of attitudes from 'survival values' towards 'self-expression values', including tolerance, sexual permissiveness, gender equality and so on. Russia, where moralistic regimentation had always been a central tool of social engineering, was now left outside this incipient development.[87]

This growing gap in norms and values must have had an effect in the Soviet Union. The flow of information between East and West had considerably improved after the Helsinki accords of 1975, and it became harder than ever to assure people, who had opportunity for comparison that their standard of living and their way of life were superior to those in the West. The doctrine of 'developed Socialism' tried to do this and hailed the 'Soviet way of life' as a more developed and dignified form of human existence, that was superior to that of any previous stage in history.[88]

It seems to be that this kind of ideological apologetics and accent on 'dematerialization', which Olga Gurova discusses in this book, was not totally without effect. People knew that the West was full of material comfort, but the capitalist way of life could be subject to doubt and criticism. The 'post-material' values could also be interpreted as signs of moral decline of the capitalist world. Certainly, capitalist society was not the haven for idlers that the Soviet Union was, according to the analysis of Alexander Zinoviev. The Soviet way of life, including collectivism, might have had some merits from the point of view of the individual. At least it was familiar and, for some time, the 'Little Deal' promised a secure everyday life. The party enjoyed a lot of prestige as long as this safety could be maintained. The moment of truth came quite suddenly, when the collapse of perestroika made everyday life unbearable and the main question was no more saving Communism or any other 'ism', but of the Soviet people.[89] As for the 'Little Deal' discussed by Olga Gurova in this book, in the early 1990s the state was no longer fulfilling its part. Only with this failure did the whole communist project very rapidly lose its mass support.[90]

The Soviet leaders who threw down the gauntlet to Capitalism in 1961 obviously could not imagine what the world would be like in just 20–30 years. But then again neither could the West.

---

86 The World Values Survey is a global network of social scientists, who investigate basic values and beliefs of almost one hundred societies for several decades. Russia has been their object of study since the 1980s. See: <http://www.worldvaluessurvey.org/index_orga nization>.

87 Inglehart (2008), 139–145.

88 *Scientific Communism* (1983), 244–247.

89 Nove (1992), 408.

90 Whereas in March 1991 as many as 40% of the Soviet people said they had "full trust" in the CPSU, in September 1991 almost nobody said so. See: Wyman (1997), 63.

The collapse of the Soviet Union did not only mean economic catastrophe. It had a terrible effect on people's happiness and their satisfaction with their life. The results of the World Values Survey show a unique drop in these indicators. Even when compared with the Eastern European socialist countries, Russia was in a class of its own.[91]

Consumerism and the End of the Soviet Union

With every year that passes since the fall of the Soviet Union, the wider the perspective allowing us to assess the place of Soviet Communism in world history. Now the communist project is a story with an end; hopes of future happiness can no longer be used to justify past or present sacrifices. Now we may try to determine to what extent it was a tragedy or whether it also resembled a comedy.

In any case, the communist experiment hugely influenced not only Russia, but the whole world. Indeed, the collapse of Soviet 'real Socialism' marks the end of an entire epoch in world history, the western countries included.[92] The end of the Soviet project was the most important single factor among those that gave rise to a crisis in world culture. This crisis has produced a wealth of new assessments of the entire world historical process. 'Postmodernism', which denied the possibility of progress and absolute values in principle, was gaining ground in the western academic world at the same time as Soviet Communism, the champion of progress and absolute values, declined materially and intellectually.[93]

Even if we cannot give a definite answer, we are obliged to ask what killed off the Soviet system, which was considered to be so stable by so many enlightened observers, both communist and non-communist alike. We may try to guess whether the system could have survived (for good or ill), if only the Soviet leadership had played its cards right.

One of the reasons for the failure of the Soviet system was its inability to fulfill its promises concerning material prosperity. In 1961, it had solemnly thrown down a challenge to the West, and had then gone on to lose the race to create the highest living standards in the world.

Especially in its last stage, the Soviet Union was not able to meet even the humblest expectations of Soviet consumers. When the crisis was at its peak,

---

91   Inglehart, Foa, Peterson, Welzel (2008), 277–278.
92   Used in this way by Hobsbawm (1995) for instance, in his *Age of Extremes. The Short Twentieth Century, 1914–1991*.
93   Hobsbawm (1995), 500–522.

the situation looked desperate and even the most elementary necessities of daily life became scarce.[94]

The catastrophic situation in the late 1980s and early 1990s was, however, not really typical for the whole Soviet period. For a certain length of time the Soviet economy showed sustainable growth and the lot of the consumer was bearable and constantly improving, with just agriculture remaining a permanent headache for the party and the people. The 'Big Deal' of the 1930s and the 'Little Deal' of Brezhnev's time, which are discussed elsewhere in this book, guaranteed the support of Soviet society for what was called 'really existing Socialism' for decades.

For several decades the Soviet Union was able to become a kind of 'anti-West', sometimes called the 'second world'. It tried hard to maintain a moralizing anti-bourgeois culture, which was anti-modern in its opposition to the popular utilitarianism that had made moral questions a private issue in the West.

It also became pre-modern in its condemnation of avant-garde modernism in cultural life since the 1930s. Bourgeois utilitarianism had gradually killed off religion in the West. In Russia, the totalitarian regime had cast out religion by force and had established its own quasi-religion, which was no less inimical to western utilitarianism as traditional Christianity had been.[95]

Despite its shortcomings, in several polls Russians have exhibited remarkable amount of nostalgia for the Soviet period. In 2003, as many as 55% of the Russian people supported the idea that it would have been better if everything in the country had remained as it had been before perestroika. In 2004 the figure was 48%.[96] The posthumous popularity of the regime was, of course, not determined just by material reasons. People tend to compare the positive sides of the past which they remember with the conspicuous ills of the present situation. Many Russians believe, for instance, that the post-communist regime is corrupt, even criminal, and alien to the popular masses.[97]

When asked in 2000 if the life of the common people was better in the Soviet Union or in the West during the 1970s and 1980s, 49% of those polled

---

94 In 1988 55% of respondents in an all-union poll told the factor, which most complicated their everyday life, was poor supplies and quality of consumer goods. 52% told that it was shortages and poor quality of food. In 1990 the respective figures were staggering 80% and 87%. See: Wyman (1997), 40.

95 Reflected, for instance in the Moral Code of the Builder of Communism, discussed above on p. 45.

96 Levada-Center (2004): Press-vypusk#30: Nostal'giia po proshlomu. Available at: <http://www.levada.ru/press/2004031901.html>.

97 Levada-Center (2005): Golov A. Vlast' sovetskaia i vlast' nyneshniaia. Available at: <http://www.levada.ru/press/2005120200.html>.

thought that it had been better in the Soviet Union, while 29% believed that it had been better in the West. In 2008 the respective figures were 38% and 30%.[98]

In interpreting these figures, we must remember that material well-being in Russia had vastly improved by 2008, after the misery of the early 1990s and the devaluation of the ruble in 1998. In November 2009, 24% of respondents said that they were living well (*blagopoluchno*), while the figure had been four times smaller, just 6%, in December 1999. Sixty two percent of the respondents in 2009 thought that their standard of living was about average (*sredne*). The figure was 46% in 1999. The amount of those who said they were 'poor' or 'very poor' had been reduced to a third (from 10% to 3% and from 3% to 1% respectively).[99]

To be sure, being 'average' in a society does not necessarily mean that one is well-off. However, the figures clearly indicate that the consumers' situation had radically changed for the better during the first decade of the 21st century. Against this background, these respondents' positive assessment of the Soviet past is striking.

'The World Revolution of Consumerism' and Russia

It seems that the chronological difference between the Soviet Union and the West in experiencing modern consumerism does not just mean that the Russians obtained more commodities to consume later than the citizens of non-communist countries.

They also came to the world of consumerism from another culture, with a different cultural package.

People's relationship to commodities and consumption is also important from the point of view of the more fundamental issue of the quest for a purpose in life, which has also been sought in religiosity and ideologies. The decline of religion and the rise of a popular culture of utilitarianism have progressed, in the West, almost simultaneously. This seems to indicate that the latter has gradually taken the place of religion as the giver of the main purpose of life. At least the correlation is clear. The growth of consumption and the waning of religion have been the simultaneous megatrends of the past 200 years. Both

---

98   Levada-Center (2008): Gde byla luchshe zhizn'? Available at: <http://www.levada.ru/press/2008031401.html>.

99   Levada-Center (2009a): Izmenenie urovnia zhizni i pokupatel'skogo povedeniia rossiian. Available at: <http://www.levada.ru/press/2009111804.html>.

have progressed in the West with special rapidity since World War II, especially since the 1970s.[100]

The simultaneity of these two processes is partly trivial: when scarcity prevails, worship of the Golden Calf cannot really be a mass phenomenon or a rewarding activity for the majority of people. The experiment of the Jews in Sinai was doomed to be short-lived. In post World War II Europe, since the 1950s, the utilitarian worship of mammon proved much more sustainable for the masses when production was steadily growing, and thus enabled greater affluence.

The World Values Survey has established that while a rise in material well-being causes a noticeable rise in happiness at a certain point of development, its marginal efficiency will later diminish and people will begin to value other kinds of things. While people adopt these 'post-materialist values', they leave behind so-called survival values, which tend to bind the individual to strict rules of traditionalism, religion and uniformity.[101]

After World War II this trend, which has grown apace with consumerism, also seems to have largely overcome such pseudo-religious movements as millennial nationalism, fascism and Communism. Larger-than-life ideological aspirations seem to have lost their appeal in comparison. Citizens of an affluent society, who have desirable objects of consumption within their reach, seem to remain happy with their consumerism and show little interest in ideologies which preach abstinence now and promise rewards a millennium later. Russia, for its part, has a low score as regards self-expression values in the World Values Survey from 1981 to 2007. Moreover, its score as regards dimension traditionalism vs. rationality has even plummeted, remarkably.[102]

This does not mean that Russians have become very religious. Religion has a low priority among the Russians' values.[103] Some historians, on various grounds, have also detected signs of an epochal change at some point in post-war history. Pierre Nora points to several simultaneous processes: the decline of the traditional countryside in France, the 'end of the Middle Ages' with its religious faith in the 1970s. Moreover, the importance of nationalism and Communism seemed to culminate in France at the same time.[104] The new phenomenon of large-scale consumerism with its utilitarian ethos has been the gravedigger of the stable traditionalism of peasant society. Thus the decay of

---

100   Judt (2005), 325–328, 485, 559–566.
101   Inglehart (2008), 139–145.
102   Inglehart, Welzel (2009), 8–12.
103   Inglehart, Welzel (2010), 559.
104   Nora (2005), 391–402.

the peasant class, which took place throughout Europe after World War II, also paved the way for the emerging new wave of consumerism.

Remarkable changes can also be detected in the sphere of high culture after the war. Peter Gay believes that the great cultural current of modernism in the arts came to a dead end somewhere in the 1960s.[105] Theoreticians of postmodernity, notably Zygmunt Bauman have also seen the late 20th century as a historical turning point. Bauman has also highlighted the importance of consumerism in this process and stressed the fact that in the new society the consumer, not the producer is the central figure.[106] Bauman's idea of 'liquid modernity', the loss of certainties and the concomitant increase of freedom is well in line with the results of the World Values Survey. It describes aptly what has happened in the western world and also what came to happen later in Russia.

Even if we do not subscribe to the tenets of the postmodernist school, it is possible to think that all this shift in values amounts to some qualitatively new phenomenon: something that from our point of view could be called the 'final' or, maybe, rather, the 'full' victory of what used to be called the 'bourgeois' way of life. The values of the proletariat, that martyred working-class, have been liquidated, not those of the bourgeoisie, as the Marxists envisaged. In recent polls, over 60% of Russians say that the most important thing about work is the salary.[107]

The new world of values means, in essence, the preponderance in society of a middle-class, whose main interests are consumerist and individual and not religious, collectivist or ideological. In the 21st century this seems to have become true in Russia also. The underclass, once politically and economically so important, now consists more and more of marginal elements, often living on welfare.

Still in the beginning of the 20th century, religion, together with traditionalism, was a pre-modern anti-bourgeois force. Later, Communism and fascism also aspired to the role of a pseudo-religion for whole nations, also under anti-bourgeois slogans. Modernism, as a cultural movement, was, in essence, also a critique of the bourgeoisie and its way of life, especially its consumerism and its utilitarian everyday culture with its concomitant *anomie*. When the bour-

---

105   Gay (2008).

106   Bauman (2007), 28–36.

107   Levada Center (2011): Otsenki sotsial'nykh problem i zaniatosti. Available at: <http://
       www.levada.ru/archive/otsenki-sotsialnykh-problem-i-zanya tosti/kakoe-iz-sleduyushch
       ikh-suzhdenii-o-tom-chto-znachi>; see also: FOM (2011c): Zarplatnyi raschet. Chto dvizhet
       liud'mi, vybiraiushchimi rabotu? Available at: <http://fom.ru/trudovye-otnoshenija/58>.
       <http://fom.ru/trudovye-otnoshenija/58>.

geois, consumerist way of life was no longer the privilege of a few, but had been adopted by the great majority of society, its critics' argument lost its poignancy.

True, consumerism is still being criticized. However, this is being done not by mighty alternative movements, but just by subcultures and individual religious zealots. With the possible exception of pre-modern Muslim fundamentalists, these are marginal groups. Environmentalists and other remaining anti-bourgeois elements do oppose the very idea of consumerism, but they have not offered any competing ideology for the masses so far. The western working class no longer shares an anti-bourgeois ideology. Workers now, in all essentials, share the popular utilitarianism and consumerist mentality which formerly used to be conceived as quintessentially bourgeois. The workers of the 21st century seem to be happy to practice the very 'bourgeois' vices which were so ardently cursed by the hungry proletarians of the 19th and early 20th century. Property is no longer a prerogative of the rich. A great majority of Russians consider the integrity of private property an important thing.[108]

In the West, as in Russia, consumerism is, in principle, now available for all. It is also the all-encompassing *Weltanschauung* and frame of reference, which has no plausible rivals in the West. The idea of the producer as the great sufferer, doomed to live without enjoying the fruits of his labor, no longer makes any sense. Those groups, within developed societies, which live in need, are not materially productive.

Russia entered this 'demoralized' utilitarian world very suddenly. In the turbulent social upheavals of the 1990s, Russia's national property was, in effect, stolen by groups of criminal elements, who operated under the flag of 'liberalism'. This bequeathed a stigma of immorality to the new order, and liberalism has not achieved any significant political support in Russia. Paradoxically, there is a lot of nostalgia for the Soviet period, but little actual desire to return there. Even during the third presidency of Vladimir Putin, the majority of Russians have obviously been happy with a stable political system that is not too liberal.[109]

Russia – a Latecomer with a Special Heritage

The collapse of Communism was an epochal event, which in Russia cleared the stage for a new ideology and way of life that had already triumphed in the West, but which only later, with a lag of several decades, was to conquer Russia.

---

108   FOM (2000): Zashchita sobstvennosti i prav sobstvennika. Available at: <http://bd.fom.ru/report/cat/business/pow_pec/dd003126>.

109   FOM (2012): Politicheskie indikatory, In: *Dominanty*, No. 39. Available at: <http://bd.fom.ru/pdf/d39ind12.pdf>.

What Russia suddenly encountered, was a brand new, developed stage of consumerism, where the dream of personal 'happiness' for the majority in a world of endless gratification had begun to seem plausible. Such a reality, even such a serious day-dream had not existed at the time of the Russian Revolution in 1917. It hardly existed for the great majority even in Western Europe before the 1950s. However, Soviet Russia had a relatively high score as regards happiness, according to the World Values Survey. This score plummeted drastically from 1981 to 1990 and further to 1996.[110] It has been rising since then but Russia still occupies quite a low position in international comparison.[111]

For decades, the Soviet model had looked a plausible alternative and it had had many admirers in Europe. Its main rival, the American dream reflected an idea of consumerist heaven earlier than its European counterpart, but before the 1950s, it hardly had much credibility abroad.

The new phenomenon of consumerism seems to have outdone not only religious and other comparable values, which belonged to the cluster of 'survival values' in the World Values Survey. In the West, it also overshadowed the values of Communism, which had promised to create a new man.

When relative scarcity still prevailed in western societies, the idea of a new man with high morals, reasonable material needs and an endless thirst for the realization of his creative energies, instead of consumption and idleness, obviously seemed more rational, plausible and alluring. By 1990 it had fallen from grace both in Russia and the West. It became absolutely nonsensical to imagine that the western allegedly exploited producer was the great sufferer and that the Soviet 'liberated' producer-hero was the model of the good life.

Gradually, since the beginning of the 21st century the material situation in Russia has fundamentally changed. Now the average Russian consumer can realistically expect to have his consumerist dreams fulfilled in the not too distant future. Well-equipped commercial centers, hypermarkets, supermarkets and mini-markets have become the standard haunt of the Russian consumer.[112]

In 2009, just 10% of the people said they had problems making both ends meet and were short even in foodstuffs, whereas, on the other hand, over 12% said that they could buy even durable goods without any trouble. In the middle, almost half of the people faced the situation of the average consumer:

110   Inglehart, Foa, Peterson, Welzel (2008), 277–278.
111   Ibid., 274–277.
112   Levada-Center (2009a): Izmenenie urovnia zhizni i pokupatel'skogo povedeniia rossiian. Available at: <http://www.levada.ru/press/2009111804.html>.

there was not enough money to enjoy every temptation available, so the consumer had to make choices.[113]

This new situation indicates that a remarkable Russian middle-class has emerged. It has become more and more realistic for the majority to get hold of material prosperity by means of working, not just by illegal or otherwise dubious means. Attitudes towards material well-being have become more positive.[114]

The consumerist mentality has been opposed both in Russia and in the West for centuries. Religion, the peasant way of life and the needs of the state and society have at different times rendered sanctions on superfluous consumption, once identifies as luxury. Luxury has also had the stigma of immorality since times immemorial. When poverty prevailed, luxury could be understood as something that had been wrongly taken from those in need.

The strange thing was that production-oriented asceticism became the ideal mentality in Soviet Russia after the revolution, even though the revolution was professedly rationalist. Instead of any kind of laissez-faire, the Soviet system developed a cult of the radiant future, which claimed sacrifices in the present. After decades, the moment of truth came and those past sacrifices, which had been made in the name of a tomorrow, were proved to have been a waste of time.

The real anticlimax for the Soviet production-oriented ideology was when liberal economists proclaimed that consumption is essentially not inferior to production. Psychologically this lowered the once sacred duty of productive work to the humble role of a means for getting money for consumption. In post-communism, production has lost its former communist glory as the lofty task of fulfilling the needs of those in need. For the younger generation, its function has become more or less ancillary, a kind of necessary evil in preparing for the feast of consumption.[115]

It has been said that consumerism is among 'the most surprising, the most unexpected developments in modern history, because it involves the most jarring clashes with the previous, traditional values'.[116] In the West, this moral revolution happened gradually, whereas, in the Soviet Union, this process was kept in check for decades. Consumerist aspirations certainly existed and to some restricted extent they were even tolerated. But the main thing was that communist ideas had many essentially pre-modern traits, including a moral-

---

113 Levada-Center (2009b): Rossiiane o svoiom dostatke. Available at: <http://www.levada.ru/press/2009111801.html>.

114 Patico (2008), 212–216.

115 FOM (2009): 'Rabotodatel' mechty' dlia molodiozhi, In: *Dominanty*, No. 39. Available at: <http://bd.fom.ru/pdf/d39rabotod.pdf>.

116 Stearns (2001), viii.

izing anti-consumerism and a pseudo-puritan accent on production. This ethos prevailed until the end of the system.

When the Soviet project crashed, Russians very suddenly encountered a brand new consumer world. Masses of consumer goods came to the country from abroad. The Russians experienced a belated and also a very violent consumerist revolution, which was reflected both in attitudes and in the availability of commodities, although these were at first too expensive for most people.

On the level of ideology, however, it was a veritable reappraisal of all their values *Umwertung aller Werte*, to paraphrase Nietzsche. In the world of morals, the consumer became king overnight and the formerly honored producer became his servant. At first, however, the average citizen, who lost his savings because of hyperinflation, was forced to live life at a subsistence level, while conspicuous consumption run riot in the criminal world. No wonder that even the career of a criminal could have seemed prestigious in those days.[117]

Nowadays, one can again speak of 'remnants of the past' in Russia, which the Bolsheviks kept seeing in Soviet society for decades after the revolution of 1917. Quite a lot of people still share a nostalgia for the past world of values. Attitudes towards the super-rich 'new Russians' have been remarkably negative in Russia.[118] However, people, who are just 'rich', were resented by just 21% of Russians in 2011. In that year, 55% of people had a positive or complacent attitude towards them and 23% had no opinion.[119]

Now, despite the specificity of Russian history, people in the former Soviet Russia seem to have become quite exemplary consumers. Anybody who visits Russia's big cities will be impressed by the amount of conspicuous consumption. Statistics suggest that the average Russian today is loath to save money. Rather, he will use the money as soon as he gets it and he will also probably choose conspicuous ways to show off his wealth. Many people have no savings at all. Just something over 20% of those polled have told to have them in the first decade of the 21st century.[120]

The right and even the duty to consume have now replaced the time-honored duty to work and to earn one's bread by the sweat of one's brow. The most

117   FOM (2011b): Populiarnye professii, In: *Dominanty*, No. 9. Available at: <http://bd.fom.ru/pdf/d09pp11.pdf>.

118   In 2002, 49% of Russians had negative feelings towards the superrich (sverkhbogatye), while as many as 38% told that they had no special feelings towards those people. See: Levada-Center (2002): Golov A.A. Massovye chuvstva k sverkhbogatym rossiianam: spokoistvie i nenavist'. Available at: <http://www.levada.ru/press/2002092001.html>.

119   FOM (2011a): Khitrost' i trud vsio peretrut. Available at: <http://fom.ru/obshchestvo/10104>.

120   Levada Center (2011): Lichnye denezhnye sberezheniia. Available at: <http://www.levada.ru/archive/uroven-zhizni-naseleniya-rossii/lichnye-denezhnye-sberezheniya/est-li-u-vas-vashei-semi-v-na>.

alluring job for Russian youth is now that of a lawyer: no less than 42% mentioned that job in 2011 (25% in 1997). A career in finance and banking was the next most popular with 41% (37% in 1997). The popularity of the entrepreneur had plummeted from 50% to 20%. But professions like an engineer (5% in 2011, 2% in 1997) or physician (12% in 2011, 7% in 1997) remained quite unpopular. Interestingly enough, the 'career' of a criminal had lost its appeal. In 1997 it had been mentioned by 13%, in 2011 only by 2%.[121]

In Russia, as elsewhere, people are now working in order to get money. It's already possible to buy any commodity with money, without using the system of *blat*. In Russia's present stage of development, an increase in money income will raise average scores for life satisfaction and happiness. Russia's score in these statistics still remains quite low.[122]

During perestroika it was joked that the longest way from Capitalism to Capitalism goes through Socialism. In Russia this process was even more complicated than it was in the other socialist countries of Eastern Europe. The specific Russian way of development meant, among other things, that both the people's consumerist instincts and the actual opportunities for them to obtain material commodities were forcibly resisted for a long time. At the same time, the state maintained a set of values, where elements of traditionalism and survival values were dominant. They inhibited the development of the utilitarian mentality, which, in the West, had developed since the 18th century. These 'post-material' values, which the authors of the World Values Survey see as the hallmark of a highly developed society, are still weak in Russia.[123]

Russia, as belated countries often do, will possibly accomplish this task within a much shorter time-span than the western countries. But it is also possible that it will not become like the West.

Bibliography

Aksiutin, Iu. (2004): *Khrushchevskaia 'ottepel' i obshchestvennye nastroeniia v SSSR v 1953–1964 gg.* Moscow: Rosspen.

---

121   FOM (2011b): Populiarnye professii, In: *Dominanty*, No. 9. Available at: <http://bd.fom.ru/pdf/d09pp11.pdf>.

122   Eichhorn (2012), 28. Eichhorn J. (2012): Context Matters. The Effect of National-Level Factors on the Relationship between Socio-Demographic Characteristics of Individuals on Their Life-Satisfaction, In: World Values Survey. Vol. 5, No. 2. Available at: <http://www.worldvaluessurvey.org/wvs/articles/folder_published/paperseries_45/files/WVR_05_02_Eichhorn.pdf>

123   Inglehart (2008), 139–145. Dmitriev-Treisman (2012), 63–68.

Andreeva, I. (2009): *Chastnaia zhizn' pri sotsializme. Otchiot sovetskogo obyvatelia*. Moscow: NLO.

Barber, B. (2007): *Consumed. How Markets Corrupt Children, Infantilize Adults and Swallow Citizens Whole*. New York: W.W. Norton.

Baron, S. (2001): *Bloody Saturday in the Soviet Union: Novocherkassk, 1962*. Stanford: Stanford University Press.

Bauman, Z. (2007): *Consuming Life*. Cambridge: Polity Press.

――――. (2008): *Does Ethics have a Chance in a World of Consumers?* Cambridge: Harvard University Press.

Berlin, I. (1982): *Russian Thinkers*. London: Penguin Books.

Bradley, J. (1985): *Muzhik and Muscovite: Urbanization in Late Imperial Russia*. Berkeley: University of California Press.

Bukharin, N., Preobrazhensky, E. (1969): *The ABC of Communism*. Baltimore, Md.: Penguin Books.

Campbell, C. (2005): *The Romantic Ethic and the Spirit of Modern Consumerism*. London: WritersPrintShop

Carlyle, T. (1843): Past and Present. In: *Thomas Carlyle's Collected Works*. Vol. XIII. Available at: <http://www.gutenberg.org/files/26159/26159-h/26159-h.htm>.

Carr E.H. (1954): *The Interregnum: 1923–1924*. London: Penguin.

Chayanov, A. (1986): *The Theory of Peasant Economy*. Madison: University of Wisconcine Press.

Chernyshevski N.G. (1975): *Chto delat'?* Leningrad: Nauka. Available at: <http://lib.ru/LITRA/CHERNYSHEWSKIJ/chto_delat.txt>

Cohen, L. (2003): *A Consumers' Republic: The politics of mass consumption in postwar America*. New York: Vintage Books.

Conquest, R. (1968): *Great Terror*. London: Macmillan.

Cross, G. (2000): *An All-consuming Century*. New York: Columbia University Press.

Dmitriev, M., Treisman, D. (2012): Discontent Grows in the Hinterlands. In: *Foreign Affairs*. Vol. 91, No. 5, Sept-Oct 2012.

Domostroi (1995): Ithaca and London: Cornell University Press.

XXII s'ezd Kommunisticheskoi Partii Sovetskogo Soiuza (1962) Tom III: Moscow: Gosudarstvennoe izdatel'stvo politicheskoi literatury.

Eichhorn, J. (2012): Context Matters. The Effect of National-Level Factors on the Relationship between Socio-Demographic Characteristics of Individuals on Their Life-Satisfaction. In: *World Values Research*. Vol. 5, No. 2. Available at: <http://www.worldvaluessurvey.org/wvs/articles/folder_published/paperseries_45/files/WVR_05_02_Eichhorn.pdf>.

Entsiklopedicheskii slovar' Brockhausa i Efrona (1890): Sankt-Peterburg: Brockhaus-Efron.

Figes, O. (1996): *People's Tragedy*. London: Cape.

Figes, O., Kolonitskii, B. (1999): *Interpreting the Russian Revolution: The Language and Symbols of 1917*. New Haven and London: Yale University Press.

Firsov B.M., Kiseleva I.G. (eds.) (1993): *Byt velikorusskikh krest'ian-zemlepashchtsev*. St. Petersburg: Evropeiski dom.

Fitzpatrick, S. (ed.) (1978): *Cultural Revolution in Soviet Russia, 1928–1931*. Bloomington: Indiana University Press.

———. (1992): *The Cultural Front: The Laboring of American Culture in the Twentieth Century*. New York, Ithaca and London: Cornell University Press.

FOM (2000): Zashchita sobstvennosti i prav sobstvennika. Available at: <http://bd.fom. ru/report/cat/business/pow_pec/dd003126>.

FOM (2009): 'Rabotodatel' mechty' dlia molodiozhi, In: *Dominanty*, No. 39. Available at: <http://bd.fom.ru/pdf/d39rabotod.pdf>.

FOM (2011a): Khitrost' i trud vsio peretrut. Available at: <http://fom.ru/ obshchestvo/10104>.

FOM (2011b): Populiarnye professii, In: *Dominanty*, No. 9. Available at: <http://bd.fom. ru/pdf/d09pp11.pdf>.

FOM (2011c): Zarplatnyi raschet. Chto dvizhet liud'mi, vybiraiushchimi rabotu? Available at: <http://fom.ru/trudovye-otnoshenija/58>.

FOM (2012): Politicheskie indikatory, In: *Dominanty*, No. 39. Available at: <http://bd.fom. ru/pdf/d39ind12.pdf>.

Gay, P. (2008): *Modernism: The Lure of Heresy*. London, New York: Norton & Co.

Gladkov, F. (1994): *Cement*. Evanston: Northwestern University Press.

Gleason, A. (1972): *European and Muscovite: Ivan Kireevsky and the Origins of Slavophilism* (*Russian Research Center studies*). Harvard: Harvard University Press.

———. (1992): Republic of Humbug: The Russian Nativist Critique of the United States, 1830–1930. In: *American Quarterly*. Vol. 44, No.1.

Gorky, M. (1919): Dve kultury. In: *Kommunisticheskii international*. Vol. 2.

———. (1902) *Meshchane*. Petrograd: Zhurnal Znanie.

———. ([1905] 1918): Zametki o meshchanstve, In: *Stat'i 1905–1916 gg*. Petrograd: Parus.

———. (1923): *O russkom krestianstve*. Berlin: Izdatel'stvo I. P. Ladyshnikova.

———. (1931): Otvet intelligentu, In: *Pravda*. May 21–22.

———. (1932): *S kem vy, mastera kultury?* Moscow: Gospolitizdat.

———. (1950): *Foma Gordeev*. Moscow, Leningrad: Detgiz

———. ([1906] 1951): *Mat'*. Moscow, Leningrad: Goslitizdat.

———. (1953): *Sobranie sochinenii v 30 tomakh*. Vol. 23. Moscow: Khudozhestvennaia literatura.

———. (1970a): *Sobranie sochinenii*. Vol. 3. Moscow: Nauka.

———. (1970b): *Sobranie sochinenii*. Vol. 6. Moscow: Nauka.

Gorsuch, A. (2000): *Youth in Revolutionary Russia. Enthusiasts, Bohemians, Delinquents*. Bloomington: Indiana University Press.

Gouldner, A. (1970): *The Coming Crisis of Western Sociology.* New York: Basic Books.

Gronow, J. (2003): *Caviar with Champagne: Common Luxury and the Ideals of the Good Life in Stalin's Russia.* Oxford and New York: Berg.

Grushin, B. (2001): *Chetyre zhizni Rossii v zerkale oprosov obshchestvennogo mneniia. Epokha Khrushcheva.* Moscow: Progress-Traditsiia.

———. (2006): *Chetyre zhizni Rossii v zerkale oprosov obshchestvennogo mneniia. Epokha Brezhneva.* Moscow: Progress-Traditsiia.

Guenther, H. (1993): *Der Sozialistische Uebermensch. M. Gor'kij und der sowjetische Heldenmythos.* Stuttgart-Weimar: Metzler.

Hessler, J. (2004): *Social History of Soviet Trade: Trade Policy, Retail Practices, and Consumption, 1917–1953.* Princeton: Princeton University Press.

Hilton, M. (2003): *Consumerism in 20th Century Britain. The Search for a Historical Movement.* Cambridge: Cambridge University Press.

———. (2012): Selling to the Masses. Retailing in Russia, 1880–1930. Pittsburgh: University of Pittsburgh Press.

Hobsbawm, E. (1995): *Age of Extremes: The Short Twentieth Century, 1914–1991.* London: Abacus.

Inglehart, R. (2008): Changing Values Among Western Publics from 1970 to 2006. In: *West European Politics.* Vol. 31, Nos. 1–2.

Inglehart, R., Foa, R., Peterson, R., Welzel, C. (2008): Development, Freedom and Rising Happiness: A Global Perspective (1981–2007): In: *Perspectives on Psychological Science.* Vol. 3, No. 4.

Inglehart, R., Welzel, C. (2009): How Development Leads to Democracy. In: *Foreign Affairs.* Vol. 88, No. 2.

Inglehart, R., Welzel, C. (2010): Changing Mass Priorities: The Link between Modernization and Democracy. In: *Perspectives on Politics.* Vol 8, No. 2.

Judt, T. (2005): *Postwar: A History of Europe Since 1945.* Penguin Books.

Kansantaloustiede (1960): Petroskoi: Valtion kustannusliike.

Konstitutsiia SSSR (1936): Available at: <http://www.hist.msu.ru/ER/Etext/cnst1936. htm>.

Kornai, J. (1992): *The Socialist System: The Political Economy of Communism.* Princeton, New Jersey: Princeton University Press.

Kostomarov, N. ([1874] 1996) Russkaia istoriia v zhizneopisaniiakh ee glavnykh deiatelei. In: *Razmyshleniia o Rossii i russkikh.* Moscow: 'Pravda International'.

Kratkii kurs (1953): Istoriia vsesoiuznoi kommunisticheskoi partii (bolshevikov). Moscow: Gospolitizdat.

Lafargue, P. (1883): The Right to be Lazy. Available at: *Lafargue Internet Archive* <http:// www.marxists.org/archive/lafargue/1883/lazy/>.

Lebina, N. (2000): O polze igry v biser. Mikroistoriia kak metod izucheniia norm i anomalii sovetskoi povsednevnosti 20-30-h gg. In: *Normy i tsennosti povsednevnoi zhizni:*

stanovlenie sotsialisticheskogo obraza zhizni v Rossii, 1920-1930 gg. Ed. by T. Vihavainen. Sankt-Peterburg: Neva.

Ledeneva, A. (1998): *Russia's Economy of Favours: Blat, Networking and Informal Exchange.* Cambridge: Cambridge University Press.

Lenin, V. ([1909] 1963): Tolstoy and the Proletarian Struggle. In: *Collected Works.* Vol. 16. Moscow: Gosudarstvennoe izdatel'stvo politicheskoi literatury.

———. ([1918] 1964): The State and Revolution. In: *Collected Works.* Vol. 25. Moscow: Gosudarstvennoe izdatel'stvo politicheskoi literatury.

———. (1971): *Izbrannye proizvedeniia.* Vol. 2. Moscow: Gosudarstvennoe izdatel'stvo politicheskoi literatury.

———. ([1917] 1972): Can the Bolsheviks Retain State Power? In: *Collected Works.* Vol. 26. Moscow: Progress Publishers. Available at: <https://www.marxists.org/archive/lenin/works/1917/oct/01.htm>.

Levada-Center (2002): Golov A. Massovye chuvstva k sverkhbogatym rossiianam: spokoistvie i nenavist'. Available at: <http://www.levada.ru/press/2002092001.html>.

Levada-Center (2004): Press-vypusk#30: Nostal'giia po proshlomu. Available at: <http://www.levada.ru/press/2004031901.html>.

Levada-Center (2005): Golov A. Vlast' sovetskaia i vlast' nyneshniaia. Available at: <http://www.levada.ru/press/2005120200.html>.

Levada-Center (2008): Gde byla luchshe zhizn'? Available at: <http://www.levada.ru/press/2008031401.html>.

Levada-Center (2009a): Izmenenie urovnia zhizni i pokupatel'skogo povedeniia rossiian. Available at: <http://www.levada.ru/press/2009111804.html>.

Levada-Center (2009b): Rossiiane o svoiom dostatke. Available at: <http://www.levada.ru/press/2009111801.html>.

Levada-Center (2011): Otsenki sotsial'nykh problem i zaniatosti. Available at: <http://www.levada.ru/archive/otsenki-sotsialnykh-problem-i-zanya tosti/kakoe-izsleduyushchikh-suzhdenii-o-tom-chto-znachi>.

Lewin, M. (1985): *The Making of the Soviet System: Essays in the Social Theory of Interwar Russia.* New York: Pantheon Books.

MacAuley, M. (1991): *Bread and Justice. State and Society in Petrograd, 1917–1922.* Oxford: Clarendon Press.

Malaia Sovetskaia Entsiklopediia (1930): Vol. 7. Moscow: Sovetskaia entsiklopediia.

Marx, K. (1978): Class Struggles in France. In: *Collected Works.* Vol. 10. London: Lawrence and Wishart.

———. ([1852] 1998): *The Eighteenth Brumaire of Louis Bonaparte.* Available at: <http://www.marx2mao.com/M&E/EBLB52.html>.

Marx, K., Engels, F. (1848): *Manifesto of the Communist Party.* Chapter II. Available at: <https://www.marxists.org/archive/marx/works/1848/communist-manifesto/ch02.htm>.

————. (2005): *Collected Works*. London. Lawrence & Wishart.

Mill, J.S. (1863): *Utilitarianism*. Available at: <http://www.utilitarianism.com/mill2.htm>.

Moral Code of the Builder of Communism (1961): Available at: <https://simple.wikipedia. org/wiki/Moral_Code_of_the_Builder_of_Communism>.

Moskoff, W. (1993): *Hard Times. Impoverishment and Protest in the Perestroika years*. M.E. Sharpe. Armonk.

Nora P. (2005): Vsemirnoe torzhestvo pamiati. In: *Pamiat o voine 60 let spustia*. Moscow: Novoe literaturnoe obozrenie.

Nove, A. (1992): *An Economic History of the USSR: 1917–1991*. Penguin Books.

Osokina, E. (1998): *Za fasadom 'Stalinskogo izobiliia'. Raspredelenie i rynok v snabzhenii naseleniia v gody industrializatsii 1927–1941*. Moscow: Rosspen.

Ostrovsky, N. (1972): *Kak zakalialas' stal'*. Moscow: Sovremennik.

Patico, J. (2008): *Consumption and Social Change in a Post-Soviet Middle Class*. Stanford University Press.

Programmy i ustavy KPSS (1969): Moscow: Izdatel'stvo politicheskoi literatury.

Pyzhikov, A. (2002): *Khrushchevskaia 'Ottepel' 1953–1964*. Moscow: Olma-Press.

Randall, A. (2008): *The Soviet Dream World of Retail Trade and Consumption in the 1930s*. New York: Palgrave. Macmillan.

Rasputin, V. ([1985] 1990): *Pozhar*. M.: Sovetskii pisatel'. Available at:. <http://lib.ru/ PROZA/RASPUTIN/pozhar.txt>.

Read, C. (1990): *Culture and Power in Revolutionary Russia: The Intelligentsia and the Transformation from Tsarism to Communism*. London: Macmillan.

Riasanovsky, N. (1965): *Russia and the West in the Teaching of the Slavophiles: A Study of Romantic Ideology*. Gloucester, Mass.: Peter Smith.

————. (1969): The Teaching of *Charles Fourier*. Berkeley, Los Angeles: University of California Press.

Scientific Communism (1983): Moscow: Progress Publishers.

Sesterhenn (1982): *Das Bogostroitelstvo bei Gorki und Lunatscharskij*. München: Sagner.

Shanin, T. (1985): *Russia as a Developing Society: Roots of Otherness – Russia's Turn of Century*. Vol. 1. New Haven, London: Yale University Press.

Shlapentokh, V. (2001): *A Normal Totalitarian Society: How the Soviet Union Functioned and how it Collapsed*. Armonk, New York, London: M.E. Sharpe.

Siegelbaum L. H. (1988): *Stakhanovism and the Politics of Productivity in the USSR, 1935– 1941*. Cambridge: Cambridge University Press.

Slovar' Akademii Rossiskoi (1789–1794): St. Petersburg: Imperatorskaia Akademiia Nauk.

Smith, S., Kelly, C. (1998): Commercial Culture and Consumerism in Late Imperial Russia. In: Kelly, C., Shepherd, D. (eds.) *Constructing Russian Culture in the Age of Revolution 1881–1940*. Oxford: Oxford University Press.

Stalin, J. (1954): *Works*. Vol. 13. Moscow: Foreign Languages Publishing House.

————. (1967): *Sochineniia*. Vol. 14. Stanford: Hoover Institution Press.

Stearns, T. (2001): *Consumerism in World History: The Global Transformation of Desire*. New York, London: Routledge.

Stites, R. (1989): *Revolutionary Dreams: Utopian Vision and Experimental life in the Russian Revolution*. Oxford: Oxford University Press.

Takala, I. (2002): *Veselie Rusi. Istoriia alkogolnoi problemy v Rossii*. Sankt-Peterburg: Neva.

The Erfurt Program (1891): Programme of the Social Democratic Party of Germany. Available at: <http://www.fordham.edu/halsall/mod/1891erfurt.html>.

The Gotha Program ([1875] 1906): *Readings in European History*, No. 2. Ed. by J. H. Robinson. Boston: Ginn. Available at: <http://history.hanover.edu/texts/gotha.html>.

Tian-Shanskaia, O. (1993): *Village Life in Late Tsarist Russia*. Bloomington: Indiana University Press.

Vihavainen, T. (2006): *The Inner Adversary: The struggle against philistinism as the moral mission of the Russian intelligentsia*. Washington: NewAcademia.

Walicki, A. (1969): *The Controversy Over Capitalism: Studies in the Social Philosophy of the Russian Populists*. Oxford: Clarendon Press.

———. (1979): *A History of Russian Thought: From the Enlightenment to Marxism*. Stanford University Press.

Voslensky, M. (1980): *Nomenklatura – Die herrschende Klass der Sowjetunion*. Wien: Molden.

Wyman, M. (1997): *Public Opinion in Post-Communist Russia*. Basingstoke, London: Macmillan Press.

Zinoviev, A. (1984): *The Reality of Communism*. London: Paladin Books.

Zubkova, E. (1999): *Poslevoennoe sovetskoe obshchestvo: politika i povsednevnost. 1945–1953*. Moscow: Rosspen.

CHAPTER 3

The Ideology of Consumption in the Soviet Union[1]

Olga Gurova

This article explores the mass discourse on consumption and official attitudes to consumer goods (mostly clothes) in Soviet Russia from 1917 to the 1980s. Through media discourse analysis this era divides into four periods based on changes in the official ideology of consumption in Soviet culture. Dominant in 1917 and throughout the 1920s was asceticism and criticism of pre-revolutionary patterns of consumption such as philistinism or the demonstration of social status by means of clothes. In the second part of the 1930s the idea of individual culture (*kul'turnost'*) emerged, and possessing material goods was rehabilitated. In the 1950s and 1960s imitating Western consumer patterns was criticised by Soviet authorities. In the 1970s and 1980s the idea of the dematerialization (*razveshchestvlenie*) of everyday life was overshadowed by the increasing demands from Soviet consumers and values of individual style and taste. In the 1990s, after the dissolution of the Soviet Union, the discourse on consumption became much more diversified; the issue of identities arose along with the discourse of repair, which continued to be topical in the context of severe economic upheavals. This article demonstrates that the ideology of consumption was neither consistent nor homogeneous during the Soviet era.

The Concept of Ideology

In this research the concept of ideology is defined according to the tradition begun by Karl Marx and Friedrich Engels in their paper called 'The German Ideology'. They defined ideology as a set of ruling class ideas aimed at promoting and preserving the existing social order. According to philosophers, the ruling class defines a particular historical epoch, and the beliefs of the ruling class dominate a particular historical period (Marx, Engels 1976). Marx and Engels also discussed 'false consciousness' or 'illusions' and used these categories as something similar to ideology. According to them, ideology can also be considered as a set of illusory thoughts of the ruling class, which relate to the existing social order and how it is organized. Such illusions as a set of beliefs legitimise

---

1 Previous version of this article was published as: Gurova O. (2006): Ideology of Consumption in Soviet Union: From Asceticism to the Legitimating of Consumer Goods. In: *Anthropology of East Europe Review*. Vol. 24, No. 2:91–98.

relationships of domination and subordination in society, and those in a subordinate position usually accept such beliefs passively.

The ideas of Marx and Engels inspired other concepts of ideology, some of which were developed by scholars of the Frankfurt School. For example, Theodor Adorno and Max Horkheimer examined ideology in the context of the critique of mass culture and the media. They considered ideology to be a false consciousness and to give a false view of social reality, which the establishment imposes by means of the media with the aim of preserving the existing social order and power relations (Adorno, Horkheimer 2002). Roland Barthes, who also analysed media and mass culture, pointed out the link between ideology and myths; he considered ideology as meanings that are ascribed to different cultural objects (clothes, images, words) by the mass media. According to Barthes, an ideology uses the bodies of 'innocent' cultural objects to give those objects particular meaning (Barthes 1993). Like Marx, Engels, Adorno and Horkheimer, Barthes considered ideology as a negative phenomenon or as a phenomenon with a negative function, such as the representation of reality in a false way according to the will of the ruling class for the purpose of promoting the existing social order, namely domination and subordination.

Some sociological concepts of ideology refuse to treat ideology as a false picture of social reality, but rather understand it as a reality itself. They also refuse to view ideology as part of public consciousness, considering it instead as collective unconsciousness. Louis Althusser, for example, considers ideology in that way; he defines it as a set of representations of social and cultural reality, a set of concepts, ideas, myths and images of reality, which form people's understanding, evaluation and experience of the real conditions of their existence (Althusser 2000).

In this paper, ideology will be treated as a set of dominant discourses that contain ideas about consumerism and attitudes to consumption and consumer practices as represented in the media in Russian society. These discourses are promoted through various forms of cultural production or cultural artefacts (magazines, newspapers, TV, cinema, material objects). These cultural artefacts contain and spread particular ideas, values and beliefs and are proliferated through everyday practices. The focus of this paper is on the ideas and concepts having information about attitudes towards clothes, fashion and everyday consumer practices in Soviet Russia from 1917 to the 1980s. These ideas and concepts are parts of official discourse, which, on the one hand, construct social reality and, on the other hand, represent that reality. Four main periods in the ideology of consumption in Soviet Russia were defined on the basis of media discourse analysis.[2]

---

2   This article is based on my doctoral research 'Ideology in clothes: A cultural history of underwear in Soviet Russia in 1917–1980s'. The following sources were used in this research: bro-

Revolutionary Doctrine of Taste and Everyday Asceticism: The 1920s

The Revolution of 1917 brought essential political, social and cultural changes to Russia and stimulated the reconstruction of everyday life. Clothing and appearance received special attention from the new authorities, and this attention can be considered as part of the nation-building policy. The reconstruction of everyday life was called 'life-building' (*zhiznestroenie*) and was based on a new revolutionary doctrine of taste.

This doctrine was in many respects based on Karl Marx theory of commodity fetishism, particularly on statement that under Capitalism the cult of consumer goods transforms relationships between people into relationships of things (Marx, Engels 1956). Marx criticized material goods for functioning as symbols of social status and prestige in a capitalist society, hence, replacing the social importance of a person with the social importance of things. Socialism, as compared to Capitalism, is also concerned with the abundance of goods; however, unlike Capitalism, the individual should be free from the oppression of consumer goods. This means that the person has to avoid evaluating others on the basis of material possessions (Zhilina, Frolova 1969:40). Objects should be treated as friends of the individual, an attitude that allows one to overcome an obsession with objects (Marx, Engels 1956:593).

In post-revolutionary times clothes, their quantity and qualities, and the attitudes to them received special attention in the context of reconstructing daily life. Svetlana Boym mentions that 'thing' (*veshch'*) had negative connotations in revolutionary discourse (Boym 1994). Ideologists criticised things as the source of a philistine, consumerism-like obsession. They actively condemned an individual's desire to obtain more things than was necessary in a functional sense. To have a lot of things, especially those produced and obtained before the revolution, meant that one was loyal to the reactionary past and to the values of the 'old world'.

According to the new revolutionary doctrine of taste, material goods should be pursued for their practical functions, not their symbolic functions; clothes

---

chures on hygiene, fashion and the art of wearing clothes, journals on hygiene, fashion journals, women's magazines, and catalogues of the clothing industry. The major source was the women's magazine *Rabotnitsa,* launched in 1914 as a magazine targeting the so-called female 'mass' (Attwood 1999:26). During the Soviet period it was one of the major women's magazines along with *Krestianka*, which first appeared in 1922. For a long time *Rabotnitsa* discussed a broad range of issues related to social and political life, urging Soviet women to enter the public realm, to become valuable citizens of Soviet society, as well as consumers (Attwood 1999:12–13).

were supposed to be functional and rational, which is why the ideology of consumption in the 1920s can be called the ideology of everyday asceticism.

After the revolution, attitudes became critical of the demonstrative effect of material consumption, 'false' beauty and the use of material things to symbolize social status: 'Have you ever been to the Bolshoi theatre? In the first row you can see ladies with make-up wearing furs. Chinchilla, arctic fox and other expensive furs. This competition by furs, jewellery came from pre-revolutionary times. To show wealth and affluence! Before, in pre-revolutionary times, people were regarded in this way' (Lin 1926:15). This citation demonstrates a critical judgement of clothes and their function as symbols of social status. According to revolutionary ideology, clothes should not differentiate people. They should provide warmth and protect their wearers from the cold, but not symbolize wealth. This last requirement was very important in a state where 'everybody was equal' according to the official ideology. It was declared that 'the revolution had destroyed the privileges that were given to someone by his or her chinchillas' (ibid.). Therefore, the competitiveness in terms of clothes came very much under criticism.

Such idealistic attitudes supposed that, in a socialist society, prices for clothes would be reasonable enough to make them accessible to everyone. Soviet fashion, it was declared, should be simple, convenient, easily made, cheap and available to working-class women. The Soviet media emphasized that clothes should be, above all, functional (*Ob odezhde* 1924:30–31). Clothes should be functional, they should not differentiate people, and what is most significant, there should be a difference between 'our' fashion and the fashion of others, in this case, those who represent pre-revolutionary bourgeois society. The post-revolutionary discourse on fashion and taste was constructed around the opposition between revolutionary society and the pre-revolutionary bourgeois society, the latter being the object of criticism.

One more noticeable thing is the use of the word 'fashion' in quotation marks in the media discourse of the time. This usage is important, because it helps to reconstruct the official attitude to fashion as something alien as well as frivolous and even worthless. In 1923 women who followed fashion were labelled as 'wretches' (*negodnitsy*).[3] According to revolutionary ideology, fashion addiction had to be excluded from the life style of working-class women. The sarcastic tone of the statements about fashion and the haughty attitude and opposition of working women to fashion addicts is typical of rather negative attitude to fashion that was promoted by *Rabotnitsa*.

---

3 'Ah, modnitsy-negodnitsy, vy seli na ezha! Pliuiut na vas rabotnitsy s sed'mogo etazha' (Step. K-na 1923:36–37).

The functional attitude towards fashion and clothes was reflected in the experiments of the Soviet fashion designers Aleksandra Ekster, Lubov' Popova and Varvara Stepanova. With the aim of producing an aesthetic transformation of everyday life based on revolutionary ideas, these designers used revolutionary symbols – sickles and hammers, tractors, screws, airplanes, and so forth. Although the quality of such prints and pictures on fabric (*agittekstil'*) was not always very good, these symbols were easily identified, and in this way the clothing propagandized the new social order in a way that was simple and clear to everyone.

The beauty of the body also came under the influence of functionality as well as fashion. Beauty was criticised and regarded as a bourgeois phenomenon, a 'deceit', or a 'scab', on one's body. One article entitled 'Young Working-class Girls Build a New Life' provides some examples of these attitudes. Working-class girls asked whether it was good to make up using powder and other cosmetics. The answer was a radical, 'Do not use any type of cosmetics. It spoils the face' (Yunye 1924:13). Finally, *Rabotnitsa* decided, 'when the cultural level of women increases, all cosmetics will logically be liquidated' (Il'ina 1927:15–16).

However, at least one type of beauty was legitimate in Soviet culture, namely 'natural beauty'. 'We, communists and komsomols, vote for a natural beauty, a graceful body. For natural beauty, instead of an artificial one' (Lin 1926:15). Natural beauty was opposed to artificial beauty, which was treated as cheating, because it promoted superficial appearances above the true essence of an individual, his or her inner personality. In contrast to bourgeois artificial beauty, Soviet beauty was associated with ideas of 'naturalness' and 'health', not with cosmetics and make-up.

Thus, clothes and personal appearance were given special attention after the revolution and throughout the 1920s. The main ideas that defined them were those of functionality and usefulness as opposed to social differentiation or the demonstration of status. According to Marxist ideas about the role of the material world in determining human consciousness, the reconstruction of everyday life had significant political value and meaning for nation-building in Soviet culture.

The Ideology of *Kul'turnost'* and Legitimating of Consumption in the 1930s and 1940s

By the middle of the 1930s, the ideology of consumption had evidently changed. Sociologists and historians have found reasons for these changes in the so-called 'Great Retreat' which meant changes in ideological orientation away from the Bolsheviks' social experiments to the conservative ideals of Stalin's epoch (Timasheff 1946). Conservative in this case are ideals understood as re-assessment of the Bolshevik ideology of the 1920s, of the anti-consumer approach to material goods, clothes and fashion and a transition from aesthetic puritanism to a tolerance for elements of the previous bourgeois life style with its glamour, luxury and pleasures.

Vera Dunham offers an analytical explanation for these changes (Dunham 1979). She speaks about the so-called 'Big Deal', which was made between the authorities and the Soviet middle class.[4] During Stalin's time, even in the most difficult periods, the regime enjoyed considerable support and did not simply impose its will through terror. Power was based on a contract between the Communist Party and the Soviet middle class. Dunham supposed that the middle class required a stable life filled with consumer goods, luxury and leisure in exchange for support of the state policy (Dunham 1979:13–14, 17). Therefore, post-revolutionary experiments with life-building were stopped in the 1930s, and life patterns that simulated the values of the Russian educated class of the mid-nineteenth century replaced radical Bolshevik ideas about the reconstruction of daily life (Gronow 1997; Volkov 1996).

A speech by Joseph Stalin in 1935 was in a sense a discursive marker of this 'conservative turn': 'Some people think that Socialism can be strengthened by achieving the material equality of people on the basis of a poor life. It is not true. This is the petty-bourgeois view of Socialism. Actually, Socialism can win only on the basis of high efficiency of labor, which is higher than the efficiency under Capitalism, and on the basis of the abundance of products and consumer goods, on the basis of the rich cultural life of each member of our society' (Rech' 1935:3–4). At that time, the Soviet discourse on consumption and everyday life was structured in accordance with three key categories resulting from the logic of Stalin's statement. The first was 'equality', the second was 'abundance', and the third one was 'cultural life'. Stalin announced a new orientation to a prosperous, cultural and cheerful life.

---

4   The term 'middle class' sounds problematic because it has sociological connotations that
    pertain to non-communist societies. In this paper I rely on the definition of Vera Dunham,
    who applies this category to diverse people, including intellectuals, professionals, technical
    and managerial specialists, white-collar workers and others. These groups have in common
    their position among educated elites and privileged groups of Soviet society. The middle class
    also have a common life style and are interested in material goods and well-being in exchange
    for loyalty to the party leaders. In the Soviet Union the middle class was the basis for the ruling
    regime, upon which the party relied (Dunham 1979:13–14; Bartlett 2004; Reid 2007).

This important structural 'turn' meant the rise of the idea of 'culturedness' (*kul'turnost'*) or an orientation towards relatively high standards of individual consumption. In the context of this change of official values, material goods were given a legitimate right to appear in the daily lives of the Soviet people. Goods even became the subject of consumer worship. The category of 'consumer' was more and more often accompanied by the category 'Soviet man' in *Rabotnitsa*. Such expressions as 'this product will have success in the consumer market' or 'according to the consumers' needs' became popular in the official Soviet discourse.

Negative attitudes towards consumption started to disappear from the discourse in the second part of the 1930s. Attitudes to consumption were changing; the media, mostly newspapers, in the 1930s became a source of so-called 'consumer pornography', according to historians (Fitzpatrick 1999:90). Articles on fashion shows, exhibitions of fabrics and the quality of consumer goods appeared again and again. New articles reported on shops overflowing with different types of consumer goods and capable of satisfying the most exacting consumer tastes (Ash-na 1935:13).

'Consumer pornography' was used to describe consumer goods that were exposed 'for show' and, thus, turned the consumer into a fetishist. The question can thus be raised: were all these consumer goods available for purchase in shops or was this just an illusion and a discursive framework? Such a question is indeed valid, because if one looks at 'real life', the consumer market was poor (Osokina 1997). Consumer pornography as well as consumer fetishism mostly emerged on the pages of Soviet magazines and newspapers rather than in real life.

Despite shortages, the idea of the Soviet man as consumer took a legitimate place in the mass discourse of the 1930s. In the context of the idea of *kul'turnost'*, many consumer values such as cosiness were rehabilitated: the pleasures of a cosy home came to life again and became an echo of pre-revolutionary bourgeois life. The rehabilitation of consumer goods in the officially approved discourse made it necessary to rethink and rewrite the meanings previously ascribed to them. Philistinism and its values, which, in the official view, had already been liquidated, were now recreated in the 'secondary' petty-bourgeois culture of Stalin's times (Boym 1994).

In his book 'An Archaeology of Socialism' Victor Buchli gives an example of how attitudes to the sofa changed, according to Marxist doctrine, from the 1920s to the 1930s (Buchli 2000:56–57). According to this doctrine, material conditions define human consciousness. What is important is not the object itself, but the cultural interpretation of the material object. Thus, for example, the sofa as a thing did not itself represent petty-bourgeois values. The value of a sofa is determined by the way it is used: if a Soviet worker used a sofa just to sleep on, but not to demonstrate his social status or wealth or love of material things, then we cannot consider the sofa as a petty-bourgeois object, as had been the case in the 1920s. Buchli explained this shift in the interpretation of things as a transition from a denotative model of understanding things, characteristic of Lenin's culture, to a contextual model characteristic of Stalin's culture. In the first case, it was easy to manipulate the values attributed to things. The focus on denotative attributes, and the judgements made on the basis of the difference between a proletarian and a petty-bourgeois attitude to consumer goods, were peculiarities of the first post-revolutionary decade. The shift to the contextual model provided justification for increasing the quantity of material objects in homes of the Soviet people.

Attitudes to fashion also changed. Whilst in the 1920s, journals were filled with criticism of fashion, the second half of the 1930s witnessed a change from negative to positive ways of talking: 'The requirements of the beauty of clothes are growing ... We can look beautiful, because we have taste and follow fashions' (*Rabotnitsa* 1937:19). The last citation from the letters of village girls show the use of such categories as 'beauty', 'style', 'taste' or 'fashion'; talking about these things in a positive way became important, not only for city girls, but also for village girls. The change in the attitude to fashion can also be seen in the opening and proliferating of Houses of Patterns (*Doma modelei*) and other infrastructure in cities 'to create the style of the Soviet costume' (Yakub 1936:18–19).

Thus, in the 1930s, the discourse on consumption became more intensive than in the previous period, and, even more importantly, had positive meaning. The reassessment of revolutionary values and the shift to 'petty-bourgeois' values such as cosiness, beauty and comfort was accompanied by a re-evaluation of the anti-consumer approach to material goods and a shift from aesthetic purism to tolerance of the 'bourgeois life' with all its pleasures.

The Ideology of Soviet Taste: The 1950s and 1960s

Changes in ideology during the second half of the 20th century affected political, economic and social spheres as well as the cultural domain. This period was characterized by an intensification of cultural contacts between Soviet Russia and the West. This 'Turn to the West' was legitimized at the Twentieth Congress of the Communist Party in 1956. From the middle of the 1950s, economic and cultural networks between the Soviet Union and foreign countries began to be rebuilt. Examples of cooperation include the International Festival of Youth and Students, the International Congress of Fashion and the

Moscow Film Festival in 1961. Owing to these and other events, crowds of foreigners visited Russia.

In the 1950s consumption was legitimated as an important part of Soviet middle-class life. One reason was that consumption became a potent political force in the peaceful competition between the Soviet Union and the West. Susan Reid (2007) called the Soviet/western competition 'Operation Abundance' or the 'Nylon War', emphasizing the deliberate strategy of the US to export its life style patterns to the USSR during the Cold War. The reasoning behind the strategy was as follows: if Russians were allowed to taste the riches of American life (nylon stockings, vacuum cleaners and so on), they would no longer tolerate masters who gave them tanks and spies instead.

This strategy would help consumption to become a real political force (Reid 2007:54–55). Even if there was more satire than truth, the strategy had reasons to exist. America might well have experienced success in exportation since the Soviet middle class was interested in consuming patterns of life styles similar to America's middle class. These patterns included financial security and the 'suburban dream' – a private house in a city suburb. In Soviet Russia people did not dream about private ownership; their dreams were of having a separate apartment instead of rooms in a communal apartment. Thus, if in the 1930s, the life style that had dominated the discourse was borrowed from the pre-revolutionary educated class, the post-war period can be characterized by the domination of values similar to western life styles, at least, in relation to consumption. The Soviet middle class adopted life style patterns that were not significantly different from the middle class in post-war America.

The dominating discursive concept, which determined official attitudes to consumer goods in the 1950s and 1960s, was the concept of Soviet taste. 'What is necessary today is taste' (Mertsalova 1964:30). 'Cultivating taste is one of the most important forms of struggle for the rise of Soviet socialist culture, for the cultural growth of the Soviet people' (Zhukov 1954). The concept of taste played an important role in regulating irrational consumer behavior in the Soviet Union and in people's choice of material goods that corresponded to a Soviet life style. Taste formed a common symbolic space for different social groups in Soviet culture and forced people to follow officially approved fashion and style.

The question of how to recognize good taste and how to acquire it surfaced regularly in the pages of newspapers and magazines: 'What are the attributes of good taste?', The answer: 'Good taste represents a combination of simplicity and a sense of moderation'. 'Too much is too bad' – this was the quintessence of the Soviet idea of taste (Mertsalova 1964:30).

The rise of a particular Soviet taste can be explained as a reaction to ideological competition from America and other so-called 'bourgeois' countries, to the infiltration of western patterns of culture and fashion and to the distribution of consumer values in the daily lives of Soviet citizens. Considering the Soviet discourse on fashion and clothes, one can argue that this discourse was built around the idea of a Soviet life style as an alternative to a bourgeois or capitalist life style at that time. This discourse became more intense when western fashion began appearing on the streets of Soviet cities. The struggle over taste for Soviet youth was carried out in campaigns against the youth subculture called *stiliagi*.[5]

The well-known Soviet writer Lev Kassil' wrote in 1958: 'Why are our notorious *stiliagi* and so-called *fify*[6] so ridiculous? The problem is not that they strongly desire to follow western fashion, always being approximately two years behind and looking the same as Parisian dandies looked last year. ... The critical point is not only in the length of a jacket, in the extreme narrowness of trousers or skirts or even in the vast width of their bell-bottom trousers! ... The point is not in the style. The problem is that such boys or girls try to look like foreigners on our streets. They have a special manner of speaking with some 'imported glamour', which they have adopted from movies that were not translated into Russian. They have developed a special weakened gait as if they have travelled all over the world with their stylish shoes on, and have seen everything. That is why everything is boring to them, and they have gotten tired. ... Good taste is a true, truthful taste. It requires everyone to be themselves, to remain honest in words and deeds' (Kassil' 1958:25–26).

However, not everyone could take the opportunity to be in fashion: the *stiliagi* were declared 'beyond morality' and 'driven from the streets' as a result of a Soviet campaign against western style. Public opinion viewed as vulgar those who wanted to be different in their clothes or appearance. Golybina's tendentious book, *Vkus i Moda* ('Taste and Fashion'), which does truly designate the position and perception of the *stiliagi* in Soviet culture, argues that: 'Some Soviet young boys and girls create ridiculous styles when they follow uncritically the latest achievements of western fashion. Instead of wearing clothes from Soviet Houses of Patterns, they copy western-style clothes' (Golybina 1974:242–243). This critical approach to western-like fashion continued into the 1970s.

---

5 *Stiliagi* are the young people who followed 'style' in their clothing and appearance. They were described as the 'youth-as-victims-of-western-influence' by the dominant discourses, and their existence was viewed as evidence of westernization (Pilkington 1994).

6 *Fify* is a female version of *stiliagi*.

In the official discourse of the 1950s and 60s, the concept of Soviet taste was thus dominant. This framework was developed in the context of ideological competition with America and western life styles as well as with signs of the previous periods of 'secondary philistinism' of Stalin's time.

The Ideology of Growing Materialization: The 1970s and 1980s

From the end of the 1960s through the 1970s when Leonid Brezhnev was General Secretary of the Communist Party, the state made its so-called 'Little Deal' with the Soviet middle class. The 'Little Deal' is understood as an agreement between the party and the middle class: the middle class supported the Soviet authorities in exchange for financial security, readiness to turn a blind eye to the black market and promise of a good life. The purpose of this deal was to ensure the stability of the existing social order (Millar 1985; Buchli 2000).

In the context of the 'Little Deal' and the relative stabilization of society, there were double standards in relation to consumer goods. On the one hand, in a speech at the xxv Party Congress, Leonid Brezhnev spoke about the growth in the supply of consumer goods and an increase in the ideological, ethical and cultural consciousness of the people of the Soviet population, further increasing the quality of life and living standards. This statement legitimized consumer goods in the daily lives of Soviet citizens, because the negative connotations were removed from the official discourse and shifted to personal attitudes. On the other hand, the idea of 'de-materialization' based on Marxist principles, according to which an individual in a socialist society should be free of commodity fetishism and dependence on material things, added to the ambivalence in the ideology of consumption during this period. It is important to emphasize again that attention moved to the individual's attitude to material objects: individuals should be conscious of such things. As a matter of fact, the aim of the Soviet state was to create a socialist post-materialistic world in which there would be consumer goods in abundance signaling the success of the socialist economy to the rest of the world, though these goods would not be of excessive significance to the individual. Soviet citizens should not be obsessed with things, although sacrificing material comfort was no longer acceptable (Paretskaya 2010:390).

In the 1970s and 1980s fashion was a legitimate part of life in the Soviet Union; people were encouraged by the Soviet media to follow fashion. The media acknowledged fashion as an international phenomenon – Soviet magazines provided designs and patterns borrowed from foreign journals; designers from the USSR participated in fairs and exhibitions abroad. International contacts were mostly carried out between the USSR and friendly socialist countries – members of the Council for Mutual Economic Assistance (Bulgaria, Czechoslovakia, Hungary, Poland, Romania, and so on). Certain fashion trends from abroad were recognized and accepted by the Soviet media: 'As far back as last year, young women abroad readily accepted the so-called 'pants suit': a fitted, lined jacket and straight, wide, full-length pants. These suits are made from various kinds of fabrics and are worn all year round as a universal outfit – for work, street, sports, and even to go out. International fashion recommends this novelty again this year' (Maliovanova 1970a:32).

Owing to further internalization of fashion, an interest in ethnic costumes and national clothing traditions as sources of inspiration in fashion sharply increased in the media discourse. Nina Golikova, an artist-designer, affirmed: 'At its core fashion is international ... Frenchmen, Poles and Russians all generally wear clothing of the same silhouette [and] length, [and] give preference to similar details. But the style of clothing and its spirit should certainly correspond to national character and living conditions. ... In the context of modern mass production clothing becomes more standardized. This is not bad at all. We aspire for everyone to be able to buy a ready-made dress, coat and a skirt at any store. But ... the role of details in an outfit ... increases. ... I believe that folk art is the inexhaustible source of discovery and small innovations which bring a bit of beauty to our everyday lives' (Mikhailova 1970:32). As the quotation shows, ethnic elements and details received not only the meaning for nation-building, but also the additional meaning of providing uniqueness to standardized, mass-produced clothing and thus contributed to the individualization and elaboration of the personal style of Soviet men and women.

Personal style and taste remained key concepts in the discourse of the 1970s and the 1980s. Style and taste served to represent the inner self and individual character. A fashionable person was someone who had mastered her or his own style and had a certain – good – personality and proper behavior: 'What is she – a well-dressed girl?' asked *Rabotnitsa*. The answer was: 'The well-dressed-girl' we remember not because of bright dresses with a big flower pattern, not because of an intricate hair-do, but because of herself – cheerful, easy-going, natural, who found her own style' (Maliovanova 1970b:13). The style should necessarily correspond to person's age, physical proportions, and daily situation (time and place). Certain styles were severely criticized. For example, a style popular among young men, the hippie style (long hair, patched jeans, platform shoes), was condemned not only for showing obsession with western consumer goods, but mostly for the asocial behavior associated with this style. Soviet youngsters who dressed like hippies were portrayed in the satirical magazine *Krokodil* as 'fast livers' who spent time doing nothing useful, but rather were smoking, drinking, dancing and lying on the sofa. *Rabotnitsa* stayed away from these extreme manifestations of youth fashion, although in the 1980s, the magazine acknowledged that young people had become a significant group of consumers and needed their own fashion distinct from that of grown-ups (Zubkova, Musina 1986:31).

In general, fashion in the dominant discourse was perceived as an 'important economic category' (Kosygova 1976). *Rabotnitsa* discussed the organizational structure of clothing production, its problems and the consequences for fashion. At that time a three-fold organizational structure of clothing production, called the 'three-level system of pattern-making' (*trekhstupenchataia sistema modelirovaniia*), was implemented. A dress was created in a House of Patterns (*Dom modelei*) by an artist – pattern maker (*khudozhnik-model'er*); then, if approved at the stage of experimental production by factories and consumers, the dress could go into mass production (Kosygova 1976:28). This system, which also included strict aesthetic commissions for approving a design, was roundly criticised for many reasons: a dress could change drastically, be simplified or lose intricate details on its way to mass production; it took about two years for the garment to get through the whole production cycle; hence, the garment had already become outdated before it could be mass produced (Kosygova 1976, Put 1978). 'A thing is planned for tomorrow what one likes and wants to buy today' (Kosygova 1976:29). As a result, Soviet-made consumer goods did not always meet the 'increasing needs' of consumers.

This far-from-efficient production system created consumer goods of questionable quality. In the 1970s *Rabotnitsa* celebrated the development of the service industry, a huge sector aimed at repairing things produced by Soviet industry. A network of service centers and repair shops for shoes, watches, clothing and home appliances proliferated around the country. This industry was seen by scholars as the state's 'repair strategy'; it was aimed at fixing the defects in and problems with Soviet-produced goods or the symbolic defects of their design (Gerasimova, Chuikina 2009:64). This can be seen as a sign of the ideology of repair, another part of which contained books, brochures and magazine rubrics devoted to home economics, which addressed issues of how to be thrifty and develop smart and practical attitudes to material things.

Thus, this period was characterized by two tendencies: on the one hand, an increase in the standard and quality of life and in people's consciousness, and, on the other hand, ideas of de-materialization. The ideas of de-materialization gradually disappeared from the discourse at the beginning of the 1980s, because of the visible contradiction between the official ideological statements and the growing demand for importation of consumer goods. A rise in the standard of living gave way to criticism of the quality of Soviet-produced goods.

Owing to these issues, the service and repair industry became topical and continued to be so into the 1990s, a time of major economic upheaval in post-socialist Russia.

After Socialism

After the dissolution of the Soviet Union and in the context of the new economic conditions (the free market, freedom of trade, private property) the media market in Russia became much more diversified, and it was difficult to talk about an official ideology of consumption. Since the mid-1990s, a significant number of magazines discussing the issues of consumption and fashion entered the media market in Russia. At the same time, the former socialist media, including *Rabotnitsa*, were forced to find a direction in the swiftly changing social reality.

Among the shifts, which require further study, two tendencies regarding the ideology of consumption can be noted. One illustrates a rather new trend, whereas the other shows an obvious continuity with the Soviet past. In the 1990s consumption and fashion were mostly connected to identities rather than to personality and the inner self, as had been the case in Soviet times. 'The business woman is the idol of the forthcoming decade', proclaimed fashion designer Viacheslav Zaitsev in 1990 (*Rabotnitsa* 1990:13). Indeed, business women, that is, the group of modern working women who were 'fairly well-off', appeared often in the discourse on consumption (Salon 1994:8). Clothes again signified class position and status, and transformed relationships between people into relationships of things, as Marx had predicted. In that sense the category of 'image' which emerged in the discourse of the 1990s implied the creation of a certain type of identity and produced a particular impression that reflects this shift in the meanings of consumer goods under post-socialism. Sexuality appeared as a noticeable category and replaced the Soviet norms of simplicity and a sense of moderation.

Because of severe economic conditions, as the vast majority of the population struggled to survive the ideology of repair dominated the discourse of *Rabotnitsa*. The magazine introduced a brand-new, quick method of pattern-making called 'Lubaks' (the name was derived from that of the method's founder Lubov' Aksionova) and introduced other crafts to readers, for example, macramé. Under the rubric 'Repair workshop' (*Masterskaia peredelok*) *Rabotnitsa* urged readers not to throw out old things – coats, jackets, children's wear: 'All these will come in handy. If you can sew at least a little, try to make vests out of them, and if you cannot sew, then use them to start learning'

(Masterskaia 1990:5). Despite the fact that sewing was mostly done through necessity, its symbolic meaning never left, and *Rabotnitsa* suggested creating something fashionable out of outdated things.

Conclusion

This paper has discussed the ideological context of consumption in Soviet culture. 'Ideology' was understood as a system of concepts, ideas, myths and images by means of which people understand, evaluate and experience the conditions of their existence. This understanding allows an investigation of the structural context of the Soviet population's daily life and the context of its attitudes to material things. On the basis of discourse analysis, four main stages were identified here. From 1917 throughout the 1920s the ideology of everyday asceticism and the revolutionary reorganization of life dominated. In the 1930s the idea of *kul'turnost'* prevailed, which promoted the rehabilitation of cosiness and consumer values. In the 1950s and 1960s ideological opposition between Soviet Russia and the West received special attention, resulting in the development of the notion of Soviet taste. The discourse of the 1970s and the 1980s was built around the framework of growing needs and consciousness and the quality of life. This article has argued that the ideology of consumption, which regulated attitudes to consumer goods, was not homogenous during this entire period, but rather that official attitudes to clothes and consumption changed at different times in the course of Soviet history. These changes in ideology and attitudes were themselves the products of changes in politics, economics, culture and daily life. In the 1990s, after the dissolution of the Soviet Union, new trends emerged, although other trends, showing an obvious continuity with the Soviet past, still remained in post-socialist culture.

Bibliography

Adorno, T., Horkheimer, M. (2002): *The Dialectic of Enlightenment: Philosophical Fragments*. Stanford: Stanford University Press.

Althusser, L. (2000): Ideology Interpellates Individuals as Subjects. In: *Identity: A Reader*. Ed. by P. du Gay et al. London: SAGE.

Ash-na, A. (1935): Vystavka tkanei. In: *Rabotnitsa*. No. 11–13.

Attwood, L. (1999): *Creating the New Soviet Woman. Women's Magazines as Engineers of Female Identity, 1922–1953*. London: Macmillan.

Barthes, R. (2000): *Mythologies*. London: Vintage.

Bartlett, D. (2005): Let them Wear Beige: The Petit-Bourgeois World of Official Socialist Dress. In: *Fashion Theory.* Vol. 8, Issue 2.

Boym, S. (1994): *Common Places. The Mythologies of Everyday Life in Russia.* Cambridge: Harvard University press.

Buchli, V. (2000): *An Archeology of Socialism.* Oxford, NY: BERG Publishers.

Chernyshova, N. (2011): Philistines on the Big Screen: Consumerism in Soviet Cinema of the Brezhnev Era. In: *Studies in Russian and Soviet Cinema.* Vol. 5, Issue 2.

Dunham, V. (1979): *In Stalin's Time. Middleclass Values in Soviet Fiction.* Cambridge: Cambridge University Press.

Fitzpatrick, S. (1999): *Everyday Stalinism. Ordinary Life in Extraordinary Times: Soviet Russia in the 1930s.* NY, Oxford: Oxford University press.

Gerasimova, E., Chuikina, S. (2009): The 'Repair Society'. In: *Russian Studies in History.* Vol. 48, No. 1.

Golybina , A. (1974): *Vkus i moda.* Moscow.

Gurova O. (2006): Ideology of Consumption in Soviet Union: From Asceticism to the Legitimating of Consumer Goods. In: *Anthropology of East Europe Review.* Vol. 24, No. 2.

Gronow, J. (1997): *The Sociology of Taste.* London, NewYork: Routledge.

Il'ina, M. (1927): V chem krasota. In: *Rabotnitsa.* No. 37.

Kassil', L. (1958): Devushka so vkusom. In: *Rabotnitsa.* No. 3.

Kosygova, T. (1976): Dialektika kachestva. In: *Rabotnitsa.* No. 11.

Lin, I. (1926): V chem krasota. In: *Rabotnitsa.* No. 27.

Maliovanova, I. (1970a): Moda vstrechaet Novyi god. In: *Rabotnitsa.* No. 1.

———. (1970b): Chto tebe idet? In: *Rabotnitsa.* No. 9.

Masterskaia peredelok (1990): In: *Rabotnitsa.* No. 4.

Marx, K., Engels, F. (1956): *Iz rannikh proizvedenii.* Moscow: Gosudarstvennoe izdatel'stvo politicheskoi literatury.

———. (1976): *The German ideology.* International publishers.

Mertsalova, M. (1964): Chto cherezchur – to plokho. In: *Rabotnitsa.* No. 11.

Mikhailova, T. (1970): Sovremennost' i traditsii. In: *Rabotnitsa.* No. 2.

Millar, J. (1985): The Little Deal: Brezhnev's Contribution to Acquisition Socialism. In: *Slavic Review.* No. 44.

Ob odezhde i modakh. In: *Rabotnitsa.* No. 3.

Osokina, E. (1997): *Za fasadom 'Stalinskogo izobiliia'. Raspredelenie i rynok v snabzhenii naseleniia v gody industrializatsii, 1927–1941.* Moscow: ROSSPEN.

Paretskaya, A. (2010): The Soviet Communist Party and the Other Spirit of Capitalism. In: *Sociological Theory.* Vol. 28, Issue 4.

Pilkington, H. (1994): *Russia's Youth and Its Culture: A Nation's Constructors Reconstructed.* London, New York: Routledge.

Put' na prilavok (1978): In *Rabotnitsa.* No. 3.

Rabotnitsa (1937): No. 5

———. (1990): No. 12.

Rech' tovarishcha Stalina na pervom vsesoiuznom soveshchanii stakhanovtsev (1935): In: *Rabotnitsa*. No. 20.

Reid, S. (2007): Gender and Destalinization of Consumer Taste in the Soviet Union. In: *Gender and Consumption. Domestic Cultures and the Commercialization of Everyday Life*. Ed. by E. Casey, L. Martens. England: Ashgate.

Salon dlia vsei sem'i (1994): In: *Rabotnitsa*. No. 2.

Step. K-na (1923): In: *Rabotnitsa*. No. 12.

Timasheff, N. (1946): *The Great Retreat: the Growth and Decline of Communism in Russia*. NY: Dutton & Co.

Volkov, V. (1996): Kontseptsiia kul'turnosti, 1935–1938 gody: sovetskaia tsivilizatsiia i povsednevnost'. In: *Sotsiologicheskii zhurnal*. No. 1–2.

Yakub, E. (1936): O novom sovetskom costume. In: *Rabotnitsa*. No. 1.

Yunye rabotnitsy stroiat novyi byt (1924): In: *Rabotnitsa*. No. 2.

Zhilina, L., Frolova, T. (1969): *Problemy potrebleniia i vospitaniia lichnosti*. Moscow.

Zhukov, N. (1954): Vospitanie vkusa. Zametki hudozhnika. In: *Novyi mir*. No. 10.

Zubkova, O., Musina, M. (1986): Molodezhnaia moda: 'firmA' ili firma? In: *Rabotnitsa*. No. 7.

CHAPTER 4

How and What to Consume: Patterns of Soviet Clothing Consumption in the 1950s and 1960s

Larissa Zakharova

A program aiming at satisfying the Soviet people's material needs is well known as one of the ambitious projects of the Khrushchev era. Public speeches of the Soviet leader on this subject (including the famous remark 'overtake and surpass the United States') contributed to some stigmatization of the political significance of this campaign in the context of the Cold War and the 'competition of two systems'. The idea of constructing a society of abundance legitimized consumption and became a way of affirming the superiority of the socialist regime. This change in Soviet policy had a number of different reasons. Firstly, during the World War II, many Soviet citizens became aware, for the first time, of the gap in living standards between the USSR and Europe. Secondly, the hardships experienced during the war and post-war period made the state pay attention to the reconstruction of the country, and the amelioration of the supply problems faced by the population regarding consumer goods. This attention can be seen in the emergence of the first project of reforms in the Central Committee of the Communist Party at the end of the 1940s.[1] Thirdly, improving living standards was seen as a way to persuade people of the advantages of Socialism, the prestige of which had been undermined by the revelations of de-Stalinization.

However, illusions were shattered rather quickly: the increase in prices announced 31 May 1962 followed by Novocherkassk events (where a meeting of protest of several thousand people encountered on the armed troupes who shot the participants) led to the obvious failure of this pretentious program in the field of food consumption. But what were its results in the field of clothing consumption? What did the state do to provide the population with clothes and what kind of clothes? How did it evaluate the consumers' needs in durable goods and which of them did it intend to satisfy? And how did the consumer

---

* This paper was written in the beginning of the 2000 and its various parts were published in Zakharova (2011); Zakharova (2013), 402–435; Zakharova (2010), 393–426 and Zakharova (2007), 54–80.

1 Pyzhikov (2002), 18.

behave in reaction to the policy of production and system of distribution of these goods?

In order to answer these questions, let's see first how Soviet economists defined the norms of clothing consumption. It is also necessary to review all the opportunities that ordinary Soviet citizens had to procure clothes. It will help us to evaluate the efficiency of the program aiming at satisfying the people's material needs to study legal and illegal consumer strategies and the state's actions to promote the former and constrain the latter. Furthermore, the correlation between socio-economic factors and the choice of consumer strategies will be analysed, essentially on the basis of income materials from the Leningrad Statistic Department (a branch of the Central Department of Statistics – TsSU which was a sort of Ministry). It is also necessary to consider the influence of cultural factors on consumer strategies. Based on interviews with consumers of the 1950s and 1960s, this part of the research aims to find some 'patterns' of consumption or consumer cultures combining different strategies. Finally consideration will be given to the relationship between mechanisms of fashion and 'patterns' of consumption.

Evaluation of Needs and the Theory of Socialist Consumption

Despite contradictory official attitudes towards consumption, which was damned and rehabilitated several times during the Soviet period, the state had paid great attention to what Soviet citizens had consumed ever since the 1930s. At that time the Statistic Department put its forces to the front of the population's budget survey.[2] This survey was continued after the war and in to the 1950s and 1960s; it had enormous theoretical and practical significance. Thus, it was necessary, firstly, for the evaluation of consumption in different professional milieus, secondly, for the elaboration of plans of consumer goods production, and thirdly, for the formulation of the theory of socialist consumption.

Such a theory was not a completely utopian project because it was based on concrete facts from Soviet reality. When some Soviet economists (Nazarov, Shvyrkov, Shnirlin and others) analysed the budget survey's data using the methods of western econometrics, they discovered that the expenditure on clothes did not increase proportionally to income growth. When income reached a certain level, expenditure on clothes stopped increasing and became stable. This observation served as a basis for economists from nineteen institutes for scientific research to elaborate a 'rational norm' of clothing

---

2   Moine (2003), 481–515.

consumption characteristic for 'healthy, cultured, conscious members of the communist society with reasonable needs'.[3] So, even if the material needs of the Soviet people had a tendency to constant growth, according to a Khrushchev's frequent statements, they could not increase endlessly. According to this theory, social and economic differences disappeared. All Soviet citizens, both in cities and the countryside, had to consume the same quantity of clothes and shoes until they had become completely worn out and regardless of the influence of changes in fashion. According to a party directive, the system of clothing production had to attain this quantitative ideal, on the assumption that the construction of communism would be achieved in twenty years. Thus the III party program, adopted at the XXII Party Congress, declared as one of the targets for the near future, the satisfaction of the Soviet people's reasonable needs. So, the qualitative characteristics of goods related to the phenomenon of fashion were not taken in consideration. Such a brutal, levelling approach to the problem of the satisfaction of consumer needs without any social and cultural distinction, resulted in the filling of shops with goods for which there was no demand.

Although the theory of reasonable needs was dominant in Soviet economic thought because it combined perfectly with the non-market, planned economy, the inefficiency of the approach based on this theory caused the emergence of an alternative scientific current represented by a Ukrainian economist Korzhenevskii.[4] He believed that in the conditions of the personal property for the consumer goods, their acquisition could not be regulated by any physiological and rational norms. He defined consumer demand as the totality of customers' requirements based upon individual tastes and needs. The goal of such a trend was to find a just correlation between supply and demand. In order to attain this, he proposed to elaborate 'differentiated patterns of consumption' on the base of budget surveys and then define plans of production and commodity circulation taking into account diverse structures of consumption proper to different economic groups.

The main difference between the Korzhenevskii theory and the concept of reasonable needs lays in its response to the question 'how and what to consume?' Obviously, Korzhenevskii observed some distinctions in the rhythm and volume of purchases, which he explained by income disparities. So, some Soviet consumers did not completely wear out their clothes but bought new

---

3   See: Nazarov, Siniutin, Shnirlin (1959); Pisarev (1959); Shvyrkov (1959); Shvyrkov (1965); *Voprosy modelirovania* (1969); Shnirlin (1961); Medvedev, Shvyrkov, Chernysh (1969); Tiukov (1960); Tiukov and Lokshin (1964); Korneev (1956); Bromlei (1966).
4   Korzhenevskii (1970); *Metodicheskie rekomendatsii* (1971); Korzhenevskii (1959).

clothes even when their old ones were wearable. But he did not question the reasons for such consumer behavior. Soviet economists underestimated the importance of the question 'how and what to consume?' In other words they could not accept the significance of fashion for clothes.

Although clothing designers invented a concept of socialist fashion[5] (in order to justify their profession and social function), economists continued stigmatizing fashion as a strictly bourgeois phenomenon related to the mechanism of market competition, whereas the socialist economy 'respected the products of human labor and could not permit the idea of throwing out some goods because they had become obsolete'.[6] An attitude to clothes based upon following fashions was considered a luxury: 'the task of providing all the population with the most fashionable clothes cannot be imposed on industry because the communist society has as its aim the satisfaction not of all the needs, but only of reasonable needs. The premature withdrawal of huge material values from the field of consumption due to the specificities of changes in fashion is out of the sphere of the reasonable'.[7] So, economists advised designers to create stable, neutral, classic forms of clothes so as not to induce people to look for novelties when they had all they needed in their wardrobe.

Even if such theoretical constructions about consumer ideals for the communist future determined the production of clothes, they went against real existing practices where elementary goods were in short supply.

Legal and Illegal Strategies of Buying Clothes

Despite the on-going efforts of the party and the government to synchronize the functioning of organizations that were part of the system of clothing production, there were some constant deficiencies in supplying the population with clothes during the whole Khrushchev period. The Houses of Clothing Design created thousands of clothes patterns every year.[8] Thus they interpreted their task as providing the Soviet people with beautiful and good-quality clothes. But clothing designers were faced with a lack of response from mass

---

5   See, for example: Efremova (1960); *Mody i modelirovanie* (1960); *Mody odezhdy na 1962–1963 gg.* (1963); *Novoe v konstruirovanii* (1963); Litvina, Leonidova, Turchanovskaia (1964); and also magazines *Odezhda i byt, Modeli sezona, Zhurnal mod* of the 1950s-1960s.

6   Braverman (1964), 19.

7   Ibid., 31–32.

8   See, for example: TsGA SPb, f. 9610, op. 1, d. 160, l. 5; op. 3, d. 35, l. 61; d. 57, l. 16, 26; d. 85; d. 87, l. 38; d. 221, l. 140; op. 5, d. 40, l. 119.

clothing production (which was interested in producing clothes according to old patterns so as not to disturb the process of plan accomplishment), and the conservatism of commercial workers who were not motivated to promote new fashion. Retailers did not take into account the influence of fashion on customer' demands: they ordered goods from factories that had been in demand the previous year. So, during the first half of 1962, 70% of the clothes made in Leningrad sewing factories were produced from obsolete patterns.[9] For this reason, the shops had no sense of fashion. Moreover, many types of clothes were constantly in short supply. For example, statistical reports on the state of trade during the second half of 1953 and the first half of 1955 in the cities of Gorky, Kemerovo, Kuibyshev, Stalingrad, Krasnodar, Molotov, Cheliabinsk, Novosibirsk, Omsk, Rostov, Vladimir, Ivanovo and other such towns, stated that there were shortages of wool and silk fabrics, knitted wear, wool coats, fur coats and raincoats, wool suits and trousers, fur hats, underwear, and leisure shoes.[10] All these goods were sold out within a few hours of their arrival on shop counters, and 'speculators' bought most of them.

The assortment of these lacking goods remained the same during the period.[11] It was characteristic not only of the provinces, but also of the capital of the Soviet Union. Consumers' remarks in 'control sheets' (*kontrol'nye listy*), which were part of the procedure for surveying consumer demand in one of two big department stores in Moscow (TsUM) reveal the lack of the same goods – suits, trousers, leather shoes, raincoats, underwear, silk and wool fabrics, etc.:

- Suits for tall persons are practically non-existent in Moscow shops. One can find them very seldom and when available there are only cheap types. It's necessary to start the supply of suits, sizes 6 and 7, not only in orders, but also in reality. I have been visiting shops since mid-December, and I could not buy a suit.
- It's inadmissible for such a big shop not to have a choice of trousers of popular sizes and at reasonable prices. There are no suits for pupils of the 9th and 10th classes that are not expensive, and decent. It's impossible to buy shoes, sizes 41–42, at reasonable prices. A pupil cannot wear fashionable shoes every day. Those who can afford them are limited.
- Why are there no short coats of good quality, except Astrakhan ones? The demand is evident and clear.

---

9   TsGA SPb, f. 4965, op. 6, d. 858, l. 24.
10   RGAE, f. 1562, op. 26, d. 219, l. 24–27; d. 433.
11   RGAE, f. 1562, op. 26, d. 783; d. 784.

- All my family have been looking for a dressing-gown for our mother for over a week, but we could not find one anywhere.
- There are no raincoats in chlorine-vinyl for women on sale. In summer these are very necessary, as these are comfortable and practical. One can put them in a hand-bag.
- Sandals are impossible to buy either in winter or in summer, either for men or girls.
- Sellers say that boots arrive once every three years. There is a demand for every day.
- There is no women's underwear in the shop. This is disrespectful to women.
- At the department selling fabrics made from discontinued fibers (*shtapel'*) one cannot find dark-blue fabric for 23 rubles 50 kopeks. Sellers say that it's a rare guest. Why?[12]

These consumers' remarks demonstrate in detail the shortfall of goods. We can see that there was a shortage of big size clothes in commercial network. The main reason was that the planned economy conditions made the production of clothes for large sizes unprofitable for factories because of the excessive use of fabrics that did not attract higher prices (on a per unit basis) for ready-made clothes. Another problem at national level which contributed to this shortfall was the out-of-season arrival of many sorts of goods, when consumers found winter clothes in summer and vice versa.

In such conditions, Soviet consumers continued to resort to other ways of 'getting' (and not simply buying) clothes, as they had done in the 1930s.[13] They adopted different strategies in order to find clothes: legal ones (purchasing in state shops, either clothes or fabrics which were meant for domestic sewing or for being used in workshops) and illegal ones (using the services of a 'domestic personal sewer', 'unregistered handicraftsmen' and 'speculators').

Deficiencies in the system of clothing production and distribution created a vicious circle: the lack of some goods aggravated shortages and resulted in complete disappearing of these goods from shops. Clerks and commercial managers organized special 'closed' networks for the distribution of these goods among their relatives, acquaintances and special clients able to pay more than the state price for these goods.[14] An informal system of distribution

---

12   TsMAM, f. 1953, op. 2, d. 238, l. 43, 44, 45, 46, 49, 59, 60, 75, 83.

13   Fitzpatrick (2002); Osokina, (1998), 5.

14   See, for example: LOGAV, f. 4380, op. 3, d. 308.

based upon *blat*,[15] was at the origin of private enterprise in the Soviet Union and involved consecutive reselling of goods for higher prices. This was officially stigmatized as speculation and was punishable by 5 years in prison according to article 107 of the RSFSR's Criminal Code.[16] This kind of abuse by commercial employees who distributed goods in short supply to their acquaintances passed mostly with impunity. Their privileged access to these goods was perceived as something natural due to their professional position. According to an informal rule, there was a sort of hierarchy in the provision of scarce goods where the shop assistants had priority. For this reason, excluding colleagues from an informal network distributing scarce goods was considered violation of this code. For example, in 1955 employees of shop No 23 of the *Lentorg* who were questioned by the militia reported with indignation on the illegal activity of two shop assistants from the ready-made dresses department: 'when Aleev and Izmailov worked, there were no plush jackets for sale. Aleev refused to acquire a jacket even for the clerk Likhacheva, for her. However 390 jackets which were delivered during the 3d and 4th quarters of 1954 were sold'.[17]

But sometimes customers who did not have any shop assistant acquaintances protested against the practices involved in the 'closed institutional distribution' of goods in short supply. For example, in 1956, in a Moscow shop, a woman saw a shop assistant wearing a silk dress and made a scandal so that this employee took off this dress and sold it to her. The next day the shop assistants asked a factory to give them the same dress in order to dress their colleague Galia.[18]

The risk of punishment was stronger when arrested private traders ('speculators') indicated their providers. In such cases the judicial organs exposed the whole network despite attempts by its members to hide from the militia:

> In Kiev a special form of speculation has spread when speculators sell not goods, but receipts that permit them to avoid the militia. The inspection

---

15   *Blat* is a system of personal relations. French specialist, Myriam Désert, defines the role of *blat* in the field of consumption in the USSR as following: '*blat* was a practice which smoothed the shortages making circulate, out of shops, goods, which were generally taken out of enterprises, that permitted to everybody to realise on the margins of legality its legal right to procure goods made to satisfy needs of all; in most of cases the transaction was part of an exchange of services, without idea of speculation (it was the difference between *blat* and the black market). It was a banal and tolerated practice, for the power as for the society'. See: (2006).

16   *Ugolovnyi Kodeks RSFSR* (1957). After the adoption of the new code in 1960, it was article No. 154 that set out the punishments for speculation.

17   LOGAV, f. 4380, op. 3, d. 172, l. 7.

18   *TsMAM*, f. 1487, op. 1, d. 75, l. 54.

of Kiev's municipal commerce revealed some cases of collaboration between speculators and clerks. For example, during this year, in shops No 1, 1011 and 1526 the dissimulation of lacking goods with the intention of selling them to second-hand dealers, was revealed.[19]

Whilst trying to be invisible to the militia, private traders were not difficult to find for customers. They did their business at the markets (which were initially intended for the sale of second hand clothes) or directly in the shops where the most prudent of them invited customers home to choose goods.[20]

Speculators got goods not only from shop assistants. Some networks functioned with the help of factory employees who stole scarce goods or materials from their enterprises.[21] Stolen materials (fabrics, furs or leather) could also be sold to handicraftsmen who made clothes and shoes at home, despite article 99 of the Criminal Code which stipulated two years of prison for these illegal activities.[22] Such homemade goods were available at markets or in commission shops (intended for second hand goods)[23] and they cost less than clothes and shoes of the same type produced in factories. Here are some examples of difference between the market prices of handicraft goods and the state prices of industrially produced goods for sale in the shops of Krasnodar during the second half of 1953.[24]

Sort of good	Market price, in rubles	State price, in rubles
Cotton-print dressing-gowns	50	80
Cotton dresses	80	95
Silk dresses	150	198
Leather hats	80	135
Men's shoes	200	240
Leather boots for pre-school children	23	40

Even people who sewed clothes at home ordered by their acquaintances were punished according to the same Criminal Code, that is article 99. But this kind of criminal activity was less frequently discovered than cases of

---

19   RGAE, f. 1562, op. 26, d. 433, l. 76.
20   See, for example: LOGAV, f. 4380, op. 3, d. 973.
21   See, for example: GARF, f. 8131, op. 28, d. 3182.
22   See, for example: LOGAV, f. 4380, op. 3, d. 5; d. 39.
23   LOGAV, f. 4380, op. 3, d. 41.
24   RGAE, f. 1562, op. 26, d. 219, l. 41.

domestic sewers who sold their products at market because of the difficulties in revealing sewers who worked only for private commissions. But in reality, instead of prosecuting such activity the state had to encourage it because it played important role in providing consumers with clothes and in this way covered the deficiencies of the state system of production and distribution of clothes.

Similarly the private traders, even if they increased the price of goods, helped the state transfer scarce goods from one corner of the country to another, given that the capacities of the national distribution system were rather limited. These goods were distributed by post or rail.[25] Thanks to these illegal private traders, workers' families in Kiev could get hold of up-to-date Tbilisi patent leather shoes and Riga wool kerchiefs,[26] and in Tashkent every Sunday thousands of people sold new clothes, shoes and knitted wear produced in Leningrad and Moscow at the market meant for second-hand goods.[27] Obviously, not only Georgian, but also Armenian patent leather shoes were in high demand because of their high quality. So, in 1954 an inhabitant of Erevan bought a lot of women's patent leather sandals in the shops of his city, went to Leningrad and together with a partner sold them at the market.[28]

Because of the huge scale of speculation, judicial bodies were confronted with difficulties in dealing with such affairs and to define speculation. Article 107 of the RSFSR Criminal Code defined speculation as the buying up and re-selling of agricultural products and consumer goods by private persons with the intention of making a profit. Persons found guilty of such crimes were subject to incarceration for a term exceeding 5 years with complete or partial confiscation of the goods. However, an occasional resale or an exchange of goods acquired initially for personal use but subsequently sold was not considered a crime.[29] This amendment can be explained by the usual practice of sponta-

---

25   See, for example: Nazarov (1957), 60; GARF, f. 8131, op. 28, d. 5117, l. 3.

26   RGAE, f. 1562, op. 26, d. 433, l. 76.

27   Ibid., l. 87.

28   LOGAV, f. 4380, op. 3, d. 86.

29   *Ugolovnyi Kodeks RSFSR* (1957), 59, 189. It's remarkable that in different republics the terms and sorts of punishment for speculation varied. This complicated the procedure for judging citizens from one republic who committed a crime on the territory of another. In 9 republics (RSFSR, Turkmen, Tadzhik, Azerbajdzhan, Uzbek, Kazakh, Ukraine, Kirghiz and Estonian) a small case of speculation committed for the first time was punished by administrative measures (detention from 3 to 15 days or a fine of less than 5000 rubles). The law provided for a penal responsibility like detention for one year, or forced labour for the same period, or a fine of less than 2000 rubles for the same crime committed the second time. In 5 republics (Georgian, Moldavian, Lithuanian, Armenian and Latvian) a

neously buying lacking goods quickly after they were put on the counter, as this often produced an immediate psychological effect on the consumer. People bought instinctively, hoping to find a use for the acquired item later. And if the merchandise was not suitable, it could be resold. This behavior was legal if the goods were resold for the same price for which they had been bought. That's why after the arrest of a person suspected of 'speculation', procedure demanded that the price of the item be estimated by merchandising experts. These experts had immense difficulty in giving exact prices. It complicated the investigation and made decisions on the culpability or innocence of the accused difficult.

Private traders mastered most of the judicial loop-holes from which they could benefit, hence claims against them were inefficient. The search for a solution to the problem resulted in efforts to make the law more severe in certain republics. In the Kirghiz republic in 1955 the resale of new goods by private persons was prohibited irrespective of the price charged.[30] But some executive committees of Belorussian Soviets of deputies went further: they forbid the resale of all sorts of goods – new and second-hand – at markets by private persons.[31] The demand for these second-hand goods can be used as an indirect indicator of the population's living standards. Some investigations, by the Prosecuting magistracy, regarding erroneous accusations against people for reselling second-hand goods, testify that the accused faced a very difficult material situation.[32] In several cases women sold their own clothes in order to have some money to buy clothes for their children. Outlawing this type of practice, the authorities deprived such people of supplementary sources of income for their daily life.[33] It is important to remember that these restrictive decisions appeared while the state was executing a program aimed at satisfying the population's needs and improving their material conditions. However, the prosecuting magistracy of the USSR considered that these decisions by republican authorities contradicted the constitutional right of the Soviet people to dispose of their personal property according to their wishes as protected by the law. Still, according to special rules for Moscow on the trade of personal goods,

---

small case of speculation was punished only by penal sanctions. In Belorussia there was no law about petty speculation. See also: GARF, f. 8131, op. 28, d. 5837, l. 169–170.

30   GARF, f. 8131, op. 28, d. 6032.

31   GARF, f. 8131, op. 28, d. 6031.

32   See, for example: GARF, f. 8131, op. 28, d. 5837.

33   This category of people could not use the services of commission shops because they had to wait that their goods would be sold before taking money for them.

defined by the government of the USSR, the private sale of new goods was forbidden at the capital's markets.[34]

The severity of the law did not extirpate the private production and distribution of scarce goods. Speculation was a permanent consequence of shortages. The real reasons for its existence were the dysfunctions of the planned economy.

However, it would be wrong to believe that the state used only police measures for the struggle against the private production of clothes and shoes. It proceeded also by principles similar to the mechanisms of market competition when it found out the reasons why consumers used the services of personal domestic sewers instead of ordering their clothes in state dressmaking establishments. One of these reasons was too big queues when the clients were obliged to come at night to order a cloth in the morning. Another problem was the very long delay for the execution of orders by dressmakers (up to 2 months).[35] For example, in Stalingrad, in 1953, dressmaking establishments took orders once a week or every two weeks. The days of opening were announced only 2–3 days before. Usually, the time announced was when the majority of the population was still at work. Moreover, the prices were not reasonable: making a silk dress in a state workshop cost 114 rubles while a private sewer could do it for 80 or 90 rubles. The price for making a *shtapel'*[36] dress was estimated at 90 rubles in state establishments (that was more expensive than the price of the fabric itself) whilst a private dressmaker would ask 40–50 rubles. State workshops refused to take orders for cotton clothes, children's coats and dresses because they were not very profitable.[37] If state workshops were to compete with and undermine private dressmakers by, these deficiencies had to be eliminated. The Minister of Trade implemented some measures in this direction. The first was aimed at the development of the state workshop network. So, in Leningrad their number increased by 6,8% between 1959 and 1963. As a consequence, the number of orders from private dressmakers had decreased by 55% in 1963 in comparison with 1959.[38] The introduction of the method of sewing clothes from semi-finished products (*polufabrikaty*) helped to reduce delays in the execution of orders.[39]

---

34   GARF, f. 8131, op. 28, d. 6031, l. 4.
35   RGAE, f. 1562, op. 26, d. 219, l. 2.
36   A type of fabric made of mixture of different short thread.
37   RGAE, f. 1562, op. 26, d. 219, l. 38.
38   TsGA SPb, f. 4965, op. 6, d. 1842, l. 11–12.
39   Zamkovskii (1960), 57–80.

The oppression of the private sector was implicitly followed by a growing regulation of fashion. When a consumer ordered an item from a private dressmaker, she/he was free to choose a pattern whereas in a dressmaking establishment her/his choice was limited to the models from Soviet fashion reviews. According to their social function, the sewers from dressmaking establishments had to educate the taste of consumers by recommending patterns designed by Soviet clothing designers.[40] *Blat* was one way of avoiding this imposition of patterns. So an actress V.N.M. remembered that she was able to have dresses made which were copied from western magazines because she had 'her dressmaker Vera', an apprentice of the young Viacheslav Zaitsev, one of the most famous contemporary Russian designers.[41]

The norms were also imposed even on the thriftiest strategy of clothing consumption, that of domestic sewing. It was largely encouraged by the state because the efficient functioning of the clothing industrial production system remained a remote prospect. The advantages of domestic sewing were emphasized in girls' and women's reviews and magazines. The organization of cutting and sewing classes, text-books for the acquisition of this know-how, and the large choice of patterns also testify to the importance of such activity:

> Every young girl ... should learn to cut and sew so she can make herself a summer dress, a sarafan, a blouse, a little dressing-gown, in short, and be independent making some simple clothes. The skill of sewing accustoms one to neatness, to assiduous work and gives a sense of satisfaction with the results achieved. Is it not agreeable to put on a dress you have made yourself or to remake something for your little sister? The skills learned when young stay with you for your whole life, and every woman regardless of her occupation always wants to be well dressed, to dress her children with taste. It can be simply achieved when you know how to do most things yourself.[42]

But, in order to achieve this, it was necessary to supply interested consumers with technical support:

> that is, a sewing machine. At the beginning of the Khrushchev period sewing machines were in short supply. Fights and the intervention of the militia accompanied the sale of a very limited number of sewing machines in Rostov shops.[43]

---

40   Semenova (1960), 102.

41   Interview with V.N.M., 8 of September 2004 in Moscow.

42   Stroev, 352.

43   RGAE, f. 1562, op. 26, d. 219, l. 27.

Numerous cases of acquiring sewing machines from private persons for exaggerated prices serve as another proof of the high demand for item. For example, in Stalingrad, second-hand manual sewing machines made by Singer cost 800–850 rubles, while the price for the same machine new in state shops was 600–640 rubles.[44] The state made some efforts to satisfy the demand for sewing machines. But there was still a shortage of them in Leningrad, in 1960. But the following year the situation seems to have improved when some machines made in the USSR could find no buyers. In 1962 there was a proposition from the Leningrad Department of Statistics to sell all sewing machines on credit to the population.[45] This proposition received a somewhat favorable reply from the government: by an order of the 18 August 1962, the Minister of Trade of the RSFSR decided to sell on credit two sorts of sewing machines produced in the USSR.[46] However, consumers were no longer interested. The growth in prices for milk, butter and meat on 31 May 1962, infected the whole structure of family expenditures. Expenditures on alimentary goods grew, while the level of acquisition of fabrics, clothes and shoes fell considerably.[47]

What kind of consumers adopted one or another strategy to procure clothes and which factors determined the patterns of consumption?

Correlation between Socio-economic Factors and the Choice of Consuming Strategies

As these strategies differed in terms of cost, it is logical to suppose that consumers with low incomes could use strategies involving low cost. But in studying the data of budget survey (individual income forms) of Leningrad teachers', doctors', nurses', ITR, workers', employees' families and retired,[48] it is impossible to determine a direct correlation between low income and the cheapest strategy that is acquiring of fabrics for the domestic sewing of clothes.

---

44   Ibid., l. 37.
45   TsGA SPb, f. 4965, op. 6, d. 858, l. 35.
46   Ibid., l. 38.
47   TSGA SPb, f. 4965, op. 6, d. 1000, l. 11, 25; d. 1842, l. 4, 5, 9, 10; f. 7082, op. 3, d. 169, l. 4.
48   My sample is composed of 469 families observed by the Leningrad Department of Statistics in the framework of the budget survey. There are ten professional groups: doctors, nurses, ITR, secondary school teachers, primary school teachers and metallurgical workers, textile industry workers, sewing industry workers, industry employees and retired. See: TSGA SPb, f. 4965, op. 2, d. 6704, 6718, 6726, 6744, 6746, 6750, 6751, 6753, 6754; op. 4, d. 1499, 1529, 1539, 1548, 1560, 1563, 1565, 1567; op. 6, d. 374, 393, 405, 422, 433, 437, 440, 442, 444; op. 9, d. 451, 469, 478, 521, 533, 538, 540, 542, 544.

Families of the first and second groups (doctors, ITR, secondary school teachers; nurses, employees, primary school teachers) devoted the same part of their expenditure on fabrics (16%) and for ready-to-wear clothes (28%). But the professional groups with the highest income that are doctors, ITR, secondary school teachers, ordered clothes from dressmaking establishments and private dressmakers slightly more often than nurses, employees, primary school teachers. The difference is really small: ordering of clothes represented 8% in the families of ITR, secondary school teachers and doctors, while nurses', employees' and primary school teachers' expenditure on this is 7% of the total amount of expenditure on clothes and related items. The rest is devoted for acquiring of shoes and clothes that could not be made in domestic conditions (like socks, tights, etc.). In the group of workers, the expenditure on fabrics represent 13% of the total expenditure on clothes and related items; the expenditure on ready-to-wear are 31%. So, in comparison with the structure of expenditures of two first groups, it is clear that workers bought more ready-to-wear than the other professional groups. The low expenditure on fabrics square with the low expenditure on making sew clothes in workers' families: 3,8% from the dressmaking establishments and 1,5% from private dressmakers. Thus the group with the lowest incomes preferred to buy ready-to-wear clothes and not fabrics.

Considering the income data of Leningrad workers' families, it can be seen that there is no direct correlation between low incomes and high expenditure on fabrics either. Instead, expenditures on fabrics and ready-made clothes do not increase proportionally to the growth of income:

Income per person in 1961	Expenditures on fabrics	Expenditures on ready-made clothes, underwear and hats
Less than 420 rubles	1,97	9,94
420,1–480,0	3,80	25,52
480,1–600	7,30	31,09
600,1–720,0	10,21	48,17
720,1–900	15,98	59,34
900,1–1200	21,75	68,40
1200,1 or greater	26,76	108,70

(Average expenditures per family member, in rubles, in 1961)[49]

As shown above, workers' families with an annual income exceeding 1200 rubles spent 13,5 times more on fabrics and almost 11 times more on ready-made

---

49   TsGA SPb, f. 4965, op. 6, d. 1000, l. 28.

clothes than families with an income of 420 rubles per person. Therefore a growth in income increases expenditure on fabrics, and these increase more quickly than expenditure on ready-made clothes. This trend can be explained by the more frequent use of workshops and private dressmakers by consumers with high incomes.

However, the socio-economic factor does not seem to be crucial for the choice of way how to get clothes. So we wonder on what principles was this choice founded? Materials from 16 interviews prompted me to take cultural factors into account, particularly attitudes towards fashion.

Influence of the Cultural Factor on the Choice of Consumer Strategies

If we use this factor to analyze the interview data, we can distinguish three types of 'consumer culture' or patterns of consumption,[50] depending on whether people take fashion into account when choosing clothes, or not. The first type of consumer culture is based upon fashion dynamics. This type was represented by seven consumers who regarded themselves as being up-to-date. They would turn to domestic sewing, to the services of workshops and private dressmakers. The second type of consumer culture can be defined as dissonant, that is, with mixed tendencies. This type was represented by five people and would follow fashion from time to time, and also buy clothes of mass Soviet production besides using the strategies of the former group. The third and last type of consumer culture is the conservative one. In this type, we put four respondents who did not follow fashion and mainly bought clothes of Soviet mass production in shops and markets. But in addition, they used the same strategies as the other groups.

The social composition of every group is rather heterogeneous. This proves once again the secondary significance of the socio-economic factor where the formation of consumer cultures is concerned. The first group included a radio engineer, an unqualified worker, a librarian, a deputy of a village Soviet, a civile servant of the Ministry of the Textile Industry (who lately became the president of the light industry department of the Moscow City Party Committee), a student of a pedagogical school and a student at theatrical institute. The second group is composed of two factory employees, a worker, a laboratory assistant and a military man. The third group comprises a technical school professor, an unqualified worker, a geography school teacher and a student of an agricul-

---

50   The terms are borrowed from the sociology of consumption. See, for example: Lee (1993).

tural school. There is no evident link between these people's social origins and their belonging to one or another consumer culture.

Regarding combinations of strategies, the first type, the one we could call 'fashionable', is an exception, because its representatives would not buy Soviet mass produced clothes. They purchased ready-made clothes from time-to-time; they were obtained mostly at markets and commission shops; they usually involved some scarce fashionable articles imported from abroad. These people avoided buying Soviet mass produced clothes because of their aesthetic requirements. So they tried to be up-to-date by other means.

How are we to explain the use of the same consumer strategies in different groups? There are some examples that offer us an answer. A woman M. N. N. born in 1932 in Leningrad, grew up in an artist's family, explains her reason for preferring domestic sewing by her wish to be up-to-date. Lacking a contact in the retail trade deprived her of the possibility of getting the goods in short supply. She could no longer buy them at the market because of her low income. Soviet ready-made, industrially produced clothes in shops did not satisfy her for aesthetical reasons. She took classes in cutting and sewing, attended fashion shows of the House of Clothing Design, looked into fashion magazines and reproduced fashionable models herself privately.[51]

An interview with another resident of Leningrad, teacher at a technical school CH.M.U., born in 1923, presents another reason for choosing to sew clothes at home. This respondent could not buy clothes in the state shops because of specificities of her body. So she made clothes herself, or ordered them from dressmaking establishments or from a private dressmaker. Choosing the patterns, she did not pay attention to fashionable novelties. The high level of conservatism distinguishes her consumer culture: she wore her clothes until they were completely worn out and then reproduced the same style with new fabrics ignoring the latest fashion. She even boasts that on one occasion she bought an old-fashion dress which was not accepted by the person who had ordered it in a dressmaking workshop.[52]

An unusual body shape as an obstacle to buying Soviet mass produced clothes is also evident in another interview – with Shch.Z.P., born in 1932 in a workers' family in Gorky region. She had no professional qualifications and worked her entire life at a factory. She started to attend cutting and sewing classes, but left because she could not buy a sewing machine of her own. For these reasons she chose to order clothes in state dressmaking establishments and from a private dressmaker. She thought that these consumer strategies

---

51   Interview with M.N.N., 31 August 2004, in Peterhof.
52   Interview with CH.M.U., 25 September 2004, in St. Petersburg.

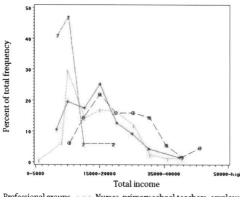

Professional groups   ⊶⊶⊶ Nurses, primary school teachers, employees
                      ┼┼┼ Workers
                      ⊕⊕⊕ Doctors, ITR, secondary school teachers
                      z z z Retired

GRAPH 1
*Repartition of families according to
the amount of their annual income
(in roubles) and their professional
category.*

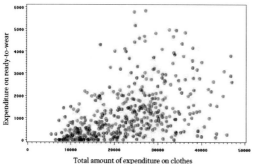

Professional groups   ⊕ ⊕ ⊕ Nurses, primary school teachers, employees
                      ⊕ ⊕ ⊕ Workers
                      ⊕ ⊕ ⊕ Doctors, ITR, secondary school teachers

GRAPH 2
*Amount of annual expenditure on
ready-to-wear of Soviet production
according to the total amount of
expenditures, per family and
professional group.*

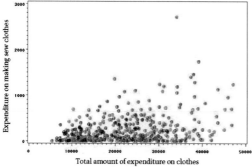

Professional groups   ⊕ ⊕ ⊕ Nurses, primary school teachers, employees
                      ⊕ ⊕ ⊕ Workers
                      ⊕ ⊕ ⊕ Doctors, ITR, secondary school teachers

GRAPH 3
*Amount of annual expenditure on
ordering clothes from dressmaking
establishments and private
dressmakers according to the total
amount of expenditures, per family
and professional group.*

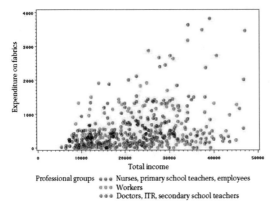

GRAPH 4
Amount of annual expenditure on fabrics according to the total amount of expenditures, per family and professional group.

helped her to be up-to-date. She trusted the professional competence of state workshop dressmakers while accepting their suggestions about patterns chosen from fashion magazines. But she had another approach with her private dressmaker: Shch.Z.P imposed her ideas on fashionable silhouette on this 'unofficial' dressmaker. This respondent searched for ideas in the crowd and when she attended fashion shows in the House of Clothing Design.[53] In this case, the consumer culture seems to have been formed under the influence of accessible strategies. Initially this person refused to consume Soviet mass produced goods not for aesthetical reasons but because of factors out of her control – lack of clothes in her size. It can thus be deduced that she would have had another consumer culture if she had been able to wear clothes made in Soviet factories.

Possessors of the dissonant culture have few aesthetical requirements regarding the merchandise in the state trade network. They would look for fashionable items only when they had to make a choice while ordering clothes in a workshop or from a private dressmaker.

So the variety of Soviet mass produced clothes did not affect the spreading of fashionable tendencies. How did consumers perceive the mechanism regarding the spreading of fashions? Were there some distinctions inside the fashionable type of consumer culture?

---

53   Interview with Shch.Z.P, 26 August 2004, in St. Petersburg.

Mechanisms in the Spreading of Fashion

Besides the factors in the spreading of fashion mentioned above (fashion shows in the House of Clothing Design, fashionable magazines and looking at other people), cinema and music played an important role in the spreading of fashions too. Many sources indicate that Soviet women drew the dresses worn by film stars during films in order to reproduce them later. The respondents named the following Soviet and foreign actresses and singers as fashion idols of the 1950s and 1960s: Tati'ana Puletskaia (especially after her role in the film 'Different fates' that she played in a 'luxurious dress with a bow on one side'); Nina Cherkasova-Vaitbreht, the wife of Nikolai Cherkasov ('fanatic of Paris fashion'); Argentine singer Lolita Torres;[54] Liudmila Gurchenko who spread a Dior style 'newlook' in the USSR thanks to Eldar Riazanov's film 'Carnival night' (1956);[55] actresses from Italian neo-realist films (for example: 'Rome at 11 o'clock', 'Naples is a city of millionaires').[56] These stars were unintentional agents in cultural transfers because they contributed to the spreading of western fashion and taste in Soviet society. Soviet actresses were not an exception as like western actresses all of them had Paris fashion as their main point of reference. The process of Soviet actors' acculturation with western fashion was facilitated by different means. For example, a 'people's' actress (*narodnaia* as a title) of the RSFSR Z. ordered several dresses at Paris workshops when she went there on tour. According to the report of the Central Committee's Commission for departures abroad, some emigrants (*beloemigranty*) covered the fee for dresses ordered from the workshops, and the actress paid the debt to their relatives in Moscow.[57] Another way of acculturation of Soviet artistic elites with western fashion is presented in a letter of the trade attaché of the French Embassy in Moscow, Jean Bernard. This document affirms that actors from the Bolshoi Theatre filled the hall of the Sport Palace 'Wings of Soviet' to look at the fashion show of Christian Dior in June 1959.[58]

---

54   Interview with M.L.V., born in 1941 (a laboratory assistant) 26 August 2004, in St. Petersburg.

55   Interview with O.T.V. born in 1944 (a student of a pedagogical school), 14 August 2004, in Novgorod.

56   Interview with O.B.M. born in 1925 (a military man), 27 September 2004, in Moscow; interview with S.G.G. born in 1924 (civile servant of the Ministry of the textile industry, then president of the light industry department in the Moscow City Committee of the Communist Party), 19 October 2004, in Moscow; interview with V.N.M. (actress), 18 September 2004, in Moscow.

57   RGANI, f. 5, op. 14, d. 19.

58   Centre des Archives Diplomatiques à Nantes. Fonds: Ambassade de France à Moscou. Série B, Carton 271. 'Opérations commerciales privées (URSS-France) 1951–1964'. Lettre de

So, artistic elites and consumers who imitated them were orientated mostly towards French and Italian fashion inspired by trends in haute couture. But such a mechanism for spreading fashions based on Spenser's and Simmel's law of imitation was not unique in Soviet society. There was a group of consumers who did not need the mediation of elites to legitimate trends in fashion. They tried to follow western street fashion and were stigmatized for doing so as *stiliagi* ('stylish people' with a pejorative sense) even if there was no unity of style in their clothing practices. They aspired to have clothes of foreign production that Soviet industry could not produce, as opposed to consumers who wore dresses inspired by French haute couture produced in the USSR that attenuated the westernized orientation. Soviet clothing designers took into account French haute couture novelties while designing 'newlines' for every season.[59] So it was simpler to imitate an actress dressed in haute couture clothes than to follow western street fashion. The officials responsible for the censure of foreign films also censured fashion styles. So if a film was officially approved, the imitation of fashionable trends from it did not present a great danger to official Soviet taste. On the contrary, the diffusion of forbidden foreign films was associated with the spreading, in Soviet society, of uncontrolled and unapproved fashions to which a pernicious influence was attributed.[60]

Nevertheless, there were several ways to get foreign goods. One of them was connected with the presence of foreigners in the USSR. Thanks to the relaxed climate of Khrushchev's 'Thaw', the number of foreign tourists increased significantly during this period. *Fartsovshchiki* – dealers specializing in selling goods bought from foreigners – facilitated the access of Soviet consumers to foreign clothes. They traded in the same places as 'speculators' and were judged according to the same article 107 of the Criminal Code,[61] but they were distinguishable from other private traders by their appearance – they exhibited on themselves the goods they were trying to sell. But they were probably less visible during the VI Festival of Youth and Students that took place in Moscow in 1957 and was followed by a real invasion of the capital's streets by more than 30,000 foreigners.[62]

---

l'Attaché Commercial de l'Ambassade de France à Moscou, Jean Bernard, au Secrétaire d'Etat aux Affaires Economiques, sur la présentation de mode Christian Dior. Le 25 juin 1959.

59   See in detail: Zakharova (2004), 34–40.

60   See, for example: a file on the exposure in Moscow, in 1957, of a group of students organizing private showings of forbidden films in Moscow Institutes and establishments: GARF, f. 9401, op. 2, d. 490, l. 357–361.

61   LOGAV, f. 4380, op. 3, d. 663.

62   RGASPI TSK VLKSM, f. 3, op. 15, d. 83, l. 42.

The festival contributed to the spreading of two types of western fashion in the USSR. It marked a big moment in the form of the discovery of the films of the Italian neo-realists. These films as well as others bought abroad with the permission of the Culture Department of the Communist Party's Central Committee, became an important channel for the transfer of western haute couture fashion to the USSR. The sale of clothes by the festival's guests, who were closely surveyed by agents of the Ministry of Interior, was a way of spreading western street fashion in Soviet society. According to the reports of the Ministry of Interior to the Central Committee of the Communist Party, Moscow was transformed into a great market during the Festival. Students from Austria, Denmark, Italy, Sweden, Finland, and socialist countries (Czechoslovakia, Poland, Hungary, Bulgaria) traded in the yards of buildings, near commission shops, and in hotels. They sold shoes, nylon stockings, men's trousers, women's blouses, suits, ties, shirts, underwear, wool sweaters, knitted hats and plastic raincoats.[63] The militia could do nothing with regard to the 'traders': militiamen told them that their actions were illegal and indicated the addresses of commission shops. Indeed, administrative measures were applied to those consumers who were arrested while buying goods from foreigners: inhabitants of provincial towns were expelled from Moscow.[64] The impunity of the traders aggravated the scale of the phenomenon: during the first Festival days the foreigners seemed embarrassed by the remarks of militiamen, but then they continued selling goods in presence of the militia.[65] Their clients were mostly Soviet students, even *Komsomol* members.[66] *Komsomol* leaders were very anxious that a certain part of Soviet youth 'began to ape, to copy the free and easy (*razviaznye*) manners of behavior of western people'.[67] According to data from the Ministry of Interior, certain students used these goods as a source of income selling them in different towns of the USSR.[68]

The warning of propagandist organs about Soviet people copying western clothes seems rather contradictory given the fact that some social groups had the right to buy clothes abroad. It was, for example, the case that sailors on merchant ships could acquire foreign goods 'for their personal use' with the salary earn during the trip.[69] But as the definition of 'personal use' was difficult

---

63   GARF, f. 9401, op. 2, d. 491, l. 257, 283, 284, 298, 299, 347, 376, 392.

64   Ibid., l. 347, 362.

65   Ibid., l. 375.

66   Ibid., l. 347, 361, 400, 407.

67   RGASPI TSK VLKSM, f. 3, op. 15, d. 83, l. 33.

68   GARF, f. 9401, op. 2, d. 491, l. 301, 348.

69   LOGAV, f. 4380, op. 3, d. 881, f. 4375, op. 3, d. 1601.

to control, the sailors could of course buy these goods in order to sell them. In such cases they could be punished for 'speculation'.

Contraband was another illegal channel for the transfer of western clothes to the USSR. The sale of contraband goods reached its height in city-ports like Odessa, for example. In this case, sailors from foreign ships played the role of agents for transfers. The objects of contraband trade were the same fashionable goods of western production: nylon clothes, shoes, blouses and shirts, wool jackets, perfumes, ties, underwear, etc. The exposure of contrabandists' and speculators' networks by judicial bodies also revealed their clientele. For example, in December 1955, in Odessa, judicial bodies discovered a contrabandist group who bought goods made in the USA from Bulgarian ships, and then sold them in big cities of the USSR. The investigation showed that some of the merchandise had been sold to a composer Bogoslovskii, and also to Moscow actors Lidia Atmanaki, Alexander Menaker, Mariia Mironova, Nikolai Rykunin and Efim Berezin during their stay in Odessa.[70]

But the passion for foreign clothes on the part of eminent personalities of culture was forgiven. They were not ranked with the *stiliagi* groups. On the contrary, in order, perhaps, to rehabilitate the moral image of a large number of Soviet consumers, Soviet designers eventually included some elements of *stiliagi* fashion in their designs. In 1959, an inert Soviet industry finally mastered the production of tight trousers – a symbol of the *stiliagi* look that had generated so much emotion at the beginning of the 1950s. And conservative customers of state shops did not miss the opportunity to voice their indignation on this subject:

- All shops, including *TsUM*, sell trousers with tight bottoms (25 cm), but not everybody likes this fashion. That's why you should produce trousers with 29–30 cm bottoms besides tight ones.
- It's preferable that the width of trousers be 28–30 cm because the fashion for tight trousers is not found beyond the capital.
- Stop making tight trousers because now one cannot buy a suit. You will make respectable people who need suits make them themselves.[71]

Conclusion

So, analyzing fashion and consumption permits to link together politics, economy and culture in Soviet society in the 1950s and 1960s. The inert system of

---

70   GARF, f. 9401, op. 2, d. 478, l. 12, 20, 29, 170–172.

71   *TsMAM*, f. 1953, op. 2, d. 238, l. 47, 115, 117.

industrial production of clothes prevented the achievement of targets set out in the political program aimed at satisfying the Soviet people's need for clothes. Various unofficial ways of obtaining clothes appeared in this context: from speculators to private dressmakers. In the process of realizing the program the private economic sector suffered from oppression. Growing regulation in the field of fashion implicitly followed this oppression. The role of Soviet designers was crucial in the promotion of a consumer culture based upon fashion dynamics in Soviet society. They encouraged essential mechanisms for the spreading of fashionable trends: fashion shows in the Houses of Clothing Design, fashion magazines, classes and text-books in cutting and sewing with patterns all enabled Soviet citizens to reproduce at home fashionable designs. The efforts of Soviet clothing designers were rather fruitful in this sense because a category of Soviet consumers chose these strategies in acquiring clothes (like domestic sewing and the use of workshops) because they were seen as up-to-date. The dream of Soviet economists of egalitarian consumption was very far from real Soviet consumer practices. The differences in how and what to consume were determined by inequalities in resources and ways of accessing scarce goods. The state itself maintained such distinctions by founding dressmaking establishments at various levels: from ordinary workshops to institutions of a higher category, so-called 'luxe' (with higher prices).

But fashionable consumer culture was not widespread in Soviet society. People who neglected fashion more or less, besides acquiring clothes in state shops (without sense of fashion), used the same strategies that people who want to be up-to-date. However the results of the Soviet designers' 'acculturating' work were numerous. Some consumers wanted to be up-to-date, profited from the partial opening up of Soviet society to the West and became rather autonomous vis-à-vis official Soviet fashion. They looked at trends in fashion abroad, using specific mechanisms for the spreading of fashion: foreign films, the presence of foreigners in the USSR, trips abroad, contraband, etc. So the official orientation to the field of consumption legitimized the construction by Soviet people of their own consumer cultures combining different strategies for obtaining clothes. Without this activity, the results of Khrushchev's program would have been less important.

Bibliography

Braverman, A. (1964): *Nekotorye voprosy razvitiia sovremennoi odezhdy. Novaia tekhnika i tekhnologiia shveinogo proizvodstva*. Kiev: Obshchestvo 'Znanie'.

Bromlei, N. (1966): Uroven' zhizni v SSSR (1950–1965 g.g.). In: *Voprosy istorii*. No. 7.

Fitzpatrick, S. (2002): *Le stalinisme au quotidien. La Russie Soviétique dans les années 30*. Paris: Flammarion.

Désert, M. (2006): Le débat russe sur l'informel. In: *Questions de Recherche*. No. 17 (May). Available at: <http://www.ceri-sciencespo.com/publica/question/qdr17.pdf>.

Efremova, L. (1960): *O kul'ture odezhdy*. Moscow: Iskusstvo.

Izuchenie sprosa i obosnovanie zakazov promyshlennosti na kozhannuiu obuv'. Metodicheskie ukazaniia (1970): Kiev: Ukrainskii nauchno-issledovatel'skii institut torgovli i obshchestvennogo pitaniia.

Korzhenevskii, I. (1965): *Osnovnye zakonomernosti razvitiia sprosa v SSSR*. Moscow: Ekonomika.

Korzhenevskii, I. (1959): Opredelenie sprosa naseleniia na otdel'nye tovary. In: *Sovetskaia torgovlia*. No. 3.

Korneev, A. (1956): K voprosu o proizvodstve i potreblenii tekstil'nykh izdelij v SSSR. In: *Voprosy ekonomiki*. No. 7.

Lee, M. (1993): *Consumer Culture Reborn. The Cultural Politics of Consumption*. London, New-York: Routledge.

Litvina, L., Leonidova, I., Turchanovskaia, L. (1964): *Modelirovanie i khudozhestvennoe oformlenie zhenskoi i detskoi odezhdy*. Moscow: Legprombytizdat.

Medvedev, V., Shvyrkov, V., Chernysh, L. (1969): *Modeli prognozirovaniia potrebitel'skogo sprosa dlia tselei planirovaniia*. Minsk: Naucho-issledovatel'skii institut ekonomiki i ekonomiko-matematicheskikh metodov planirovaniia pri Gosplane Belorusskoi SSR.

Metodicheskie rekomendatsii po sostavleniiu i obosnovaniiu zakazov promyshlennosti na shveinye izdeliia (1971): Kiev.

Mody i modelirovanie (1960): Moscow: GosTorgLit.

Mody odezhdy na 1962–1963 gg: Moscow: GosTorgLit 1963: Moscow.

Moine, N. (2003): Le miroir des statistiques. Inégalités et sphère privée au cours du second stalinisme. In: *Cahiers du Monde Russe*. Vol. 44, No. 2–3.

Nazarov, R., Siniutin, V., Shnirlin, Iu. (1959): *Potreblenie v SSSR i metodika ego ischisleniia*. Moscow: b/i.

Novoe v konstruirovanii i modelirovanii odezhdy i napravlenie mody na 1963–1964 gg. (1963): Simferopol': b/i.

Osokina, E. (1998): *Za fasadom 'Stalinskogo izobiliia'. Raspredelenie i rynok v snabzhenii naseleniia v gody industrializatsii, 1927–1941*. Moscow: ROSSPEN.

Pisarev, I. (ed.) (1959): *Metodologicheskie voprosy izucheniia urovnia zhizni trudiashchikhsia*. Moscow: Sotsekgiz.

Pyzhikov, A. (2002): *Khrushchevskaia 'Ottepel'*. Moscow: Olma-Press.

Semenova, E. (1960): Po stranitsam zarubezhnykh zhurnalov mod. In: *Mody i modelirovanie*, Moscow: GosTorgLit.

Shnirlin, Iu. (1961): *Nauchno obosnovannye normy potrebleniia*. Moscow: Vysshaia shkola.

Shvyrkov, V. (1959): *Metodologicheskie voprosy izucheniia struktury potrebitel'skogo biud-zheta*. Moscow.

———, (1959): *Pokazatel' elastichnosti potrebleniia i ego prakticheskoe znachenie pri izuchenii urovnia zhizni trudiashchikhsia*. Moscow.

———, (1965): *Zakonomernosti potrebleniia promyshlennykh i prodovol'stvennykh tova-rov*. Moscow.

Stroev, A. (ed.), *Podruga*. Moscow [the year and the publisher are not mentionned].

Tiukov, V., Lokshin, R.A. (1960): *Planirovanie roznichnogo tovarooborota. V pomoshch ekonomistu i planoviku*. Moscow.

Tiukov, V., Lokshin, R. (1964): *Sovetskaia torgovlia v period perekhoda k kommunizmu*. Moscow.

Ugolovnyi Kodeks RSFSR (1957): Official text with corrections and additions on the 1st of March 1957. Moscow.

Voprosy modelirovaniia potrebitel'skogo sprosa (1969): Part 1, *Metodika prognoza sprosa i planovogo rasscheta roznichnogo tovarooborota*. Minsk.

Zakharova, L. (2004): La mode soviétique et ses sources d'inspiration occidentales (années 1950–1960). In: *Matériaux pour l'histoire de notre temps* 76 (October-December).

———, (2007): Sovetskaia moda 1950–1960-kh godov: politika, ekonomika, povsed-nevnost. In: *Teoria mody: odezhda, telo, kul'tura*. No. 3.

———, (2010): Sur le chemin de l'abondance matérielle dans l'URSS khrouchtchévienne. Consommer rationnellement ou suivre la mode ? In: Capelle-Pogăcean A., Ragaru N. (eds.) *Vie quotidienne et pouvoir sous le communisme. Consommer à l'Est*. Paris: Editions Karthala, CERI.

———, (2011): *S'habiller à la Soviétique. La Mode et le Dégel en URSS*. Paris: CNRS Editions.

———, (2013): Soviet Fashion in the 1950s-1960s: Regimentation, Western Influences, and Consumption Strategies. In: Gilburd E., Kozlov D. (eds.) *The Thaw: Soviet Society and Culture during the 1950s and 1960s*. Toronto, Buffalo, London: University of Toronto Press.

Zamkovskii, D. (1960): Novye formy obsluzhivaniia v atelie. In: *Mody i modelirovanie*. Moscow.

Archival Materials

GARF

f. 8131 'Prosecuting magistracy of the USSR. Inquiry direction',

    op. 28,

        d. 3182 'Inquiry into the affair of the plundering of fur goods at the 2nd Moscow fur factory. March 23 1956–November 28 1957';

d. 5117 'Materials of the control of the Odessa region's prosecuting magistracy's work for the struggle against speculation and fraud of customers.
1957', l. 3;

d. 5837 'Materials on practices of the struggle against speculation and violation of rules regulating trade. April 24 1958–November 29 1958', l. 169–
170;

d. 6031 'Presentation to the first vice-chairman of the Council of Ministers of the BSSR, Klimov I.F., on the prohibition to sell individually new
and secondhand goods at markets. January 27 1958–January 21 1959', l. 4;

d. 6032 'Presentation to the president of the Council of Ministers of the
Kirghiz SSR, Dikambaev K.D., on the abolition of point 5 of the resolution
of November 12 1955 'On the strengthening of the struggle against speculation in the republic' that forbids citizens to sell new goods at the markets. January 30 1958–June 3 1960'.

f. 9401 'Special file of Khrushchev N.S.',

op. 2,

d. 478, l. 12, 20, 29, 170–172;

d. 490, l. 357–361;

d. 491, l. 257, 283, 284, 298, 299, 301, 347, 348, 361, 362, 375, 376, 392, 400,
407.

LOGAV

f. 4380 'Prosecuting magistracy of Leningrad',

op. 3,

d. 5 'Case of Gurfink D.G., Abakshina R.A., Efremova N.F. 1954';

d. 39 'Case of Baraev E.I., Kosterin A.S., Vasiliev M.E. 1954';

d. 41 'Case of Rudeleva V.D. October 8–October 13 1954';

d. 86 'Case of Okun' F.D. and Oganesian Zh.O. June 7–July 8 1954';

d. 308 'Case of Romanov D. V., Balashov P.S., Shirokov
P.I., Rubchin F.I. 17.3–30.4.56);

d. 172 'Case of Mamrukov I.M. and Bakhtin V.N, article 107 of the Criminal
code of the RSFSR. March 29 – April 30 1955', l. 7;

d. 663 'Case of Abramson L.G. June 15–July 17 1959';

d. 881 'On the delivery of carpets as contraband on the steamer 'Pskov'.
May 6–June 28 1960';

d. 973 'Case of Saleev A.Kh., Sadaikin Sh.P., Tuishev A.M. October 10—October 14 1960'.

f. 4375 'Leningrad municipal court',

op. 3,

d. 1601 'Case of Skvortsov N.N. and others accused of crimes according to articles 59–9, 59–12 and 107 of the Criminal code of the RSFSR. January 28–February 26 1959'.

RGAE

f. 1562 'TsSU SSSR',

op. 26 'Department of income statistic. Section of statistics of workers' and employees' incomes',

d. 219 'Reports of Departments of statistics on the acquisition of non-food merchandise from private persons by workers' families, and also on using private persons' services in making and repairing clothes and shoes during the 3d and 4th quarters of 1953', l. 2, 24–27, 37, 38, 41;

d. 433 'Notes of the Department of statistics 'On the volume of the acquisition of non-food industrial goods from private persons by the workers, engineer and technical employees (ITR) and employees' families during the 1st and the 2nd quarters of 1955', l. 76, 87;

d. 783 'A study on the acquisition of industrial goods from private persons, on the sewing, repairing of clothes and shoes by private persons in the questioned families (list of goods bought from speculators and handicraftsmen) in regions, krai, ASSR of the RSFSR during 1959'. (Part 1);

d. 784 'A study on the acquisition of industrial goods from private persons, on the sewing, repairing of clothes and shoes by private persons in the questioned families (list of goods bought from speculators and handicraftsmen) in regions, krai, ASSR of the RSFSR during 1959'. (Part 2).

RGANI,

f. 5 'Apparatus of the Central Committee',

op. 14 'Commission for departures abroad',

d. 19 'About serious demerits in the work of the Ministry of Culture in sending on missions of artists. January 9 1960'.

RGASPI TsK VLKSM,

f. 3 'International events and organizations',

op. 15 'The 6th World Festival of Youth and Students',

d. 83 'Reports on the results of the festival. June-October 1957', l. 33,42.

TsGA SPb,

f. 9610 'Leningrad House of Clothing Design'

op. 1, d. 160 'Tekhpromfinplan of the House of Clothing Design for 1954',

l. 5 ;

op. 3, d. 35 'Tekhpromfinplan for 1958', l. 61;

d. 57 'Schedule of personnel and income, 1958', l. 16, 26;

d. 85 'Annual report of the principal activity of the Leningrad House of Clothing Design during 1959', l. 1;

d. 87 'Orders of the Sewing industry Department, 1960', l. 38;

d. 221 'Annual report of the principal activity of the Leningrad House of Clothing Design during 1963', l. 40;

op. 5, d. 40 'Annual report of the principal activity of the Leningrad House of Clothing Design during 1964', l. 119.

f. 4965 'Leningrad Department of Statistics, Department of Trade Statistic',

op. 2, d. 6704, 6718, 6726, 6744, 6746, 6750, 6751, 6753, 6754;

op. 4, d. 1499, 1529, 1539, 1548, 1560, 1563, 1565, 1567 ;

op. 6, d. 374, 393, 405, 422, 433, 437, 440, 442, 444;

op. 6, d. 858 'Analytical notes of 1962 (reports, information on trade statistics)', l. 4, 5, 9, 10, 24, 35, 38.

d. 1842 'Analytical notes, reports, information on income statistics in 1963', l. 11–12.

d.1000 'Analytical notes of the department on the results of study of personal incomes of the workers of the Leningrad industry in 1962, on the acquisition of non-food goods by the Leningrad workers' families, on the results of the study of Leningrad workers', kolkhozniks', ITR and employees' incomes in 1961', l. 11, 25, 28;

op. 9, d. 451, 469, 478, 521, 533, 538, 540, 542, 544.

f. 7082 'Cheif Trade Direction of Leningrad,

op. 3, d. 169 'Conjuncture survey of the state of the trade in Leningrad in 1963 with some materials', l. 4.

TsMAM,

f. 1953 'Moscow TsUM'

op. 2,

d, 238 'Information on the results of exhibitions-sales of the TSUM at the Moscow fair in Luzhniki, on the sale at industrial enterprises in 1959. There is an analysis of the customers' demand and a reference on the sale at the 1st Moscow Clock factory. August 1959 – December 1959', l l. 43, 44, 45, 46, 47, 49, 59, 60, 75, 83, 115, 117.

f. 1487 'Mosodezhda',

op. 1,

d. 75 'Notes of the meeting of the shop managers on the 24th of January 1957 on the results of work in 1956', l. 54.

CHAPTER 5

The Soviet Consumer – More than Just a Soviet Man

Elena Bogdanova

Comrade, who's last?

Probably me, but there's another woman in a blue coat behind me.

So that means I'm behind her?

Yes. She'll be back soon. Meanwhile, wait behind me.

And you're going to wait?

Yes.

I'd like to leave for a moment, really, just for a moment ...

It's probably better to wait till she comes back. What shall I say if some-one else comes? Just wait. She said she'll be back soon ...

All right. I'll wait. Have you been standing here for long?

No, not really.

Do you know how many they're giving everybody?

Hell knows ... I didn't even ask. Don't you know how many they giving everyone?

I don't know how many they're giving today. I heard they gave everyone two yesterday ...

∴

That is the beginning of the novel 'The Queue' by Vladimir Sorokin, which he wrote in 1985. People queued up in the boiling sun and pouring rain, waiting for products day after day, got to know each other, flirted, swore at each other, spoke about products they had bought in other shops, fell asleep and woke up. In short, life took its normal course and people were standing in a queue. And not everyone standing there knew what the queue was for. The plot could not be more absurd, and exactly describes Soviet everyday life and, especially, the later Soviet years.

Queues, worn-out mothers with shopping bags, and endless squabbles be-tween buyers and retailers became symbols of daily life in the Khrushchev and Brezhnev era. The planned distribution system led to unfavorable conditions for the ordinary customer. The centralized system of delivering goods to shops was subject to frequent failures and shortages of goods were a general problem. After the War and in the 1950s domestic industry developed slowly. The scale of production was insufficient to fulfill the people's needs. Even the most elementary goods of mass consumption were not easy to find and obtain. To get them you had to stand in a queue. Goods like light bulbs, toothbrushes and salt were constantly sold out. These and others circumstances displeased the Soviet consumers quite often.

The misfortune of Soviet consumers vividly characterizes later Soviet daily life, but the fight of the consumers against the injustice of Soviet retailing remains in the dark. The most important official way of defending the interests of citizens in Soviet society was to complain to various authorities. Under Khrushchev and Brezhnev official petitions for help in solving consumers' problems were extremely popular. The peculiarities of the Soviet system of consumption defined the special strategies used by consumers, which will be explored and analyzed in this article.

The analysis is based on consumer complaints which were sent in to the editorial offices of newspapers.[1] Many of these complaints were published in the newspapers 'Vechernii Leningrad' and 'Leningradskaia pravda' in the 1960s and 1970s. Besides these, complaints filed in the State Archive of the Russian Federation (GARF), the Russian Government Archive of Economic History (RGAE), the Central State Archive of St. Petersburg (TsGA SPb), the Leningrad Regional State Archive in Vyborg (LOGAV), and interviews with people who had worked in jobs connected with receiving complaints (a head of a shop, a deputy, a member of the newspaper's editorial board), and with people who had experience in petitioning in the 1960s and 1970s were used.

Complaints as a means of exposing violations of the Soviet citizen's interests were legitimate and widespread in Soviet times. As a means of addressing a superior person, complaints displayed in the clearest fashion the traditional hierarchical model of cooperation between citizens and agents representing the authorities in Russian and Soviet society. Moreover, complaints displayed the paternal model of dependence of the citizens on the authorities, which was an organic part of the idea of Soviet societal structure.

Complaints from citizens were interesting for the authorities in so far as they provided valuable informal information 'from below' for the state administration, and gave citizens the illusion of taking part in important political processes. Both points were extremely important for the existence of the Soviet system. This is why the authorities paid a high degree of attention to letters and complaints from citizens. There were organizations, departments and centers for dealing with citizens' complaints at all levels of Soviet, party, trade

---

1   The article is based on the materials of PhD thesis. See: Bogdanova (2006)

union and economic authorities, which led to a highly developed bureaucracy with exact working principles.

As complaints were a universal means of interaction, it gave citizens the opportunity to enter into a dialogue with the authorities where their civil rights and interests had been violated. It was this interaction which led to the defining peculiarity of Soviet complaints – their pragmatism. The aims and opportunities open to the authors of the complaints were closely linked with the aims and opportunities of the authorities addressed. In order to communicate, the author and the addressee of the complaint tried to use a system of symbols comprehensible for both sides – the descriptions of the parties involved, the basis of the complaint, the methods used for justifying the complaint and the way the people involved are characterized. The citizen had to know the corresponding system of signs to make a complaint.

Formal rules for making complaints, spread by numerous manuals and propagandistic literature, turned out to be insufficient for Soviet society.[2] These rules, which were supposed to regulate the defence of civil interests and interaction with the authorities in the event of judicial problems, did not really clarify the situation. In reality, a complex system of norms, values, and moral and ethical reference points accepted in Soviet society often took the place of these rules. In order to make the text of the complaint pragmatic, the author needed knowledge of difficult, complex and often contradictory unwritten rules to defend his own interests.

Possibilities of complaining were open for everyone. At the same time the options for expressing criticism and dissatisfaction with the existing system were severely limited. As a rule, complaints informed representatives of authoritative structures about failures in the system or cases of social unfairness. At the same time, Soviet ideology did not admit the existence of citizens who were not satisfied with the system. Writing in genre of a complaint required further justification. It was always matter what about a person complains, to whom he addresses the text, what words and arguments he uses, etc. The opportunities for drawing up and submitting complaints were further restricted by the limitations connected with contradictions in the Soviet system of consumption. In order to achieve some result of their complaint, the consumers should be sufficiently knowledgeable in the field of informal rules of life in Soviet society.

---

2 See: *Zhaloby passazhirov na vagony-restorany* (1934); Kazakevich, Kuz'min (1975); Kozlov (1959); *Kuda zhalovat'sia na neporiadki* (1926); *Kuda, na chto i kak zhalovat'sia* (1931).

The Contradictions of Soviet Consumption

The very word 'consumption' was ambiguous in Soviet ideology. Consumption in a general sense was an important element in Marxist-Leninist theory and Socialist ideology. According to these, production develops the need for produced goods and entails consumption, which finally determines the level and structure of production. On the other hand, consumption also influences production. As existing needs are satisfied, new needs develop. That is the core of Marx's theory of the growth of needs (Marx 1955:144–145).

There are two specific features about this Marxist-Leninist interpretation. Firstly, production and consumption are co-dependent. And according to this understanding of consumption, the word 'consumer' is used almost synonymously with the words 'citizen' or 'worker' and went far beyond the limited understanding of consumption as simply the satisfaction of personal needs. Secondly, Marxist-Leninist theory entailed an alternative to the classical understanding of consumption. In Aristotle's understanding, needs themselves were a measure of consumption, but in the Marxist-Leninist conception, the measure of consumption was industrial capacity (Marx 1955:128). Thus, according to Marxist-Leninist theory, productive forces were the most important factor in defining the volume and character of needs.

The understanding of consumption as the satisfaction of personal needs existed in Soviet discourse as well, but bringing it into conformity with the dominant broad theory caused Soviet ideologists no small amount of effort. In particular, they created the concept of 'reasonableneeds', which can be divided into two groups. In the first group were reasonable needs which could be regulated by using scientific standards. These standards were to be worked out scientifically by institutes of hygiene and medicine (Strumilin 1961:361; Zhilina, Frolova 1969:120–122; *Kommunizm i sotsial'nyi protsess* 1973:130–132). In the second group were reasonable needs which could be regulated by bringing material needs into line with the level of production so far attained (Arzamastsev 1980:78–85). The bases for defining the level of needs in both cases were artificially created standards, determined by Soviet production capacity. The standards set out what quantity of meat, milk, bread, refrigerators, pairs of winter boots, and so on should be consumed by the average Soviet citizen within a certain period of time.

Using levels of consumption as a guide, a clear ideological position was worked out which was used as a further means of making sure these standards were observed. The ideology encouraged consumption, but only as long as it did not exceed certain limits. Much of the philosophical and ideological literature of the 1960s, 1970s and 1980s sets out standards, imperatives for the socialist way of life, and the Soviet model of the relationship between the citizen and material values. A model of consumption unlimited by anything save subjective desire is severely criticised.[3]

Personal consumption which exceeded state norms was presented as a pathological desire for enrichment and the use of material goods. In the Soviet lexicon, this was denoted either as 'consumerism' or *veshchizm*, materialism (in the sense of excessive devotion to material objects) (Motiashov 1985; Motiashov 1988; Kogan 1987). As a consequence, in Soviet discourse the words 'consumption' and 'consumer' had negative meanings. The existence of such a contradiction within one discourse explains the change of concepts which were used to define personal consumption in the Soviet years. The word 'consumer' is often substituted with 'buyer', 'visitor', 'client', 'citizen', 'customer', and so on. Depending on the context it could be interpreted as good or evil.

One more contradictory attribute of Soviet consumption was the relationship between the consumer and the retailer. This can be easily explained: from the point of view of the market economy, the Soviet model of interaction between consumer and retailer does not look entirely natural. The formal and informal principle of the market is that 'the customer is always right'. However, in the Soviet system this principle was reversed: 'the retailer is always right'.

According to the Hungarian scientist Janos Kornai, when there is a shortage of goods, the interaction between consumer and retailer goes as follows: 'Buyers compete against each other to get the good which is in short supply. The retailer behaves in an unfriendly and impolite fashion, while at the same time the buyer tries to please the retailer and to get his sympathy. The buyer is ready to pay more to get the product article item he wants. The range of products is small, the packaging careless and haphazard, the buyer has to arrange for the delivery. The producers or retailers, working to order, fix long terms for the fulfillment of the orders, which they, however, often do not carry out' (Kornai 2000).

The social status of the professional shop assistant was comparatively high. Participation in the distribution system provided them with opportunities to re-distribute goods through informal networks. For many, such forms of re-distribution were the only means of acquiring scarce goods. In a popular film shot in the final years of the Soviet regime, the heroine tells an anecdote: 'Communism, Mum, is when all Soviet people have their own butcher at the shop'.[4] Those who organized re-distribution were guaranteed an important and respected position within the network. Alena Ledeneva, a researcher into *blat*, notes the significance of these informal networks in the organization of daily consumption and the functioning of Soviet society (Ledeneva 1998).

3   See: Arzamastsev (1980); Zhilina (1988); Sadikov, Vetrov (1974); Tarasenko (1977), etc.
4   *Rebro Adama* (1990) Film Director is V. Krishtofovich.

People with access to scarce goods were seen as separate social and professional groups. *Torgashi* and *blatnye*[5] contrasted with ordinary people who had to put up with the poor assortment available on Soviet shop shelves. 'Mere mortals' took a very antagonistic stance towards those involved in *blat*. At the same time, a large number of citizens were involved in these informal redistribution networks.

A lack of competition between state-owned retailers, dependence upon the retailer, and a number of other factors often left consumers defenseless. Sending complaints directly to retail employees turned out in most cases to be absurd or useless. In addition to complications connected to the search for or acquisition of goods, consumers regularly ran into problems with service. The standard, stereotypical behavior of Soviet shop assistants and service personnel was rudeness and boorishness. The behavior of workers in the Soviet retail trade and the service sector regularly became the theme of criticism, reflected in satire, film, and the press. The informal requirement for recruitment into the retail sector introduced with the beginning of the market economy is fairly telling in this respect, that is, 'to have never worked in retail trade in Soviet times', and 'to have never worked in service in the Soviet era'.

One of the most widespread problems of the Soviet retail trade and service – cheating in weighing – is reflected in the caricature.[6] A telltale demonstration of the model of interaction of the Soviet consumer and the shop assistant appears in a cartoon created in the 1960s by the well-known *Kukryniksy*[7] group of cartoonists. Above the counter hangs a sign marking the official principle of Soviet service: 'Be mutually polite'. A conflict breaks out in which the shop assistant exhibits aggressive, arrogant and even dangerous behavior. The customer is left with one option: submission. The shop assistant raises a bottle of milk to the customer: 'You wanted to see this bottle? Didn't you want a bottle?'[8]

The consumer's desires conflicted with the opportunities open to him from the end of the 1950s to the 1970s. The authors Natal'ia Lebina and Alexander Chistikov, in the conclusion of their book 'The Citizen and Reforms' note that besides the surging phenomenon of shortages in the 1950s and 1960s, there was another circumstance that affected the behavior of consumers in the late

5   *Torgash* – slang word, issued from the Russian words *torgovat'* (to sell), identifying a salesman, and keeping meaning of not very honest and civilized forms of sale. Te word *blatnye* identifies people, belonging to the non-formal network of distribution, named in the Soviet discourse *blat*.

6   See Picture 1 (Magazin of caricatures *Krokodil*, (1969)).

7   The title of group of cartoonists *Kukryniksy* was formed out the first syllables of the group members names: **Kupriianov**, **Krylov** and **Nikolai Sokolov**.

8   See Picture 2 (Caricature of the famous Soviet group of caricaturists *Kukryniksy*, 1964).

— Раз уж вы взвесили свой палец, то заверните и его!

Рисунок О. КОРНЕВА

FIGURE 1
– Pack your finger also, since you have weighed it!

FIGURE 2

Soviet years: 'In the 1950s and 1960s the rigid ideological diktat in the realm of fashion disappeared' (Lebina, Chistikov 2003:308). From the end of 1950s to the beginning of 1960s, new patterns of consumption from the West began to appear. Imported goods showed Soviet consumers a completely different standard of quality and a different notion of the variety of goods. Leonid Ionin pays attention to the phenomenon of '*stiliagi*'[9], who appeared at the end of 1950s like an omen of the end of a single 'asceticism from above', a forced drabness and dullness in clothing, and notes the sharp social resonance created by the appearance of such alternatives (Ionin 2004:194).

---

9   Young people given to extravagant displays of clothing and manners.

The Soviet consumer of the 1960s was not only seduced by novelties. Oleg Kharkhordin, a researcher into Soviet society, notes that, roughly at the beginning of the 1960s, material objects began to play an important stratifying role in society (see: Kharkhordin 2002). All in all, thanks to Khrushchev's famous statement: 'We will catch up and surpass the USA in milk and meat production', consumer abundance expressed a distinctive symbolic measure of national might. There was a burning desire to have fashionable, beautiful things despite the essentially limited opportunities for obtaining them, as many who lived during those years remember:

> – I remember when I bought my first jeans. They were not the right size for me – too small. Somebody in the Institution told us that jeans were available in 'Sportivnyi' department store. And we forgot about the lectures, and ran there. The jeans coast about 30 rubles. That was a full scholarship for a month. There was a horrible crowd.

> – And could you try on the jeans?

> – Oh! That was out of the question! I gave my money to somebody, through the crowd, and somebody gave me back a bag with jeans. And size? They were about three sizes too long for me, and too tight. I could hardly pull them on. And the length <...> I saw that guys roll them up, and I've also got to do that. There was some kind of label on the jeans. Not a proprietary label, but ordinary. After the first washing that peeled off, and I was almost crying.[10]

The narrow ideological limits open to Soviet citizens for the expression of discontent and the protection of one's interests further limited the Soviet consumer. The ambiguity in the ideological appraisal of consumption and the status of the consumer created complications in representing consumer problems and status. The ideological and social contradictions of Soviet consumption required additional explanations and grounding, without which a complaint turned out to be insufficiently legitimate and had little chance of success.

---

10 Interview 3 (see list of quoted interview after bibliography).

What They Complained About

Endless Combat – We Can Only Dream of Peace[11]

Looking at the complaints submitted we can see that the spectrum of consumer problems common in the 1960s and 1970s was extraordinarily broad. Consumers complained about the lack of goods, the poor service at the dry-cleaners and in restaurants and stores, and about the rudeness, boorishness, and indifference of shop assistants. They complained about the poor quality of shoes, clothing, cloth and materials, about the low quality of furniture and toys, about paint which 'doesn't paint', and about skis to which it was impossible to fasten bindings. They complained about the shortage of fresh flowers in city stores, about queues and the violation of queuing rules; about poor work transport, and so on.

Some features of these complaints allow one to suppose that Soviet consumer believed that there was some hope of correcting not only the behavior of retail employees, but even the system of distribution. Not uncommon among consumers' complaints are protests about the lack of the most basic goods in stores: 'Recently one cannot find small enameled pans. One has to use a large pan to cook porridge for a child. Lenhoztorg[12] has to take care about the consumer's needs'.[13]

Deficiencies in the organization of commerce were also reflected in complaints. The common Soviet-era practice of selling goods 'as a bundle'[14] often attracted consumer protests, as in the following case:

Dear comrade editor! Imagine please that you have to buy a saddle for a bicycle, and they tell you to buy also a handle bar, otherwise they will not sell you a saddle. What could you say to a shop assistant in reply? May be you don't believe us, but this is a fact. In the Slantsy district, B. Luchki city, in the supermarket one can buy a bicycle cover just in set with an inner tube and a wheel. It is a question: what should I do with the wheel when what I need actually is a cover?!![15]

Or in another revealing instance:

---

11   From Alexander Blok's poem *'Na pole Kulikovom'*.

12   Lenkhoztorg – **Len**ingradskoe **khoz**iaistvo **torg**ovli, which means Leningrad trade economy.

13   Vechernii Leningrad, 1963, 3 April, p. 2.

14   This rule of selling, widespread in the late Soviet period, permitted buying scare commodities just in set with some another commodities (often ordinary, easy accessible).

15   LOGAV, f. P. – 3553, op. 7, d. 9, l. 80.

<...> The other day we visited a medical equipment store at Nevskiy pros-
pect, 69. There were rubber gloves on sale – this good is necessary not
only for surgeons but also for women who do the house work and want to
keep their hands healthy. Imagine our amazement when we discovered
that in this store one can buy these gloves only if one also buys photo-
graphic film. The price of the gloves is 42 kopeks, price of a film is 35
kopeks, and consequently, together it costs 77 kopeks. We wanted to take
the gloves very much, and we bought several sets without a dispute. However, we suppose that the sale of goods with such the compulsory accom-
paniment is worth complaining about.[16]

Consumers complained about the lack of goods of a certain size or colour,
about the lack of clothing or shoes of a certain style, or the production shortage of a certain enterprise. For example, in a complaint published in the newspaper 'Evening Leningrad' in 1963, a consumer poses a question: 'Why don't
Leningrad furniture factories produce dark brown cupboards?'[17] In their book
Ntal'ia Lebina and Alexander Chistikov note that 'at the end of the 1950s the
most serious event in shoe fashion was the abrupt change from round to pointed toes' (Lebina, Chistikov 2003:195). However, judging by complaints, none of
the consumers were satisfied with this innovation. Among complaints published in the beginning of the 1960s are the comments of consumers about the
difficulty of buying shoes with round toes, the production of which had been
abruptly reduced: 'There are fashionable shoes in stores, but my age doesn't
allow me to wear them. My feet get tired and sore'.[18]

Soviet complaints practically never refer to laws and regulations. Nonethe-
less, this does not mean that consumers were not familiar with them. The complaints show quite clearly ideas of the rules of trade organization and service,
about the supposed selection of goods, about the rules of supply, and about
certain standards of quality of goods and services.

The authorities dealing with complaints classified them according to their
grounds. The Trade Committee of the Leningrad Region Executive Committee
listed the following headings in its 1961 report about complaints and declara-
tions: 'the lack of food products; the lack of industrial goods; infringements of
the rules of trade; unsatisfactory quality of goods; unsatisfactory organization
of trade'.[19] The list of the trade department of the Executive Committee of the
Leningrad Regional Soviet of Workers' Deputies is slightly different, but ex-

16   *Perchatki s 'nagruzkoi'.* Vechernii Leningrad, 1964, 25 November, p. 2.
17   Vechernii Leningrad, 1963, 24 April, p. 2.
18   Obuv' ne po vozrastu. Vechernii Leningrad, 1963, 23 April, p. 2.
19   LOGAV, f. P – 3551, op. 7, d. 181, p. 1.

presses a similar situation: 'rudeness; short change, incorrect weight or measurement; the use of glass crockery; badly prepared food; slow service; refusal
to give out the book of complaints'.[20] Other reports make points relating to the
shortage of certain goods and services, for example, 'the lack of paper', 'the lack
of toothpaste', 'insufficient clothing in large sizes' and so on.

Judging by documents held by other authorities dealing with complaints,
counting and classifying were obligatory elements of the work involved in
dealing with complaints. Reports to higher authorities generally contained an
analysis of the complaints received. This allows us to conclude that the principle of collecting complaints and their capacity to influence the planning and
distribution system worked. Without doubt, there were failures in the work of
the bureaucracy in that the statistics given did not always accurately reflect the
true state of affairs. However, in a number of cases consumer complaints really
were taken into account in the adoption of administrative decisions, in the
processes of planning and distribution.

When consumers turned to the authorities at various levels and repeated
the same complaint about the same product, or described the 'incorrect' behavior of the same shop assistant, this could have serious repercussions for
those involved. According to the interview with the former head of a shop, and
other materials available, serious reforms were undertaken as a result of the
complaints received. If complaints reached a critical mass, goods could be
withdrawn from production. For example: 'There were other negative remarks
about production from the 'Red Triangle' (*a factory producing rubber – E.B.*), as
a result of which the administration decided to stop producing rubber boots
No. 118-SFD'.[21] New enterprises might even be set up, for instance:

> as a response to the large number of complaints about the lack of laundry
> facilities in their area emanating from the inhabitants of the 3rd to 9th
> Lines, Vasil'evskii Island[22], the deputy director of the directorate for ser-
> vice of the Leningrad Region Executive Committee, S.M. Levin,
> announced that it was planned to open a laundry at number 62, 4th Line,
> Vasil'evskii Island[23] in the next quarter.[24]

---

20   LOGAV, f. P – 3551, op. 5, d. 14.

21   Neudovletvoritel'nyi otvet. Vechernii Leningrad, 1964, 30 November, p. 2.

22   The 3rd and 9th Lines, Vasil'evslkii Island are street names in Leningrad (recently St.
       Petersburg).

23   62, 4th Line, Vasil'evskii Island is the address in Leningrad (recently St. Petersburg).

24   Mery priniaty. Vechernii Leningrad, 1970, 2 February, p. 2.

Where They Lodged Their Complaints

According to the formal rules, consumers could file a complaint with any level of authority. The higher the level at which the complaint was examined, the better chances it had of being addressed. Complaints about bad service, poor quality of goods, and so on, were examined not only by specialized trade organizations, but also by 'organs of common competence', which included supreme organs of Soviet and party power, government and regional executive committees, party organs, the Workers' Bureau of Complaints and Suggestions, the editorial staffs of newspapers and magazines, and so on.

Given such an enormous bureaucratic structure, the authorities receiving complaints were not equal in their capacity to deal with complaints. According to one interview, the most effective complaints turned out to be those sent to the party organs:

> It was possible to complain to the higher organs, but the Soviets did not have this power <...> this competence in the restoration of justice which the party had. The party sector was, of course, much more powerful, offered more opportunities. That is why, so to say, a secretary of the district committee was always more important than a chairmen of an executive committee. That means that the formal head of a district or a city was nothing in comparison with the party committees. For example, everybody knew who the secretary of a party district committee was, but far from everybody knew who the managers of the city were.[25]

Among archival documents it is possible to find confirmation that complaints by ordinary consumers were examined at high levels of power. For example, an ordinary complaint, sent to the address 'Moscow, The Kremlin, Chairman of Ministers Kosygin', was examined in the Ministry of Trade in March 1968:

> For the attention of a chairman of ministers, Kosygin, from Feoktistov Nikolai Sergeevich who lives at the station Ashukino, the North Railway. A complaint. Comrade Kosygin, the black market is located in the stores. Anywhere you go, you meet deception. Here are the facts. On the 11th of March I bought a kilogram of sausages in the store number 35 which is situated on Masha Poryvaeva Street. They cheated me by 40 grams of weight of Liubitelskaia (*the sort of sausages* – E.B.). They have not returned me my money and did not give me the complaint book. I asked what the family name of the store manager was and they answered:

---

25   Interview 4.

'Bubnova Raisa Vasil'evna'. The shop assistant was Vasil'eva Natasha. I have applied to the general administration several times, but nothing changes. I do not have a great pension, and service in the stores is worse than on the black market, and when you ask for the complaint book, they say rude things like: 'You have nothing to do, and you count the kopeks'. I have a question: what do they do in the general administration?[26]

Complaints forwarded to high levels of power turned out to be more effective because the process of reviewing turned out to involve all the levels of bureaucracy. Officially, local executive committees[27] were in charge of receiving and investigating the complaints of ordinary people. Executive committees did in fact receive a high number of complaints, for the most varied of causes. They were inundated. For example, according to the article of Theodore Friedgut, in the first four months of 1962 alone, the executive committee of the Kirov region of Moscow received 11,803 complaints (Friedgut 1978:466). To ensure that complaints were not lost among the enormous number of letters but were in fact examined, additional resources were often required. Representatives of peoples' authorities such as people's deputies, activists, famous public and cultural figures, and so on were often recruited for collaboration:

> She was helped by Nina Vasil'evna Peitser. She was a ballerina at our musical theatre. And Nina Vasil'evna was a deputy. A people's deputy. That was what it was called. And Nina Vasil'evna got mother a permit <...> Sometimes these actors who were also deputies <...> you went to them, and if they were good, responsive people, they could get you something like that.[28]

The Department of People's Inspection[29] and the Workers' Bureau of Complaints and Suggestions also received a great deal of complaints. Where problems of consumption arose, complaints in the press turned out to be especially effective.

---

26 GARF, f A – 410, op. 1, d. 2130, l. 49.

27 Local executive committee (*Raionnyi ispolnitelnyi komitet*) – middle level of the Soviet power hierarchy, empowered to solve citizens' problems on the city districts level.

28 Interview 1.

29 People's Inspection (*Narodnyi kontrol'*) is a form of control in the Soviet society, combining the state control with peoples' control. The main function of this organization was to control activity of different shares of economy and management, including the trade industry.

Complaints of Soviet Consumers in the Press

The press played a special role in the organization of Soviet consumption. The press fulfilled a unique role as an intermediary between producers, consumers, and the authorities. In the conditions of a planned economy this was a very important role.

Seminars and conferences were devoted to discussing the problem of the mutual dependence of consumer goods and the press. They discussed in detail the characteristics and qualities of newly developed products, problems related to the rise in the quality of goods, the rise in the quality of production, safeguarding material resources during their transport and storage and dozens of other themes (*Proizvodstvo tovarov narodnogo potrebleniia i zadachi pechati* 1979:53–60).

In the 1960s and 1970s the popularity of consumer subjects in the press – particularly locally – was extraordinarily high. Ninety percent of the coverage of the popular newspaper was devoted to consumption. In medium-sized regional newspapers 80% of their space 'Vecherniaia Moskva' was devoted to similar materials, and republic-wide newspapers devoted 58%, 'Pravda' and 'Izvestiia' – 48% (Inkeles 1961:679). Local newspapers, as a rule, ran regular columns in which they placed texts of complaints, correspondence with readers, and replies to previously published letters.

In the newspapers 'Leningradskaia pravda' and 'Vechernii Leningrad' there were headings such as 'Measures Taken', 'You Wrote to Us', 'On the Trail of Your Letters', and so on. Such materials and others touching on problems of consumption are encountered in practically every issue of Soviet newspapers in the 1960s. By the middle of the 1970s the popularity of the theme had only slightly abated. The regularity of columns featuring consumer complaints or references to them varied from newspaper to newspaper.

According to materials of correspondence between citizens and authorities, found in the archives, the press often became the transmitter of a complaint, or the addressee of a recurring complaint, after an unsuccessful appeal to a different authority. Among archival documents are many complaints forwarded from the editorial offices of newspapers to executive committees, regional executive committees, trade organizations, and other decision-making authorities.

There were three elements in the effectiveness of complaints sent to the press. First, it was an additional channel. A letter forwarded to the proper authority on a newspaper's special form[30] enjoyed priority. Second, a complaint

---

30   Newspapers used special headed not-papers forwarding complaints to the other authorities.

which had been published in a newspaper signaled that the problem was now part of political discourse, increasing its significance, and it was a weighty argument in favor of the consumer in the case for further examination. Third, where rules stipulating how the complaint should be examined or where the period given for a reply had been broken, or where the complaint had not been given sufficient attention, critical remarks about the work of the authorities could appear on the pages of the paper, which was extremely undesirable for employees.

In this interview, striving for such levels of effectiveness is described in the following manner:

> Any negative publication <...> that is, so to say, the publication of a complaint in a newspaper, or the presentation of that on TV <...> this kind of complaint was very effective and fruitful. We had a newspaper 'Leningradskaia pravda', and there was not a manager who wanted to be in the news. Never. Because that could entail various negative consequences, even removal. Publication in the newspaper of the regional party committee <...> and our newspaper was a newspaper of the regional party committee <...> even a publication in a local newspaper could involve the sack. So, at least, a reproof.[31]

The book of complaints and suggestions was a specific means of making a complaint.

The Book of Complaints and Suggestions

A Soviet version of a book of complaints and suggestions was established in the Soviet state immediately after the revolution. Lenin ordered that: 'In every Soviet establishment there must be a book for notes, in the shortest form, with the name of the complainer, the essence of his statement and the action taken' (Lenin 1973:366–367).

The complaints book was a sewn brochure with numbered pages. The shop's stamp and the date of the first entry appeared on the cover. There was a clear procedure for filling in the book: after the notes of the consumer, the shop management had to respond indicating any measures taken.

According to the interview with the former head of shop, there was a hierarchy of complaints depending on their importance. Complaints were ranked according to their importance or 'seriousness' during inspections of individual

---

31   Interview 5.

shops by agents of the trade inspectorate and the trade directorate, and by people's inspectors:

> They made complaints against the rudeness, of course. Against deception, or as they called it, against 'giving short weight'. This complaint was also serious. And there was a very serious complaint, when there was a deficit, and there was a problem of concealment of goods. That was a most serious complaint.[32]

Complaints that were 'not very serious' were settled by the store management. More serious complaints were transferred to higher levels of authority.

The ability of the customer to make notes in the book of complaints in times had a certain disciplining influence on workers in the retail and service sector. In one of these complaints, published in a newspaper, a consumer noted that: 'After the rude response of store attendant L. Eriomina, I requested the book of complaints and suggestions. At once followed an apology'.[33]

Judging by the information to be found in complaints, an entry in the book of complaints and suggestions was extremely undesirable for store employees: 'Basically you did everything to make sure that they didn't write anything down in the complaint book'.[34]

Avoiding entries being made in the complaint book was possible. For this the employees of the retail and service sectors developed different methods. Books turned out to be 'away for examination', or in the process of being replaced at the moment when a buyer requested it. Even if the book was where it should be its rightful place was, a consumer's request for it was often refused. To get the book of complaints and suggestions was sometimes problematic.[35] Refusal to give out the book of complaints was considered an offence. Judging by the fact that workers in the retail and service sector were prepared to commit such a violation, we can see that a complaint in the book really could entail certain consequences.

The book was checked by the shop management. People's inspectors also checked the book of complaints as part of their inspection of goods, food and everyday services, to see if there were any complaints, if they had been noted

---

32   Interview 2.
33   Pochemu nuzhny ugrozy? Vechernii Leningrad, 1970, 13 March, p. 2.
34   Interview 2.
35   Difficulties in getting access to the complaint book were one of the most favourite topics of Soviet caricaturists. See picture 3 (Magazine of caricatures, *Krokodil* (1964)).

FIGURE 3

down correctly and if the rectifying measures indicated in the book had been put into practice (*Narodnyi kontrol' v sfere obsluzhivaniia* 1983:25–30).

The book of complaints and suggestions was used most frequently in enterprises dealing with trade and everyday services. The books were used by the Soviet citizens. Sellers and waitresses often invented strategies that allowed them to avoid writing complaints into the books. That can probably serve additional evidence, that complaints, recorded in the books, were significant. According to interviews with former sellers, punishments in the form of warnings, fines, and even court examinations may have occurred as a consequence of complaints.

Strategies Used when Writing Consumer Complaints

Soviet complaints differed from place to place. Pragmatism meant that the consumer had to choose the basis for the complaint carefully, so as to avoid numerous ambiguities and contradictions. As a rule, we can distinguish five elements in the texts of complaints: an address to the reader, an outline of the basis of the problem, forms of justification, a description of the guilty party and a description of the author of the complaint.

Strategies Used for Describing the Problem
When presenting the problem which had led to the complaint, Soviet consumers often used generalizations. An individual problem such as a faulty bicycle, vegetables of low quality or the rudeness of a shop assistant are interpreted as a symptom of a greater problem, which affects a whole group of consumers or the even the state.

L.I. Boitman, a consumer, was faced with bad service in a drycleaner's and expressed her complaint as follows:

> Consumer services are important. Indifferent staff cannot be tolerated. Today, when one of the main tasks facing the Communist Party is to provide Soviet citizens with high quality services, there is no room for indifference in consumer services.[36]

A second example is the complaint made by L.S. Baianov, who was unsatisfied with his purchase of eau-de-cologne: 'The struggle for the quality of production is a matter of great state-level importance, a matter of honor for the staff of every enterprise'.[37] According to a complaint made by L. Kuranov after he bought a faulty tape measure:

> The struggle for the honor of factory produced brands, for well manufactured products, for the reliability and durability of appliances, is one of the conditions for the successful creation of the material-technical base of Communism and elevation of the standard of living of every Soviet citizen.[38]

Generalizations are made not only concerning the scale of the problem but also concerning the number of people affected. The number of people who made a complaint, or who were affected by the problem, impacted on the success of the complaint. The mechanism for resolving complaints depended on the number of 'signals' received that something was wrong. The greater the number of people included in the complaint, the greater the complainer's chance of getting the result he or she wanted. A complaint could be made by one consumer in the name of a group, or on behalf of a group in society, as for example, in the following complaints:

> The type of photo album costing 2 rubles 80 kopecks enjoyed great demand among shoppers. Unfortunately this kind of album is not on sale now. It turns out that the 'Svetoch' factory has stopped producing them. It's a pity. G. Orlov, amateur photographer.[39]

---

36   Servis ne terpit ravnodushnykh. Leningradskaia pravda, 1963, 29 March, p. 2.

37   Pokupatel' zhdiot. Leningradskaia pravda, 1963, 10 March, p. 2.

38   Otvetstvennost' i kachestvo. Leningradskaia pravda, 1964, 21 November, p. 2.

39   Vechernii Leningrad, 1963, 24 April, p. 2.

Or:

> People who like sport have noticed with pleasure that there is a fairly
> wide range of skis available in Leningrad shops today. I didn't imagine
> there would be great difficulty in buying excellent slalom skis for my son.
> I bought boots as well however, and now both boots and skis are lying
> unused in the cupboard. The problem is that it is impossible to buy bind-
> ings for slalom skis anywhere in Leningrad. There are none this year,
> there were none last year. Surely one of the enterprises in Leningrad, per-
> haps the 'Sport' experimental factory, could come to the aid of skiers.[40]

Collective complaints about problems affecting many people were also written. Such complaints often mention the number of people who have signed:

> We, the drivers of the second Leningrad taxi fleet, have been forced to
> publish a complaint in the newspaper. Up until now, we have eaten in the
> fleet's canteen. The range of food there always left something to be
> desired, and there was never enough room for more than one shift. There
> were often queues and we had to wait for a seat. The management raised
> our hopes that next year they would turn their attention to staff catering.
> And what happened? Our canteen has been completely shut down <...>
> (107 signatories).[41]

There were also other ways of presenting the problem. The problem is quite
often presented as if by an observer from the sidelines. The author of the complaint therefore takes on the role of a sympathetic bystander who cares about
others. We see this for example in a complaint printed by 'Izvestiia' in 1962:

> For the attention of the editor of the newspaper 'Izvestiia' VTsIK SSSR.
> Citizen editor, please, publish my note in your newspaper. A settlement,
> Lakhta, Olgino, which is situated in the Sestroretskii district, is consid-
> ered a resort region. But there is a problem. This year we were thoroughly
> badly prepared for the welcome of the summer residents and children
> from Leningrad. Especially, bread and rolls were inadequate for our
> needs, as well as other products, especially at weekends. The water sup-

---

40   Lyzhi v kladovke. Vechernii Leningrad, 1963, 26 February, p. 2.
41   V tesnote i v obide. Leningradskaia pravda. 1964, 12 December, p. 2.

ply was also insufficient. People stood in queues, but, all the same, a number of inhabitants remain without bread and without water.[42]

A certain playing down of the problem was typical of Soviet complaints, and particularly of consumers' complaints. The problem is presented as an isolated fault against the backdrop of the values and achievements of the socialist society. In the complaint detailed above, the author employs the following means: ' <…> cultural conditions of the settlements Lakhty and Olgino look bad. Although, they have constructed many standard fences, and these fences were colored, but various slops flow from the courts and create a stench'.[43]

Strategies of Self-Presentation

An indication that the author possessed a certain social status could increase the complaint's significance. This is indicated by the notes highlighting the author's status which were made directly in the margins of the complaints by those reading and sorting them.

We can highlight three groups of signatories who warranted particular attention. The first group enjoyed social approval, for instance, 'candidate of economic sciences'[44], 'engineer' or 'research assistant, University of Leningrad'. The second group was made up of people who had performed specific services for society, such as 'veterans of the Great Patriotic War'. The third group consisted of people who could lay claim to a particular level of protection by society, such as 'pensioner', 'disabled of the second group',[45] 'mother of three children'.

Strategies for Justifying the Complaint

When writing a complaint, the most difficult part was to justify it. Here the consumer was faced with the greatest number of obstacles. The consumer had to show that he really did need help and that he was deserving of help.

Many researchers of the Soviet society note that status of a citizen is indistinguishable from his status as a 'Soviet citizen', with all the associated moral qualities. For this reason, the consumer often demonstrated the correctness of his position by testifying to his own positive moral and social qualities. It was also important to show that any claims made by consumers were moderate,

---

42   TsGA SPb, f. 7384, op. 30, d. 53, l. 2.

43   TsGA SPb, f. 7384, op. 30, d. 53, l. 2.

44   'Kandidat ekonomicheskikh nauk' is the postgraduate scientific degree in Soviet and contemporary Russian system of education.

45   Disability in the Soviet and contemporary Russian systems of the People's Social Protection is divided into three groups. Belonging to each of them depends on illness.

and to show that the interests of the consumer had been affected while he was engaged in pursuing those interests and that they did not exceed certain limits.

A widespread technique for justifying complaints was appealing to the state's promise of care for its citizens. This meant the problem could be viewed using the Soviet concept of legality. Typical phrases for complaints employing this 'paternalistic' strategy, such as 'Why does the state not take care of us?'[46] and 'What has become of the care for consumers' interests which the state promised?'[47] can be found in the newspaper 'Leningradskaia pravda'.

The resources which the consumer could use to justify the complaint were very limited. Sometimes the consumer tried a type of 'blackmail' by describing the kind of serious damage that had been brought about by for example an inadequacy of some kind in the health care system, or even just in everyday life. For instance, a quote from a complaint made to the executive committee of the Leningrad region in 1959. The reason for the complaint was constant noise in a flat:

> <...> two weeks or a month's holiday in a 'house' held – can lead to a serious breakdown <...> Some of us, having reached the last limit of patience, having exhausted his nervous system just cannot stay at home and are forced to be away from home so as not to get sick.[48]

An example of a complaint from a hospital says: 'The patients are half-starving in the hospital. As a result you can observe emaciation and collapse'.[49] Complainers frequently resorted to the justification that isolated disruptions in the workplace could engender serious damage to the whole system. For example, in one of the documents, the consumer says that workers are forced to spend their working time sorting out their consumer problems instead of working for the good of the state:

> I would like to draw the attention of the party and state authority to the low quality of the clock-work toys, produced by the plant of metal wares. Lately I have bought a toy boat in the Lenkulttorg's store, No. 19. Its clock-work mechanism worked for just during 15 minutes and then broke. I applied to the manager of the store with a claim for the poor toy. He explained that I cannot return the toy to the store, and advised me to 'Go to the plant where the toy was produced. They will exchange it'.

---

46   Ni kupit' ... ni sshit'. Leningradskaia pravda, 1964, 24 November, p. 2.

47   Pochemu procherk v meniu? Leningradskaia pravda, 1981, 3 April, p. 2.

48   TsGA SPb, f. 7384 op. 30 D. 53 d. 2633 1. 58.

49   TsGA SPb, f. 7384 op. 30 D. 53 d. 1565 l. 101.

I don't have time to go to the factory, and I don't have a guarantee that the new toy will work longer than this one. Talking with the manager I learned that the plant systematically delivers defective goods, and sometimes workers come from the plant to the store to repair the defective toys.[50]

Strategies Used when Representing the Guilty Party

These kind of strategies often consisted of attributing negative characteristics to the guilty party. Exposure of the guilty is a standard technique when complaining. Soviet complaints are unique in the techniques used and the labels which are assigned to the perpetrator.

To aid our analysis of the labels used, we can turn to the ideal of the 'model' Soviet citizen (*Sovetskii prostoi chelovek* 1993:15). The ideal qualities of the Soviet citizen were outlined at the XXII Congress (1961) and were included in the Communist Party's new program as a 'Moral Code of the Builder of Communism'. According to this ideological construct, the Soviet citizen should possess the following traits: 'conscientious labor for the good of society, the care of each individual for the conservation and augmentation of social achievements, humane attitudes and mutual respect between people, honesty and correctness, intolerance of injustice, parasitism, dishonesty, careerism, acquisitiveness etc' (*Moral'nyi kodeks stroitelei kommunizma* 1962:5–6).

In order to describe the guilty party, consumers use characteristics which are contrary to those outlined in the code:

> The canteen staff at the Gostinyi Dvor and Passazh department stores allows abuses to take place in the sale of juices and mineral water.[51]

> In the No. 2 Lenmebelmorga[52] furniture store, home delivery is organized in a very strange way <...> A group of moonlighters in state-owned cars offer to deliver your purchases.[53]

---

50   Nuzhny li takie igrushki? Vechernii Leningrad, 1963, 15 March, p. 2.

51   Mery priniaty. Vechernii Leningrad, 1970, 8 January, p. 2.

52   **Len**ingradskaia **mebel'**naia **torg**ovlia, which means 'The Leningrad furniture trade economy'.

53   Po sledam nashikh vystuplenii. Vechernii Leningrad, 1964, 29 December, p. 2.

In order to wrap goods, the assistants use very thick sheets of paper. They shouldn't take such a cavalier attitude to material and use expensive paper in such a wasteful manner.[54]

I was made very uncomfortable in 'Chaika' when I began to choose something I needed. The assistants answered my questions indifferently and it was clear that they did not have the slightest desire to help the customer. The assistants were inattentive and discourteous. I was deeply offended by their attitude. I left without buying anything.[55]

A dichotomy is created between desirable traits and the traits actually being described: conscientious labor for the good of society contrasts with 'taking a cavalier attitude'; 'care by each individual for the conservation and augmentation of social achievements' contrasts with 'using in a wasteful manner'; 'humane attitudes and mutual respect between people' contrasts with 'inattentive', 'unsolicitous', 'indifferent' and so on.

The strategy consisted in highlighting how incorrect the guilty party's behavior was in relation to the ideal of the Soviet citizen. By achieving his aim (the satisfactory resolution of his complaint), the consumer was also underlining the legitimacy of the 'Code for the Builder of Communism'.

Strategies Used when Addressing the Reader

The basis of the complaint as a genre of text is the asymmetry between the complainer and the addressee. The complaint is always addressed to someone stronger, who has more resources at their disposal. Techniques are therefore used which increase the status of the recipient and at the same time show the lowly status of the complainer. As well as the official salutation to the addressee, we also find constructions such as 'dear', 'beloved', 'you can do anything', 'you are our last hope', 'it's in your power to solve my problem' and so on. Il'ia Utechin, a researcher into the stylistics of Soviet complaints, notes this characteristic and gives examples where the merits of the recipient are outlined in detail, for example, 'Comrade Kosygin, I'm appealing to you as a manager and senior comrade, who is respected by more than 200 million people and all the workers in the world!'[56]

The complaints often contain elements of personalization. Utekhin (2004) interprets this as an attempt to reduce social distance. A second possible inter-

---

54   Narushiteli pravil torgovli nakazany. Vechernii Leningrad, 1964, 12 December, p. 2.
55   Kak ia pokupala plat'e. Vechernii Leningrad, 1964, 4 December, p. 2.
56   TsGA SPb, f. 7384, op. 42, d. 1005, l. 269.

pretation is that this creates a model of paternalistic relations with 'the authorities'. According to this model, 'the authorities' and 'the people' should be close to one another, like members of a family. It is possible that this is why the complainer uses forms of address such as 'father', 'brother', 'son', 'you are my last hope', 'you are like a member of our family' and so on. A personal meeting with the civil servant in question is presented as being a pleasant opportunity. The author of one complaint regrets that one meeting did not take place: 'As I was in the town of Kirishi I came to your offices. You were on a business trip. I therefore have to communicate in writing'.[57]

Hence, a result was achieved first and foremost by demonstrating loyalty to the Soviet system and appealing to well-known aspects of official ideology, such as the values of collectivism, the care promised by the state, the moral qualities of the 'real' Soviet citizen and so on.

Conclusions

Being a Soviet consumer was not easy. You could not just go shopping in order to get everyday goods for yourself and your family. You needed time and patience to stand in queues. You needed the right contacts to get hold of goods which were difficult to obtain and in short supply. You needed to know when goods would be delivered and the rules of trade, so as to be able to find what you wanted. Dealing with shop assistants and customer service authorities sapped your strength. Everyday consumption became something more than simply consumption. For some it was a problem which complicated the everyday existence of ordinary Soviet people. For others it was like a hobby or sport. For both it represented a system of relations, stratified according to special rules. Every Soviet consumer found himself caught up in a number of complementary hierarchies: the consumer as opposed to the shop assistant, or the consumer who was in a network of unofficial distribution as opposed to the consumer who was not, and so on.

Status as a consumer was connected with a range of difficulties. The accessible, official means of lodging a complaint with high-level institutions was well-known. That said, limited opportunities to influence the situation forced the Soviet consumer to turn to another system of hierarchical relationships, that of complainer as opposed to the recipient that had been granted powers by the authority. The complainers inevitably occupied a lower position in the hierarchy.

---

57   LOGAV, f. P-4514, op. 1, d. 38, l. 1b.

In order for a complaint to be successful, the consumer needed to know which authority he should address his complain to, so that it resulted in his request being satisfied. The consumer also had to have a detailed knowledge of the rules (such as the existence of hierarchical relationships, the system of moral and ethical norms which were current, and the difficult and contradictory theses of Soviet ideology) in order to speak the same language as the authorities. In comparison with any other type of complaint, the consumer complaint needed to demonstrate moderation in consumption, and to include additional explanations and justifications connected with the ambivalent status of consumption, the consumer and problems of consumption in Soviet society.

Bibliography

Arzamastsev, A. (1980): Chto ponimaetsia pod razumnymi potrebnostiami? In: *Nauchnyi kommunizm*. No. 1.

———. (1980): *Istoriko-filosofskoe issledovanie problemy razumnykh potrebnostei*. Avtoreferat na soiskanie uchionoi stepeni doktora filosofskikh nauk (09.00.03) Moscow.

Bogdanova, E. (2006): *Obrashcheniia grazhdan v organy vlasti kak opyt otstaivaniia svoikh interesov v usloviiakh pozdnesovetskogo obshchestva (1960–1970-e gg.)*. PhD (kandidat nauk) thesis in Sociology. St. Petersburg [unpublished].

Friedgut, T. (1978): Citizens and Soviets: Can Ivan Ivanovich Fight City Hall? In: *Comparative Politics*. Vol. 10, No. 4.

Kharkhordin, O. (2002): *Oblichat' i litsemerit': Genealogiia rossiiskoi lichnosti*. Moscow, St. Petersburg: Letnii sad.

Inkeles, A. (1961): *Soviet Citizen. Daily Life in a Totalitarian Society*. Cambridge, Mass.: Harvard University Press.

Ionin, L. (2004): *Sotsiologiia kultury*. Moscow: Izdatel'skii dom GU-VShE.

Kazakevich, N., Kuz'min, E. (1975): *Poriadok rassmotreniia predlozhenii, zaiavlenii i zhalob trudiashchikhsia*. Moscow: Profizdat.

Kerimov, D. (1956): *Obespechenie zakonnosti v SSSR*. Moscow: Gosudarstvennoe izdatel'-stvo iuridicheskoi literatury.

Kogan, L. (1987): Potrebitel'stvo i veshchizm pri sotsializme: sushchnost' i puti bor'by s nimi. In: *Filosofskie nauki*. No. 12.

Kornai, J. (2000): *Sotsialisticheskaia sistema*. Moscow: Voprosy ekonomiki.

Lebina, N., Chistikov, A. (2003): *Obyvatel' i reformy. Kartiny povsednevnoi zhizni gorozhan v gody NEPa i khrushchevskogo desiatiletiia*. St. Petersburg: Dmitrii Bulanin.

Ledeneva, A. (1998): *Russia's Economy of Favours: Blat, Networking and Informal Exchange*. Cambridge: Cambridge University Press.

Lenin, V. (1973): Nabrosok pravil ob upravlenii sovetskimi uchrezhdeniiami. In: *Polnoe Sobranie Sochinenii*. 5th edition. Vol. 37. Moscow: Izdatel'stvo politicheskoi literatury.

Marx, K. (1955): Nemetskaia ideologiia. In: Marx, K., Engels, F. *Polnoe Sobranie Sochinenii*. 2nd edition. Vol. 3. Moscow: Izdatel'stvo politicheskoi literatury.

Moral'nyi kodeks stroitelei kommunizma (1962): Dushanbe: Tadzhikizdat.

Motiashov, V. (1985): *Vlast' veshchei i vlast' cheloveka*. Moscow: Molodaia gvardiia.

———. (1988): *Mify i realnost' obshchestva potrebleniia*. Moscow: Znanie.

Narodnyi kontrol' v sfere obsluzhivaniia (1983): Riga: AVOTS.

Proizvodstvo tovarov narodnogo potrebleniia i zadachi pechati (1979): Vos'moi vseso-iuznyi seminar zhurnalistov. Moscow: Gazeta Izvestiia.

Sadikov, I., Vetrov, B. (1974): *Obshchestvennyi kontrol' za rabotoi predpriiatii torgovli i obshchestvennogo pitaniia*. Moscow: Profizdat.

Sorokin, V. (2002): Ochered'. In: *Collection*. St. Petersburg: Ad Marginem.

Sovetskii prostoi chelovek: opyt sotsial'nogo portreta na rubezhe 90-h. (1993): Ed. by Iu. Levada. Moscow: 'Mirovoi okean'.

Strumilin, S. (1961): *Problemy sotsializma i kommunizma v SSSR*. Moscow: Nauka.

Tarasenko, G. (1977): *Zakon vozvysheniia potrebnostei i zhiznennyi uroven' trudiashchikh-sia*. Kiev: Vishcha shkola.

Utekhin, I. (2004): Iz nabliudenii za poetikoi zhaloby. In: *Studia Etnologia*. St. Petersburg: EUSPb.

Zhaloby passazhirov na vagony-restorany (1934): Moscow: Izdatel'stvo. ob'edineniia vagonov-restoranov.

Zhilina, L., Frolova, N. (1969): *Problemy potrebleniia i vospitaniia*. Moscow: Mysl'.

Zhilina, L. (1988): *Potrebnosti, kultura potrebleniia i tsennostnye orientatsii lichnosti*. Moscow: AON.

List of Quoted Interviews

Interview 1 – Interview with a woman, 1959, the journalist. Her mother used a complaint mechanism seeking a permission to return to Leningrad after repression in 1960s.

Interview 2 – Interview with a woman, 1951, the former head of shop.

Interview 3 – Interview with a man, 1951. Memories about his studentship in the late 1960.

Interview 4 – Interview with a man, 1945, worked as a university lecturer in 1960s–1970s.

Interview 5 – Interview with a woman, 1957, having an experience of complaining in 1960s–1970s.

CHAPTER 6

Meshchanstvo or the Spirit of Consumerism and the Russian Mind

Timo Vihavainen

The Concepts of the Study

The concepts of *intelligentsia/intelligentnost'* and *meshchanstvo* (the philis-tines/philistinism) played an important and very special role in the discourse of pre-revolutionary Russia and the Soviet Union.[1] These two concepts have been and, to some extent at least, still are, understood as antipodes, as the clas-sic chronicler of the Russian *intelligentsia*, Ivanov-Razumnik supposed about one hundred years ago: 'The struggle against philistinism (meshchanstvo) and for individualism <...> this is a point of view, which is general enough to give us the opportunity to examine the whole two-hundred year history of Russian consciousness'.[2]

Ivanov-Razumnik defined philistinism as a suppressive force, a brake on historical progress, which tried to suffocate the creative *élan* of the *intelligent*. An *intelligent* was not supposed to live 'as everybody does' but to be a free spir-it and the real force of historical progress. The *intelligent* occupies a very prom-inent place in Russian history. Nowhere has he been as respected and honored by his admirers or been as despised and bullied by his detractors. The friends of the *intelligentsia*, including its own representatives, praised its moral eleva-tion and unselfishness. By some others, the *intelligent* was considered to be an impractical and effeminate creature, who, in fact, was a good for nothing. Still others sometimes accused the *intelligenty* of counterproductive sabotage and unconstructive criticism of the powers that be.

Maxim Gorky, the high priest of socialist realism, tried to create a new syn-thesis by fusing the exemplary and progressive qualities of the proletariat and the *intelligentsia*, as has been shown in chapter 2 of this book.[3]

The group of *intelligentsia* has played a very special role in the history of Russian culture and society. More often than not, Russians consider that *intel-ligentsia* is an exclusively Russian concept and maintain that no comparable

---

1 Vihavainen, (2006).
2 Ivanov-Razumnik (1907), 14–15.
3 More detailed discussion in my book: Vihavainen (2006), 60–70, 180–184, and passim.

groups exist or have existed in other countries.[4] This opinion has been cherished not only by those who believe in the idea of an exclusive Russian road of development and the singularity of the Russians. Many westernizers have also shared this opinion, and after the collapse of the Soviet regime many of them have maintained that the history of the *intelligentsia,* as an exclusive Russian phenomenon, is now coming to an end.[5] This would be an inevitable result of the process of 'normalization', which was supposedly taking place in Russia. The country seemed to be becoming more and more like the western countries, where no *intelligentsia* proper exists or is needed.

The *intelligentsia* has sometimes been understood as an ersatz civil society, which has pretended to the role of the brain of the inert masses and been their tribune and guardian against the brutal state.[6]

In a new, post-communist Russia, there is supposedly no place for this class, which has excelled not only with its prowess and virtues but also in its self-complimentary pathos. The intelligent has devoted his life to the people, and been prepared to suffer for it. In this role, he has voluntarily entered the ranks of the martyred and exploited masses. According to this opinion, such a role is no longer needed or even possible. Therefore, *intelligentnost'* should also already be a waning concept. Instead, people should rather begin to speak about 'intellectuals' or 'specialists', terms which refer rather to the spheres of activity of certain people than to their specific moral qualities and role in society.

The Russian word *meshchanstvo* has also meanings which have been considered specifically Russian. *Meshchanstvo* can be translated into most other languages (as 'philistinism' in English, for instance) and it is not uncommon to meet scornful attitudes towards philistines and their lifestyles also in the West. However, this concept has a very specific history in Russia.[7]

During one and half century of turbulent Russian history, the concept of *meshchanstvo* has changed its meaning. Obviously, the specific Russian way of development attached to it connotations which varieties of 'philistinism' did not have in other societies that had a different history.

The Russian bourgeoisie proper before the revolution was a relatively thin layer in a predominantly agrarian society and the estate of petty bourgeoisie (*meshchanstvo*) was also quite small. It did not excel in material well-being. However, for the Russian *intelligentsia*, it became the symbol of an inferior state of mind where material values prevailed over spiritual ones.

---

4 See: Gasparov (1999), 9–12.
5 See: Gessen (1997).
6 Stepanov (1999), 20, 30.
7 See: Vihavainen (2006), 18–21.

Both the concepts, which refer to the groups and their supposed mindsets (*intelligentsia/intelligentnost'* and *meshchanstvo*) are very complex and vague. This is due to the dramatic changes in Russian social and political history. They denote or have denoted both certain rather tightly defined social groups and also more or less vague ideal types, or lifestyles, which have had different meanings for different groups of society.

The author of this study believes that after the collapse of the Soviet Union it is especially interesting to research mentalities and attitudes reflected in the use and understanding of such key concepts as *intelligentnost'/intelligentsia* and *meshchanstvo*. Both of them have a history that goes far beyond the communist regime and both have been getting new meanings after the collapse of Communism.

In Putin's time, a renaissance of pre-revolutionary discourses has been taking place. One of the most active champions of specifically Russian values has been Sergei Kara-Murza, director of the 'Centre of Problem Analysis and Projects of State Administration' think-tank. In 2014, Kara-Murza published 'Crash of the USSR' (*Krakh sssr*), in which he maintained that the collapse of the USSR was in fact a revolution of *meshchanstvo*. It happened that since the 1970s the Soviet *intelligentsia* had adopted the values of *meshchanstvo* itself and betrayed the new Soviet man, a unique cultural-historical type of human being which had been created during the Soviet rule.

The Soviet man, by nature inimical to *meshchanstvo*, was now forced to retreat to *the catacombs*, Kara-Murza declares, but has not been annihilated; it is still there and can be called back to the fore.[8]

According to Kara-Murza, the 'retreat of the *intelligentsia* in the face of *meshchanstvo*' was fatal for Soviet society. It was also a paradox, because the Soviet system was intelligent-centred (*intellektotsentrichnym*) and the *intelligentsia* and *meshchanstvo* have traditionally been understood as diametrically opposed. The bourgeois had once been a creator, but the *meshchanin* was just the reverse of high culture. His was a philosophy of 'the autocracy of property' (*samoderzhavie sobstvennosti*).[9]

The Intellectuals and the *Intelligenty*. Some Comparison

Intellectuals, as a social group, have been much researched, both in the West and in Russia. Outstanding analyses of western intellectuals can be found in

---

8 Kara-Murza (2013), 219- 226.
9 Ibid., 222.

the works of Karl Mannheim, Julian Benda, Paul Hollander, Paul Johnson, Richard Posner, and many others. Usually the analyses purport to sort out some typical social characteristics of this group, which has become a more and more influential factor in western societies since the Enlightenment. This group gained much visibility in France in the beginning of the 20th century. In the West, intellectuals have been renowned for their social and political role, as innovators, champions of radicalism, and defenders of the oppressed.

Because of his radicalism and the moral furor which has usually been attached to him, the archetypal western intellectual has rather played the role of a blasphemous rascal than a saint. It is not easy to think of western intellectuals as models of a moral personality or models of gentlemanly behavior. Rather, *épatage* has been the norm for intellectuals, whose often libertine ways of living and thinking have often effectively cut them off from the masses, which have been considered retrograde.

Gustave Flaubert considered that a hate of the bourgeois was essential for the intellectual and the Bloomsbury intellectuals believed themselves to be 'new people', whose lifestyles were above the level of comprehension of the masses. In general, it may be said that western intellectuals have very seldom adored the 'masses' or believed in their elevated moral nature. In Russia, on the contrary, this has been the standard starting point since Herzen and the *narodniks*. The Russian *intelligentsia* did not believe that the masses were inferior, because their understanding was underdeveloped. This, after all, was not their fault.[10]

As regards the Russian *intelligentsia* as a corporate institution, Russians themselves have tended to underline its uniqueness. Frequently, it has even been maintained that there has been no '*intelligentsia*' in the West at all, just 'intellectuals', which allegedly are very different.

The Russian *intelligentsia*'s specific plight has been determined by the fact that it has functioned in a society where the relations between the government ('the power', *vlast'*) and the people have been different from those in the West. Not all western researchers share this opinion. Paul Hollander, for instance, believes that the terms 'intellectuals' and '*intelligentsia*' can be used interchangeably, even if there may be a slight difference in emphasis due to certain historical factors.[11]

Hollander argues that especially 'two groups, the French Enlightenment intellectuals and the 19th-century Russian *intelligentsia* represent the core of historical tradition and the principal models, to which contemporary western

10   See: Vihavainen (2006), 6.
11   Hollander (1981), 43.

intellectual sensibilities reach back, consciously or not'.[12] According to Hollander's unsympathetic opinion, the factor which unites both groups is 'exclusion from politics, inexperience and the resulting propensity to grand illusions and beliefs divorced from social and political realities'.[13]

This unflattering conclusion about intellectuals has been shared by some others. Paul Johnson puts it bluntly: 'One of the principal lessons of our tragic century <...> is: beware intellectuals'.[14]

The main delusion of intellectuals, as formulated by Johnson, is that they forget the elementary truth that 'people matter more than concepts and must come first. The worst of all despotisms is the heartless tyranny of ideas'.[15]

The list of this kind of negative assessment of intellectuals, both as a group and as individuals, could easily be continued. After the collapse of Soviet Communism, intellectuals in the West are nowadays considered by many as a suspect group, which is being held responsible for its support of the most tyrannical regimes of the past century. At least in conservative circles, the stigma of violence is now tightly associated with western intellectuals. Apparently senseless violence was the central thing the riots of 1968. Adoration of violence has later been the hallmark of several groups of 'warriors', from the Red army Fractions and the Black Panthers to many other self-professed friends of progress.

In Russian history idealized nature of political violence, preached and practiced by the 19th-century *intelligentsia* has been still more flagrant. The Soviet authorities hailed the assassins and plotters against the tsars and presented them as moral examples. The fanaticism of the tsars' murderers was supposed to be the moral ideal for all the oppressed, but naturally not a model to be emulated in the new socialist society, where no oppression existed.

But social role of intellectuals aside, what kind of personal qualities have the western intellectuals, as individuals been supposed to have?

Paul Hollander underlines the importance of a certain 'mindset' for qualifying somebody as an intellectual.[16] He remarks that intellectuals are supposed to be generalists rather than specialists, with a 'special concern with ideas which ultimately springs from disinterested sources <...> creative, playful, sensitive, inquisitive and somewhat impractical'. From the moral-ethical point of view, intellectuals have been depicted as 'idealistic, critical, irreverent, icono-

---

12   Ibid., 51.

13   Ibid.

14   Paul Johnson (2000), 342.

15   Ibid.

16   Hollander (1981), 48.

clastic, imbued with altruistic-ameliorative impulses, deep moral concerns and commitments'. Socially they are usually regarded as 'outsiders, yet the conscience of society, the upholders of its true values and ideals'.[17]

Richard A. Posner further analyzes the concept by pointing out that an intellectual need not have 'highbrow' tastes, and a person with such tastes need not be an intellectual. In his definition an intellectual is 'not a synonym for cultured, cultivated, creative or even bookish, though the last is close'.[18] It goes without saying that an intellectual is not a synonym for intelligent in the sense of an adjective in the English language that is an intelligent person. Posner argues that an important quality of an intellectual is that he 'applies general ideas to matters of public concern'. He is not just a reporter or a technician; he is interested in the principles, not just in the practical result.[19] Hollander quotes Julien Benda in saying that a 'clerk' (intellectual) is essentially not pursuing practical aims or looking for material advantages. Accordingly, an intellectual could 'in a certain manner' say 'My kingdom is not of this world'.[20]

A vast literature about the Russian *intelligentsia* exists and anyone acquainted with it will certainly recognize that practically everything that has been said about the western intellectuals above, has, or could also have been said about the Russian *intelligenty*.[21]

The main difference seems to be one of emphasis. One dimension, which is less conspicuously present in depictions of western intellectuals as compared with their Russian colleagues, is guilt. Before the revolution, (social) guilt was something very characteristic for the Russian *intelligent*.

This feeling is by no means absent from depictions of today's western intellectuals, but in the Soviet Union it has been almost absent, for certain reasons. Why should a Russian (or Soviet) *intelligent* feel guilty? Since the 19th century the typical Russian intelligent was not rich or privileged. In fact he was often poor and oppressed. Only a few writers like Alexander Solzhenitsyn have said that good reasons for guilt existed. This was especially the case during the Soviet period, when everybody had his share of guilt for living in a lie. But, after all, this was a variety of guilt quite different kind of guilt from that resulting from unearned social privilege. The Soviet *intelligentsia* had reason to feel oppressed rather than to feel guilty for being an oppressor.

---

17   Ibid.
18   Posner (2003), 18.
19   Ibid., 19.
20   Hollander (1981), 43.
21   See Vihavainen (2006), 1–9, and the sources used there.

One of the specialties of the Soviet period was that the Soviet regime wanted to remold and redefine the *intelligentsia*. It conducted an experiment in social engineering on educated people and it also purported to redefine the whole idea of *intelligentnost'* –the qualities understood to be typical for an *intelligent*.

Immediately after the Bolshevik Revolution, the word *intelligent* definitely had pejorative connotations in the official jargon. The *intelligentsia* was mostly very critical of the Bolsheviks' methods.[22] Very typical of this was Lenin's phrase that the *intelligentsia* was not the brain of the people, but its shit. In short, Lenin was furious about the *intelligenty* lacking ruthlessness and their inclination to defend those persecuted by the new regime.[23]

But, in the early 1930s, Stalin made peace with the *intelligentsia*. He declared that the *intelligentsia* had now developed a new class nature. It no longer represented the bourgeoisie as had been the case at the time of the revolution, now it was with the working people. Therefore, the *intelligentsia* was now declared to be an equal partner of the toiling classes, the workers and the peasants. The *intelligentsia* was their flesh and blood and served them. In itself, the *intelligentsia* was not a class, but received its class-nature from the masses.

The criteria used to define the *intelligentsia* were also changed. The *Intelligentsia* was no longer supposed to be a caste which was critical of the regime and defended its victims. Now it was to be understood as an integral part of society and thus it could be inimical only to the enemies of the regime. Technically, the *intelligentsia* was defined just by degree of education. Anybody with a secondary education was now counted as a member of the *intelligentsia*, that is, an *intelligent*. This implied that all kinds of elites, including the *nomenklatura* were also part of the *intelligentsia* and similarly borrowed their class-nature from the workers and peasants, whom they supposedly served.

It is perhaps needless to say that in spite of these reformulations the traditions of the old Russian *intelligentsia* survived this Stalinist simplification. *Intelligent* and *intelligentsia* began to have two meanings. There was the official one, which just had a technical denotation, and there was the traditional one, which retained its former moral content. What was being meant could be only understood from the context.

When we compare the role of the Russian *intelligenty* and western intellectuals today, it will be necessary to bear in mind their different historical experience. The Russian *intelligentsia* in its classical era was quintessentially radical,

22   Burbank (1986), 19–40, and passim.
23   Lenin (1970), 134–135.

never constructive, but an instrument of destruction.[24] It was the first group of its kind in European history: oppositional, bellicose, loud, moralistic, and well-known for its inclination to terrorism. But all this changed after the revolution. The historical experience of the Russian *intelligentsia* during the past 90 years has been very different to that of its western colleagues, and this quite probably has also affected both its outlook and its image.

The historical example of rebellious radicals, who were partly canonized by the communists and elevated to the Soviet Pantheon, was a terrible heritage for new generations of *intelligenty*. They could see the unintended impact of the past radicalism in their everyday life. The Soviet *intelligenty* lived in a country which had built a cult of violence and which had shown in practice that it was ready to go to extremes, not shirking innocent blood, if that served the supposedly great cause.

Hecatombs of blood proved to be unable to create a paradise. With this terrible experience in their mind, the Soviet *intelligenty* obviously had a different perspective on violence in political issues than their western colleagues.

As regards western intellectuals, their predicament also changed profoundly during the 20th century. The cult of violence and the glorification of revolutionary, 'ultimate' solutions for social problems became the hallmark of many western intellectuals especially since the Russian Revolution. This radical faith was then put in doubt with the collapse of the Soviet Union.

It would be wrong to underestimate the impact of the latest Russian Revolution of the early 1990s. It was the moment when even western intellectuals had to swallow the uneasy truth about the reality of Soviet Socialism. The ethos of 'postmodern' intellectuals is much more skeptical and less fanatical than the spirit of the champions of the great cultural revolution of the 1960s once was. 1968 probably marked the high point of radical chic in the West, while Russia had had its own anticlimax fifty years earlier.

It is possible, even probable, that the social and intellectual surroundings of both western and Russian intellectuals are now converging also on this issue; both their ideas and their mindset will become increasingly similar. This will also affect the image of these social groups and their members.

So far, however, as representatives of the former Soviet *intelligentsia* are still alive, we have reason to consider that the difference between the Russian *intelligentsia* and its image on the one hand and western intellectuals on the other still lingers on. This image in Russia was studied by me in the beginning of the 21st century.

---

24   Szamuely (1974), 143–144.

The Aim of the Study

The aim of the study was to find out which kinds of meanings the terms *intelligent, intelligentsia* and *meshchanin, meshchanstvo* have in post-Soviet Russia. The informants were also asked to remember what role these concepts had had in the Soviet period. The informants were asked both to define the concepts of an *intelligent* and a *meshchanin* and to give concrete examples that would illustrate their definition. Some questions were made to check the informants' reactions to certain classic remarks about the 'essence' of the *intelligentsia* and *meshchanstvo*. The researchers were also interested in finding out what those concepts meant for the informants personally.[25] It was expected that at least some remnants of past values would still linger on and that the values which the Soviet Union had tried to impose on its citizens would still to some extent determine the value orientations of people in the older age cohorts. On the other hand, it might be expected that the rapid socio-economic changes, together with the collapse of the Soviet economy and ideology, would arouse some reactions against the 'false gods' of Communism.

On the other hand, both *intelligentsia* and *meshchanstvo* lie outside rather than inside the central tenets of Soviet ideology. Even though the Communist Party every now and then attempted to define them, they always also bore 'unofficial' meanings, which could be, and were, used against the ideological orthodoxies: for example *intelligenty* were often thought to be not, or not just, representatives of the social stratum which got its class character from the workers and the peasants and which was doing intellectual work, as the party would have it. In practice the word could denote dissidents or independently minded people, probably with a strong moral character, who did not conform to the party's dictates. In the same vein, *meshchane* were, for many, not just selfish and dull people, who did not care about the common good, as the party would have them be, or semi-criminal speculators, who hoarded scarce goods or foreign fashions. Some people were also ready to use the word also about the party elite and/or the rank and file of the party, who spoke about the virtues of collective work and altruism, while they themselves exploited their social position in order to better their own material well-being.

In other words, both *intelligentnost'* and *meshchanstvo* have had both neutral and value-laden, official and unofficial, meanings. They belong partly to the world of morals and denote ideals, but partly they also concern the world of everyday lifestyles and attitudes. The words have meanings and connotations concerning attitudes to consumption and hoarding, attitudes towards

---

25   See questionnaire in the appendix.

fellow citizens and moral values, towards erudition or the lack of it, value-orientations concerning high culture and cheap entertainment, refinement of manners and tastes or the lack of them.

The interviewers did not pressure the informants to confine themselves to any particular sphere of meanings, although they urged them to give some concrete examples and to assess the meaning of the concepts for the informants themselves, personally.

The Techniques and the Sample

The interviews were structured and the interviewers used two slightly different sets of questions: formula A for those who defined themselves as *intelligenty* (members of the *intelligentsia*) and formula B for those who did not consider themselves to be part of that category. The questions in each set differed slightly from each other, in that they had to be relevant for those who regarded themselves as members of the *intelligentsia* and, on the other hand, for those who did not consider themselves to be members of that group. Both groups were asked to present their ideas concerning the qualities of the *intelligenty* and the *meshchane*. It was not presupposed that those interviewees who were not *intelligenty* would necessarily be *meshchane*. In general, the interviews were not tightly-knit, and the informants did not always give answers that were easy to classify. Instead, the informants were given more room for their own understanding of the issues, which may give a more valid idea about the nature of the problem.

The role of the interviewer usually affects the results. In this research, several interviewers were used, two in St. Petersburg and four in Petrozavodsk.

As regards the sample, its size was 55 persons, 37 were from St. Petersburg and the remaining 18 from Petrozavodsk. The sample was taken by the 'snowball-technique': the interviewers chose the informants from their surroundings, trying to get a rather even distribution of age groups, sexes, and type of profession (axis *intelligent* – non-*intelligent*). There were 24 male and 30 female informants. About a half of the males (13 out of 24) had been born before 1950. The women were slightly older (18 of 30). The median age was high: 61–62 (born in 1939).

In general, the older generations were overrepresented, if we compare the sample with the age pyramid of Russia in 2000–2002, when the interviews were made.[26] On one hand, this ensured that the voice of genuine Soviet generations would be heard. On the other hand, there were also young people: 5 men and 6 women were born after the 1960s. The oldest man had been born in 1911 and the oldest woman in 1906, while the youngest man had been born in 1982 and the youngest woman in 1983.

As regards the distribution between *intelligenty* and non-*intelligenty* (self-definition), the distribution is not quite even, among both sexes the *intelligenty* are somewhat overrepresented: 12 males identified themselves as *intelligenty* and 8 as non-*intelligenty*, while 4 cases are more or less problematic: for instance a professor and a holder of two university degrees, who did not want to use the label of an '*intelligent*'.

Among the women, 17 identified themselves as *intelligenty*, while 9 were non-*intelligent* and 4 cases remain problematic.

The sample is not representative, but it can give in-depth information both about the older generations (including the Brezhnev-generation) and also about the youngest adult cohort. The sample comprises only urban dwellers, but not only from metropolitan St. Petersburg, but also from the middle-size provincial center of Petrozavodsk.

'*Intelligent*', '*Intelligentnost*" as Moral Categories

It turned out that the concept of *intelligentnost'* was considered to denote first of all a moral category. Over a half (26) of the informants named moral qualities as the only or the predominant criteria of an *intelligent*.[27] Sixteen other informants mentioned both moral qualities and education/upbringing,[28] and only 13 clearly thought that belonging to the *intelligentsia* was determined by one's work, schooling or social position.[29]

Age did not determine people's opinions on this matter: there were both young and old, rather evenly distributed in each of the groups, who believed *intelligentnost'* to be a moral category, a professional category, and who put stress on both of them.[30]

---

26 In 2000, no more than 23% of the males and 32,9% of the females were 50 years old, or older. See <http://www.census.gov/cgi-bin/ipcd/idbagg>.

27 Informants 31, 34, 4, 1, 18, 14, 15, 5, 6, 13, 11, 48, 35, 41, 37, 46, 39, 17, 47, 43, 42, 54, 27, 40, 20, 45.

28 Informants 2, 3, 16, 28, 9, 12, 25, 36, 30, 33, 55, 32, 51, 52, 44, 50.

29 Informants 21, 10, 7, 29, 38, 8, 53, 19, 22, 26, 23, 24, 49.

30 15 of the 1st group were born before 1950, 9 after that and two cases were unknown. The oldest in the group had been born in 1909 and youngest in 1982. Within the group

The interviewees' hometown, St. Petersburg or Petrozavodsk, seems to have had no clear influence as regards their stressing of the moral or professional dimension of the concept. Almost half (15) of the informants from St. Petersburg stressed the moral dimension, 'professional' definition was rarer (10) and another 10 named both factors. In Petrozavodsk 10 out of 19 informants stressed the moral factor, only three laid stress on the professional/cognitive dimension, and 6 named both. While it is true that *intelligentnost'* was more seldom understood to belong to the professional/cognitive sphere, it may be stated that in both towns the clear majority also named the moral dimension (25 out of 35 in St. Petersburg, 16 out of 19 in Petrozavodsk). So, according to our material, it is obvious that there are no essential differences in understanding dimensions of the concept of *intelligentsia/intelligentnost'* that are dependent on living in a metropolitan (St. Petersburg) or provincial (Petrozavodsk) center. It is possible that interviews in the countryside proper could give other results.

As regards correlation with the category, to which the informants placed themselves (axis *intelligent* – non-*intelligent*) the results were as follows: 16 out of the 31 self-defined *intelligenty* stressed moral qualities,[31] and 22 named them among the attributes of an *intelligent*.[32] Seven informants stressed the professional/cognitive dimension. Seven out of 18 non-*intelligenty* stressed the moral dimension[33] of an '*intelligent*' and 12 named it together with other things,[34] while '*intelligentnost'*' had just a professional/cognitive meaning for 6.[35] Additionally, there was a problematic group of 6 people, whose identity on the axis '*intelligent* – non-*intelligent*' was not clear.[36] All of them named moral qualities, while 3 also named the professional/cognitive dimension.[37]

Thus we can safely conclude that for the majority, to be an *intelligent* has a moral meaning, not dependent on whether they consider themselves to be part of that category.

While for most of the informants to be an '*intelligent*' was a good thing, some did not share this view. As many as 7 informants had a negative idea about the

---

stressing professionalism 6 were born before 1950 and 7 after it. The oldest within the group had been born in 1906 and the youngest in 1983. In the mixed group 10 had been born before 1950 and 6 after it.

31   Informants 4, 1, 18, 14, 15, 5, 6, 13, 48, 37, 47, 37, 47, 27, 40, 45,
32   Informants 25, 27, 40, 48, 51, 52, 54.
33   Informants 11, 41, 39, 17, 43, 42, 54.
34   Including also informants 28, 9, 12, 33, 50.
35   Informants 10, 29, 38, 53, 22, 49.
36   Informants 46, 35, 20, 36, 55, 32.
37   Informants 36, 55, 32.

intelligentsia.[38] Interestingly enough, only two of these identified themselves as non-*intelligents*,[39] while another was 'objectively' a stereotypic *intelligent*: a philosopher, writer, and professor.[40] Just one respondent (born in 1972) believed that the category of *intelligentsia* had become obsolete.[41] The age distribution of those informants who gave a negative assessment of the *intelligentsia* corresponded rather well with the average of the whole group (3 were born before the war,[42] one during it,[43] and three after it).

As regards the qualities of an *intelligent,* 14 informants considered that an *intelligent* must carefully mind his fellow-men.[44] Five named self-restraint as a quality of an *intelligent*.[45] Good behavior was mentioned by 19 informants.[46] Spirituality (*dukhovnost'*) or non-material interests were mentioned by 12 informants.[47] Other qualities of the intelligent mentioned were 'cultural interests' (11 times),[48] 'conscientiousness' (5 times),[49] 'broadness of views' (5 times),[50] 'justness/morals' (10 times),[51] 'inner independence' (3 times),[52] and 'sociability/ tact' (7 times).[53] Nineteen informants mentioned schooling/erudition as a condition for '*intelligentnost*'.[54] Only two mentioned that an *intelligent* was supposed to be in opposition towards the powers that be,[55] whereas one thought that the *intelligenty* are likely to stay outside politics[56] and another believed that being interested in politics to be typical for an *intelligent*.[57]

---

38   Informants 44, 7, 8, 19, 46, 55, 38.

39   Informants 38, 46.

40   Informant 46.

41   Informant 26.

42   Informants 7, 8,38.

43   Informant 46.

44   Informants 2,4,6,7,10,15, 18, 20, 34, 42, 44, 46, 47, 50 named taking into account other people.

45   Informants 10, 14, 15, 17, 36.

46   Informants 4,10,12,14, 21, 26, 27, 29, 31, 33, 35, 37, 41, 43, 45, 52, 53, 54.

47   Informants 1, 11, 10, 12, 13, 16, 20, 30, 32, 39, 42, 45.

48   Informants 4, 9, 22, 23, 32, 33, 35, 36, 39, 40, 45.

49   Informants 6, 12, 20, 45, 48.

50   Informants 3, 14, 34, 43, 48.

51   Informants 6, 25, 27, 40, 46, 47, 48, 51, 52, 54.

52   Informants 5, 30, 41.

53   Informants 14, 25, 29, 39, 40, 51, 52.

54   Informants 5, 8, 9, 12, 13, 24, 25, 28, 32, 33, 35, 36, 37, 44, 45, 49, 50, 51, 53.

55   Informants 20, 30.

56   Informant 48,

57   Informant 41.

Obviously most of the informants understood that they were being asked to describe some phenomenon, which really exists and they also gave examples of 'real' *intelligenty*, they knew personally. Some informants probably thought more about an ideal type, which was mostly believed to be something worth emulating.

As we can see, the qualities of an *intelligent* have mostly a moral character in some way or another, but not only that. An *intelligent* was mostly supposed to have both erudition and education, which was reflected in his social relations and lifestyles. If we look for a common denominator for the qualities which were associated with an *intelligent*, it would obviously be 'personal development'. An ideal *intelligent* is somebody who has grown more than his less developed fellow-citizens. He is someone who knows more and who understands more about the world and its values than others. Therefore, he is not likely to waste his time on superficial interests like hoarding material things, which fills the world of the so-called 'grey' people, who quarrel, swear, and cheat. The ideal *intelligent* is just and refined. The world of culture is his realm, both in the sense that he knows how to behave in a 'cultured' way and in the sense of reading, attending theatres and exhibitions and so on.

Here are some typical descriptions of *intelligentnost'*, the necessary qualities of an *intelligent*:

> *Intelligentnost'* is defined by an ability for unselfish spiritual interest. 'An *intelligent* is <...> one who thinks three times, before he hits'.[58] 'The first and most necessary quality: it's a person who is able to put himself in the place of another human being and sympathize with him (*soperezhivat' drugomu*). Even goodness and fairness (*dobrota i poriadochnost'*) are not most important; the main thing is to be just even when it goes against one's own interests. This is impossible for a philistine'.[59] 'Besides spirituality, an *intelligent* must have kindness of heart, although, spirituality does mean a certain kindness of heart (*serdechnaia dobrota*)'.[60] 'There are consumers and there are those who give ... An *intelligent* person must first think about society and only then about himself'.[61] 'An *intelligent* cannot work in business. The same thing with the power structures (*vlast'*) – an *intelligent* cannot be so cruel'.[62]

---

58   Informant 1.
59   Informant 6.
60   Informant 12.
61   Informant 13.
62   Informant 50.

It was also thought that *intelligentnost'* is something typically Russian: 'They are using our word, 'the *intelligentsia*' <...> and they concede that, in fact, they do not have the phenomenon. [At the University of Durham] I kept a diary <...> during two months I wrote two times 'An interesting discussion'. Mostly discussions there are no discussions at all'.[63] 'I think that it is a purely Russian concept <...> in the West, when they speak about *intelligentsia*, they mean just education, if I can tell by the films and books which I have seen and read'.[64] 'My son was in Germany and understood that morals is the most important thing for Russia. For us'.[65] 'He was in the USA. There no *intelligentsia* exists. In the USA, 90% think about nothing <...> about 3% are interested in international politics'.[66]

The moral aspect of *intelligentnost'* was quite dominant and in one way or another it was almost always present in the answers. Sometimes morality and *intelligentnost'* were even understood to be almost synonymous; one of the informants thought that the Soviet regime had been 'very *intelligent*' because it had taken care of the poor.[67] Another informant believed that goodness (*ser-dechnaia dobrota*) is the decisive quality of *intelligentnost'*, and, since this is a trait typical of Russians, there is 'a grain of *intelligentnost'* in every Russian'.[68]

Being an *intelligent* is very much like being a gentleman in the sense that an *intelligent* is supposed to behave in a restrained manner and to take into account other peoples' feelings even at one's own loss.[69]

Among those who highly esteem *intelligentnost'*, there are also people who think that things were better under communist rule. One informant thinks that philistinism is coming from the West and *intelligentnost'* is fading away.[70] Another sees that the youth has been corrupted and believes that the real *intelligentsia* were the old Peterburgians, not the contemporary mass.[71] Another informant, in turn, thinks that during the Soviet era, there was a 'colossal lowering of the moral level'.[72]

---

63   Informant 1.
64   Informant 17.
65   Informant 5.
66   Informant 7.
67   Informant 6.
68   Informant 12.
69   Informant 6.
70   Informant 12.
71   Informant 15.
72   Informant 16.

Sometimes it was remarked that belonging to the *intelligentsia* did not mean that somebody was *intelligentnyi* (has the attribute of *intelligentnost'*).[73]

When the informants were asked to give examples of *intelligenty* and were asked whether the Soviet leaders might be considered such, the answers were quite varied. Mostly the informants did not like the idea that Soviet leaders, even Lenin, could be classified as *intelligenty*. Some did, however, accept this idea,[74] and one even named the Cheka-chief Felix Dzerzhinsky as an *intelligent*. Other people named *intelligenty* were Joseph Stalin, Gennadii Ziuganov, Galina Starovoitova, Vladimir Putin, Dmitrii Likhachev, and Leo Tolstoy (a relative of the writer, who lives in St. Petersburg), Alexander Tvardovskii, and Daniil Granin. By way of explanation, it should be added that Putin was said to know foreign languages and to be a restrained person, who 'does not quarrel'. Stalin and Lenin were put into the *intelligentsia* by a person who believed that the concept is about a social category ('the leaders'/*rukovodiashchii sostav*).[75] Another informant believed that an *intelligent* is a free spirit, who never bows before any kind of hierarchy.[76]

On the basis of the interviews it is possible to sketch ideal types of an *intelligent* and a philistine. These types share qualities that different informants attached to them and are likely to be recognized as typical representatives of their genre by all of the informants.

An ideal *intelligent* is, first of all, a person with personal warmth and cordiality. He dwells in the world of true values, not appearances. He has creative potential and is not a slave to conventions. He is capable of understanding others and empathizing with their position. He has a strong sense of justice and he will be true to its imperatives, even to his own detriment. An *intelligent* is tactful and restrained. It is possible to tell, almost at first glance, and certainly after a conversation that a person belongs to this category. The *intelligent* is at home in any company, for he is capable of understanding different people. He is also well read in classical literature and also probably knows foreign languages or has other exclusive knowledge. The *intelligent* has unerring taste and does not feel the need to display his wealth or outstanding qualities; he is inwardly independent and does not care about the opinions of others. The *intelligent* may be critical of the regime, but first of all he is someone, who is not afraid to speak

---

73   Informant 23.

74   Informants 11, 15.

75   Informant 11. Incidentally, this informant also considered that an intelligent is a 'warm person' (dushevnyi chelovek).

76   Informant 30.

out against any wrongdoings, not for his own sake, but for others, even risking his own interests.

The *intelligent* is, however, not primarily a representative of a social category nor does he have primarily the social function of a critic of the powers that be. Rather, the *intelligent* is the ideal man, the full-fledged person. His personality very much resembles the ideal type, which the psychoanalyst Erich Fromm has coined, with his Freudian jargon, as the 'productive type', denoting the ideal of a fully developed human personality, who has a positive, beneficial attitude towards his fellow-men and who is prone to giving, not taking. Russians believe that this type can most likely be found in Russia.

Meshchanstvo –the Spirit of Consumerism

When the informants were asked about *meshchanstvo*, the concept proved to be even more vague and problematic than was the case with *intelligentsia/intelligentnost'*. Three informants did not know of the concept at all,[77] and as many as 11 said that they did not use it or that it is obsolete.[78] Seven abstained from defining it at all.[79]

However, it was clear to the majority that the concept had negative connotations.

Thirty two informants mentioned the morally dubious qualities of the *meshchane*,[80] 6 mentioned also bad taste,[81] and 7 referred only to tastes.[82]

It happened that those who did not consider themselves to be *intelligenty* mentioned almost exclusively the moral dimension (13 cases),[83] whereas the *intelligenty* also named vulgarity of tastes also quite often (11 times),[84] while morals was also predominant (19 times).[85]

As regards the preponderant meaning of the concept, the following results were obtained: 20 informants said that the term refers to selfishness or the

---

77 Informants 19, 22, 33.
78 Informants 17, 20, 25, 26, 27, 28, 36, 37, 40, 43, 47.
79 Informants 1, 2, 14, 29, 32, 41, 54.
80 Informants 34, 18, 15, 5, 6, 11, 13, 35, 17, 27, 20, 1, 2, 3, 16, 12, 30, 26, 23, 39, 47, 42, 40, 45, 55, 51, 52, 44, 50, 38, 53, 49.
81 Informants 5, 27, 26, 45, 51, 52.
82 Informants 14, 33, 21, 19, 24, 48, 36.
83 Informants 35, 20, 55, 11, 39, 17, 42, 12, 50, 38, 53, 49, 34 (36 and 33 mentioned tastes).
84 Informants 5, 27, 45, 51, 52, 26, 14, 48, 21, 19, 24.
85 Informants 1, 18, 15, 6, 13, 47, 40, 2, 3, 16, 30, 44, 23, 5, 27, 45, 51, 52, 26.

narrow-minded pursuit of personal gain.[86] Nine said that it refers to the preponderance of 'material' values, consumerism;[87] four said that it was connected with false self-aggrandizement;[88] and four mentioned lack of culture or creativity.[89]

Obviously *meshchanstvo* had negative overtones, but at the same time many informants referred to its 'naturalness'. As many as 10 informants said that *meshchanstvo* was not a bad thing or that it was 'normal'.[90] Two said emphatically that *meshchanstvo* was a good thing.[91] When asked whether an *intelligent* can be a *meshchanin*, 11 informants gave an unequivocally negative answer,[92] 10 gave a positive answer,[93] and 6 answers were ambiguous.[94]

Over one third of the informants (21) obviously considered the concept more or less alien or did not know it at all. As regards the rest, most informants understood it to denote a morally dubious or in other ways defective personality. On the other hand, it was largely understood that it had to do with a certain 'normal' disposition of the human personality. While *intelligentnost'* was clearly a positive quality, quite many thought that it could be united with *meshchanstvo* in the same person. On the other hand, about as many people did not believe this to be possible. It seems to be that this division primarily reflects the fact that certain people were thinking about *intelligenty* and *meshchane* as ideal types, while others were referring to people they knew.

There were also other signs of *meshchanstvo*, such as the use of serviettes, lampshades, tiny elephants, and the like, some even called guitar a philistine instrument. As examples of a *meshchanin,* one informant named Hitler, another recalled (the wartime pop-singer) Klavdia Shul'zhenko's songs. One informant said that 'an officer's wife' was a quintessential type of *meshchanin*.[95]

A *meshchanin* was described in the following typical ways: 'Meshchanstvo means the ability to see only one's own profit, one's own benefit'.[96] 'It is the primitive life <...> without any rising into the spheres (*parenie*), without art. A

---

86   Informants 3, 4, 5, 7, 8, 9, 53, 47, 39, 38, 35, 34, 10, 12, 13, 16, 17, 18, 26, 30.

87   Informants 9, 23, 42, 44, 47, 50, 51, 52, 55.

88   Informants 6, 21, 24, 27.

89   Informants 13, 42, 44, 49.

90   Informants 11, 15, 45, 55, 19, 20, 25, 43, 48, 55.

91   Informants 31, 46.

92   Informants 14, 11, 16, 12, 30, 29, 23, 24, 41, 52, 49.

93   Informants 4, 35, 25, 33, 37, 39, 43, 50, 38, 54.

94   Informants 34, 18, 46, 45, 36, 44.

95   Informant 12.

96   Informant 1.

grey life, without creativity'.[97] 'It's more or less a closed circle, where people are tied by some rules of conduct. In everyday life it was manifested for example in a love of serviettes, of decoration, maybe even in tidiness'.[98] 'A *meshchanin* cannot be just if it is to his own detriment <...> The will to display (*pokazushestvo*) <...> He cannot drive a small car. He needs the latest model'.[99] 'A *meshchanin* is self-sufficient <...> just a man of the period of natural economy'.[100] 'Low-mindedness (*poshlost'*) and *meshchanstvo* –they are very near to each other <...>. A consumer's attitude to the world is the main trait of a *meshchanin*'.[101] 'They are people who are nothing by themselves, but who want to have all the good things, to look beautiful. In fact they are just the grey people'.[102] 'They are people who only care about themselves <...> they can cheat you at every step'.[103] 'Taking care of just one's little, personal interests'.[104] 'It's the home (*the Domostroi*) <...> Science is not interesting, politics is not interesting, one is living just on the surface. First of all, one's own everyday life is interesting'.[105]

If we try to sketch the archetypal *meshchanin* (philistine), recognized as such by all the informants, he would be something like this: a *meshchanin* is a restricted, egotistic, and self-centered person, whose interests are restricted to satisfying his own, primitive needs. He has no higher needs nor does he understand others who do have them. Consumption, attaining riches, and commanding posts and displaying them to others are the aim of his life. Sensations on the everyday level are the life of the *meshchanin*, who consumes cheap entertainment and has an undeveloped taste. The Russians often believe that Russia is less philistine than the West, but is rapidly getting more so.

All in all, the concept of '*meshchanin*' was believed to be more or less old-fashioned. One informant recalled that Soviet power had fought philistinism, but this was because this had been a 'land of fools'(*strana durakov*).[106] Another thought that the word had gradually disappeared, having lost all meaning.[107]

---

97   Informant 2.
98   Informant 5.
99   Informant 6.
100   Informant 7.
101   Informant 13.
102   Informant 14.
103   Informant 15.
104   Informant 16.
105   Informant 17.
106   Informant 8, who considered himself an intelligent and had been active in politics.
107   Informant 10.

One concluded that people in the West are philistines and that this phenomenon had now also arrived in Russia from the West.[108]

As a whole, it seems to be that as ideal types, *intelligentnost'* and *meshchanstvo* (philistinism) are to this day generally understood to be incompatible and
even diametrically opposite qualities. Even so, there is also a certain inclination to understand philistinism, which, after all, is a normal propensity of human beings. The meaning of ideal *intelligentnost'* comes near to altruism,
which is preferred to egoism, but even the latter is believed to have its rightful
place in society.

Conclusion

All in all, the survey shows that the concepts of *'intelligentsia/intelligentnost'*
and *'meshchanstvo'* still had a definitive place in Russian post-communist discourse. They were recognized by townspeople irrespective of their age and
education. In many respects, an ideal *'intelligent'* represents an ideal human
being both for those who themselves consider to belong to the *intelligentsia*
and for those who consider themselves to be outside that category. *Intelligentnost'* is understood to be, first of all, a moral category, even though the ideal
intelligent is also erudite. Obviously, the answers presuppose a hierarchical
idea of the human personality, where more developed individuals are generally respected. An ideal *intelligent* is rich spiritually, irrespective of his material
belongings or his status in society. It even seems to be generally believed that
ideal *intelligenty* cannot be found among those who are in power or those who
are rich.

In comparison, *meshchanstvo* seems to be a slightly more ambiguous concept. It is also understood somewhat differently in different circles. While
meshchanstvo is also a preponderantly moral concept, it seems to be harder to
define or recognize for certain people. For most informants, *meshchanstvo* also
means an underdeveloped personality; it denotes restrictedness, egoism, false
pretensions. On the other hand, members of the *intelligentsia* obviously understand this concept somewhat differently than those who do not consider
themselves to be members of that category. For the non-*intelligents*, the moral
dimension is clearly the decisive and almost sole dimension which identifies
the *meshchane*, while the *intelligenty* often also refer to the development of
tastes.

Both *'intelligent'* and *'meshchanin'* were concepts which the Soviet regime
used for its own purposes. However, the Soviet discourse was not totally able to

---

108   Informant 12.

determine the content of these concepts and it does not look likely that they will be rapidly rendered obsolete by virtue of today's new surroundings, in which Soviet ideology has become marginal.

While material well-being is a generally recognized goal for human beings, it does not mean that Russians highly esteem people who have a lot of money, but are spiritually poor. There may no longer be a cult of the *intelligentsia*, but there still seems to linger on an ideal image of the *intelligent*, a hero, whose realm is 'not of this world', one who recognizes genuine, real values and lives up to them, one, who is uncorrupted and sincere, even though not necessarily an active opponent of the powers that be.

I have no relevant comparable material about the image of an 'intellectual' in a western society, but it seems to me that we have reason to expect that the image would be quite different. This would be almost inevitable, given the different social roles which intellectuals have played in both societies. Probably the image of the benign, calm *intelligent*, who abhors any kind of violence and is not ready to hit back, is a very distinctive characteristic of the Russian *intelligent* today. Obviously, he is a different personality than the tsar's murderers. It is also hard to imagine that such qualities would be associated with western intellectuals, given their leading role in most violent movements of the past century.

On the other hand, the *meshchanin* seems to be considered even in Russia as a more and more normal phenomenon, even though not one deserving respect. A sizable contingent keeps on despising this restricted and underdeveloped being, while others are ready to recognize at least some rights for human frailty, which this type represents.

Some informants recognized and mentioned the importance of the Soviet legacy which was attached to the concepts of *intelligentnost'* and *meshchanstvo* and some thought that the concepts, especially *meshchanstvo* were obsolete or becoming obsolete. However, it does not seem that the majority of any age cohort would consider either concept to be empty of content or artificial. So it seems that the cultural content of these two key concepts will linger on. Obviously the concepts are subject to constant change, but they are likely to preserve some ideas of Russian culture through the ages for future generations.

While this survey has no pretensions to being statistically representative for the whole of Russia, it is based on a rather heterogeneous sample and obviously gives results which are not dependent on the personality of the interviewers or the place of residence of the informants (St. Petersburg or Petrozavodsk).

It seems to me that understanding the special dimensions of the concepts *intelligent* and *meshchanin* gives added value to any foreigner who wants to understand Russian culture. They witness the degree to which the tenets of moralizing, anti-bourgeois currents, which were influential both before and during the Soviet regime, have survived in Russia. It is obvious that the collapse of Communism dealt a mighty blow to the prevailing mentality, which was to a remarkable degree influenced by specific economic and ideological surroundings. The sudden change of social system has obviously changed the mentality as regards consumerist values.

The popular utilitarian culture of capitalist society, which downplays moral considerations and tends to make them private issues, is obviously reflected in these results. The moral hero seems to be losing his traditional position also in Russia. Still, he enjoys a fair degree of admiration, probably more so than comparable figures in the West.

Bibliography

Burbank, J. (1984): *Intelligentsia and Revolution. Russian Views of Bolshevizm 1917–1922*. Oxford, Now York, Toronto: Oxford University Press.

Gasparov, M.L. (1999): Intellektualy, intelligenty, intelligentnost. In: *Russkaia intelligentsia, istoriia i sudba*. Moscow: Nauka.

Gessen, M. (1997): *Dead again. The Russian intelligentsia after Communism*. London and New York: Verso.

Hollander, P. (1981): *Political Pilgrims: Travels of the Western Intellectuals to the Soviet Union, China and Cuba 1928–1978*. NY and Oxford. Oxford University Press.

Ivanov-Razumnik, R. (1907): *Istoriia russkoi obshchestvennoi mysli. Individualizm i meshchanstvo v russkoi literature i zhizni XIX veka*. St. Petersburg: Tipographiia M.M. Stasiulevicha.

Johnson, P. (2000): *Intellectuals*. London: Phoenix Press.

Kara-Murza, S. (2013): *Krakh SSSR*. Moscow: Izdatel'stvo Algoritm. Available at: <http://problemanalysis.ru/doklad/2013/publicazia/Kpax_CCCP.pdf>.

Lenin, V. (1970): *Polnoe sobranie sochinenii*. Vol. 51. Moscow: Izdatel'stvo politicheskoi literatury.

Posner, R. (2003): Public Intellectuals: A Study of Decline. Cambridge, Mass. and London: Harvard University Press.

Stepanov, Iu. (1999): 'Zhrets', narekis' i znamenuisia: 'Zhertva'. In: *Russkaia intelligentsia. Istoriia i sud'ba*. Ed. by T. Kniazevskaia. Moscow: Nauka.

Szamuely, T. (1974): *The Russian Tradition*. New York, etc.: McGraw-Hill.

Vihavainen, T. (2006): *The Inner Adversary: The Struggle Against Philistinism as the Moral Mission of the Russian Intelligentsia*. Washington, DC: New Academia.

CHAPTER 7

Afterword

In this volume the problems, which consumption and consumerism caused for the Soviet Communism, its ideology and practices, have been approached from various angles.

Soviet Communism was, in principle, inimical to consumerism. It purported to create a culture of producers, of the liberated *homo faber*, who created society as his image, finally reaching communist society, where scarcity would be overcome and everybody was happy to give his contribution to the common good without special compensation.

Communist society was very much like the anarchists' utopia as Lenin aptly said. People would be cooperating instead of competing, they would be helping each other instead of struggling with each other and they would be interested in the production of goods and not in their consumption.

The fundamental achievement of the communist society was to be that people were to lose interest in commodities for their own sake. Consumer goods would be given gratis to everybody; there would be no classes of rich and poor. Envying the neighbor's living standards would be absurd in that kind of society.

However, this expected end of material interest could be possible only if there was enough production. This 'enough' was thinkable only if people were supposed to ask no more products after their needs had been satisfied at a certain point. Nothing would be enough, if people, in fact, were insatiable.

Was it possible to think that some amount of products would be 'objectively' enough to satisfy people? The Soviet answer was, yes, people had certain 'reasonable needs', which could be satisfied.

In some sense the idea of building communist society in Russia resembled the Russian *narodniks'* idea of building socialist society right on the foundations of the existing rural commune. The great majority of Soviet citizens had not been spoilt by bourgeois consumerism. It could be expected that their material needs were not excessive. This seemed to get support from polls, which were conducted in the 1960s.

In 1961, the Communist Party of the Soviet Union solemnly promised that those 'reasonable needs' of the Soviet people would be fully satisfied by the year 1980. This meant, in other words, that the material basis of the communist society would have been created.

© KONINKLIJKE BRILL NV, LEIDEN, 2016 | DOI 10.1163/9789004303973_008

Certainly, communist society was something, which the CPSU had been prepared to build from the very beginning. The Bolshevik Party had adopted its new name in 1918 to underline the importance of this goal. It was the justification of its power.

However, the CPSU realized quite soon that it was necessary to pay much attention to the consumers' needs. Although western kind of consumerism already had made its influence known in pre-revolutionary Russia, the great mass of the people were peasants, who tended to be indifferent and even inimical towards consumerism. Also the leading *intelligenty* preached against the viciousness of human greed. The materially simple life with high level of spirituality and justice was considered to be the opposite of the philistine's mean aspirations, which concentrated on material well-being.

In the 1920s the CPSU still concentrated in liquidating social inequality by leveling, which meant scarcity for everybody. In the middle of the 1930s, when the socialist society was supposedly constructed, the party rehabilitated material well-being and 'cultured' consumption in principle. A society of abundance, where life had become better and merrier, was proclaimed to have been born. At first, it comprised only a small amount of people.

During the Khrushchev era, consumption became one of the central themes of the day. The USSR was to construct communist society, which meant greatly surpassing the USA in material well-being. Thus, consumers' goods were, paradoxically, to attain great importance for people before they would become uninteresting and gratis for everybody.

It turned out that the basic tenets of the communist ideology were flawed. The authors of this book show that the concept of 'reasonable consumption' proved to be an illusion. Production and consumption of clothes, which have here been studied by several authors, were especially sensitive issues. Changes of ideology were immediately reflected in the discourse concerning clothes. The ideal of the perfect Soviet woman changed together with her clothes.

Clothes also proved to be tightly associated with undomesticated economic natural forces. Production of the right quantities and qualities of clothes for 'reasonable consumption' proved to be unrealistic. The phenomenon of fashion was a real problem for both the Soviet ideology and practice. In principle it was tolerated within certain limits, but in practice it proved one of the most awkward stumbling stones of the Soviet society.

In the real world, the Soviet consumer's lot was hard. Instead of being able to enjoy the services of competing producers and retailers, he had to defend his most basic rights as consumer on the daily level. Often he was obliged to produce himself items, which were not available. When the sales clerks and retailers did not try to sell more, but, on the contrary, tried to keep things away from the reach of the customers, an important element of modern consumerism was absent. The system of *blat* –mutual favors- tended to transform the anonymous consumer market into a network of personal connections. This was another factor, which sapped the growth of consumerism in the Soviet Union.

The CPSU put all of its authority into play, when the XXII Party Congress in 1961 solemnly promised that communist society would be built by the year 1980. Unavoidably, its credibility soon waned and its further support in the 1970s and 1980s was largely based in increased oil revenues and in the so-called 'Little Deal' with the Soviet middle class. This purported to ensure security and stability for both the middle class and the state.

However, the party's ideological prestige waned, when the consumers' needs proved impossible to satisfy. To some extent at least, negative consequences of missing consumerism made themselves felt. Lack of material impulses in the everyday life of many workers in the Soviet Union proved to be not developing any public-minded citizens of the communist society. Rather, it was begetting lifestyle of the *Liumpenproletariat*, with no interest for improving its own lot, not to speak about voluntary work for the society.

Development of consumerism in the Soviet Union was complicated by the fact that many items of consumption were extremely scarce. By the middle 1980's it was clear for everybody that the end of scarcity was not to be expected in the foreseeable future. This was reflected even in the practices of the Soviet state as regards its attitudes towards foreign items, such as fashionable clothes.

However, the traditional Soviet ideas concerning the ideal man, the *intelligent*, for whom material things always remained of secondary importance and his opposite, the mean consumerist-oriented *meshchanin*, still lingered on ten years after the Soviet system had collapsed. These were ideas, which the Soviet ideology had inculcated since the revolution and they obviously they had to some extent filled the place of religion, whose importance had waned during the years of Soviet power.

When the Soviet Union suddenly collapsed, the Communist Party very rapidly lost almost all support among the people. This revolution left the Soviet people in an awkward situation both economically and intellectually. Now, in the early 1990s, there finally were enough commodities for sale and nobody prevented from buying them, but most people did not have money. This situation was fundamentally changed only in the 2000s.

Nowadays, the extent of consumerism in Russia is a striking phenomenon. The Russians do not like to spare money and they like conspicuous consumption. This means that a fundamental revolution both in norms and values of the older generation has taken place within a very short time-span. The whole material and intellectual environment of the Russian people has changed totally.

Even though the contemporary Russian material and intellectual environment is quite different from that in the Soviet time, it is to be assumed that some remnants of the Soviet heritage will, in some way or another, still linger on for years in Russia, even though the environment of the Russian consumer very much resembles that of his colleague in the West.

The Soviet experiment to overcome consumerism by restricting consumption to the fulfillment of the consumers' 'reasonable' needs was not unpopular in the beginning, but it met unexpected difficulties and ended in disgrace. This story needs to be studied by all those, who for some reason may consider the necessity of comparable policies in the future for environmental or other reasons.

Appendix

Questionnaire

The introductory question is: "Do you consider yourself to belong to the category of the *intelligentsia*?"[1]

If the answer was positive, the informant was given a set of questions called 'Type A' (*intelligent*), which were relevant for this group. If the answer was negative, another set of questions 'Type B' (non-*intelligent*) was used.

Type A (*Intelligenty*)

1. To which generation of *intelligenty* does your family/ you belong? Please, relate briefly the history of your family and about the social status of two to three generations of your ancestors.

2. Please, talk briefly about your life history and your professional career. What do you do today (if the informant is retired, ask what he did retiring)? Is the concept '*intelligent*' connected with a certain profession?

3. What do you think are the main, most characteristic qualities of an *intelligent*, especially a Russian *intelligent*? Which well-known persons or literary heroes would fulfill the criteria of an *intelligent*? Are there typical *intelligenty* among your friends and acquaintances? If there are, could you describe (you do not need to give any names) and explain why you consider them to be *intelligenty*?

4. In what way have attitudes towards the *intelligentsia* changed during your life? How would you assess the mutual relations between the state (vlast') and the *intelligentsia* during different stages of the Soviet period?
   (if the informant assesses the relations between the state and the *intelligentsia* to be totally antagonistic, he can be reminded about the cooperation of many *intelligenty* with the state in the USSR (Gorky, A. Tolstoy, Pasternak, Mayakovsky, Chukovsky, Meyerhold and so on, the interviewer may choose the names: How will the informant assess this phenomenon? Do those individuals and their like belong to the category of the *intelligentsia*?)

5. How did representatives of other social groups (workers, peasants and so on) evaluate the *intelligentsia* during different periods of Soviet history? Did you personally, or your relatives or friends, ever have conflicts on these grounds? Did you suffer from any unjustness, estrangement, or discrimination on these

---

1　In Russian: 'относите ли Вы себя к категории интеллигентов', which gives some weight to the concept of '*intelligent*' as an individual, not just a representative of a social group.

grounds in some concrete life situation? Or, on the contrary, can you remember any instances of a positive, friendly attitude towards yourself as an *intelligent*?

6. How would you respond to the idea that there are "working-class *intelligenty*?[2]

7. How would you define the concept *meshchanstvo*? Has the content of this concept changed during different phases of your life? Which well-known people, politicians or literary heroes would fulfill the criteria of a '*meshchanin*'? Are there typical *meshchane* or people with their relevant qualities among your friends or acquaintances? If there are, could you describe them and explain why you consider them to be *meshchane*?

8. Do you remember any periods of ideological,[3] government-sponsored, or other forms of struggle against *meshchanstvo* in the USSR? When was *meshchanstvo* most hated and despised? And, on the contrary, were there periods of a patronizing, indulgent attitude towards *meshchanstvo?*

9. Were there in the collective where you worked, any campaigns against *meshchanstvo*? If yes, when? Could you talk about them and give an example of a campaign against *meshchanstvo*?

10. What symbols of *meshchanstvo* you have encountered in newspapers, journals, literature, and films? (For instance: lampshades, tulle curtains, a mountain of pillows on one's bed, little elephant figurines on a bookshelf, furniture with carvings, and so on). Have the symbols of *meshchanstv*o changed during your lifetime?

11. How would you characterize the concepts of *meshchanstvo* and *intelligentsia* in the Soviet Union during different periods of its development? Were there periods when these concepts came close to or distant from each other?

12. Can an intelligent be a *meshchanin* or the other way round? Do you remember cases when the same person was both an intelligent and a *meshchanin*?

13. P. V. Ivanov-Razumnik wrote that one of the basic tasks of the *intelligentsia* is to struggle against *meshchanstvo*. Maxim Gorky, on the contrary, in his article 'Comments on *meshchanstvo*' accused the *intelligentsia* of *meshchanstvo*, for its 'passive role in the struggle of life'. Which one of these two thinkers is right in your opinion?

Type B (*For those who do not consider themselves to be* intelligenty)

1. Please, talk briefly about your life history and professional career. What do you do today? (If the informant is retired, what did he do before retirement).

---

2 'рабочий интеллигент'.

3 Идейный.

2. Are there, among your relatives, friends, or acquaintances, people whom you would put in the category of *intelligenty*? What qualities do you think this person (these persons) has that make him an *intelligent*?

3. What are, in your opinion, the main characteristic qualities on an *intelligent* and, especially, of a Russian *intelligent?* Were Lenin, Trotsky, or Stalin *intelligenty*? Is it possible to consider the present leaders of the state *intelligenty*?

4. Would you like to become part of the category of the *intelligentsia*? What do you think is bad and what is good in being an *intelligent*? What would be needed for a worker or a peasant in to become an *intelligent*?

5. Which kind of role, positive or negative, has the *intelligentsia* played in the history of Russia? If the role has been negative, what is the problem with the *intelligenty*, what have they done wrong?

6. How would you assess the relations between the *intelligentsia* and the state[4] during different periods of the Soviet era? Do you think that the *intelligentsia* made common cause with the state, served it, or was in opposition to it? Did the *intelligentsia* suffer as a result of the policies of the state. If yes, during which periods of Soviet history and why? In which way did this happen?

7. What were and what are the attitudes towards the *intelligentsia* and the *intelligents* among the workers and the peasants? In which ways, concretely, have the positive or negative attitudes been reflected? Has there been respect or contempt? Do you remember any personal concrete cases of conflicts with the *intelligenty,* why have they taken place?

8. Is the *intelligentsia* needed in Russia at all? If it is, why?

9. How would you comment on the concept of a working-class *intelligent*?

10. How would you define the concept *meshchanstvo*? Which well-known politicians, literary heroes, or film heroes would you like to call *meshchane*? Are there typical *meshchane* or people with the qualities of a *meshchanin* among your friends and acquaintances? If yes, can you describe them and explain why you consider them to be *meshchane*?

11. During what time was there the most active struggle against *meshchanstvo* in the Soviet Union? When was *meshchanstvo* regarded as especially odious and despised? And on the contrary, were there periods of patronizing, indulgent attitudes towards *meshchanstvo*?

12. Were there in the collective where you worked any campaigns against *meshchanstvo*? If yes, when? Can you talk about them and give some examples about the struggle against *meshchanstvo*?

---

4 власть.

13.   Can an *intelligent* be a *meshchanin* and the other way round? Why? Do you
      remember any instances, when the same person was both an intelligent and a
      meshchanin?

14.   Alexander Solzhenitsyn wrote in one of his articles that the *intelligentsia* was
      'philistinized'[5] during the Soviet period. Do you agree with this?

---

5   'omeshchanilas'.

Index